D1446239

THE CHIEF EXECUTIVE:

and business growth

A Comparative study in the
United States, Britain and Germany

THE CHIEF EXECUTIVE
and business growth

A Comparative study in the
United States, Britain and Germany

by George Copeman

LEVIATHAN HOUSE
LONDON & NEW YORK

By the same author

LEADERS OF BRITISH INDUSTRY

PROMOTION AND PAY FOR EXECUTIVES

THE CHALLENGE OF EMPLOYEE SHAREHOLDING

THE ROLE OF THE MANAGING DIRECTOR

LAWS OF BUSINESS MANAGEMENT

PART AUTHOR: HOW THE EXECUTIVE SPENDS HIS TIME

FIRST PUBLISHED 1971

SBN 0 900537 00 0

PRINTED IN GREAT BRITAIN
BY W & J MACKAY & CO LTD, CHATHAM

CONTENTS

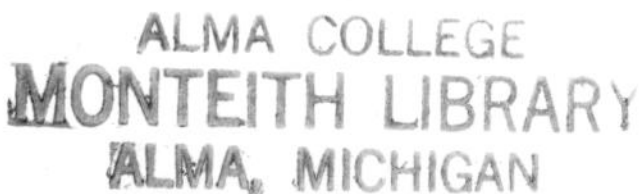

ACKNOWLEDGEMENTS

I wish to express my gratitude to all who have helped me with this study, and especially to the following:

1. The 103 American, British and German chief executives who, by the nature of this study, cannot be named. They gave me generously of their time, ideas and experience.

2. The 27 American, German and British chief executives, amongst the 103, who volunteered to read part or all of the draft manuscript and send me their comments.

3. Dr. J. R. Perrin, Wolfson Professor of Financial Control, and Professor S. B. N. Shimmin of the Department of Behaviour in Organizations, University of Lancaster, for discussion and comment at each stage of the project—drafting of the questionnaire, preparation of the interview sample, analysis of results and finally, reading of the draft manuscript. Since this was not academic supervision as would be entailed in a higher degree course, it must be made clear that the final text is entirely my own and they cannot be held responsible for any ideas, etc., which it contains. Fortunately Professor Perrin's working experience takes in both sides of the Atlantic. Considerable effort has been made to overcome the problem of differences in American and British business and financial terminology, in this English-language text. If there are any remaining causes for misunderstanding, they must be my responsibility, and I would be grateful if readers could draw my attention to them.

4. Mr. Dick H. Brandon, whose personal friendship and business association with us at Business Intelligence Services Limited brought about the actual circumstances under which I was able to obtain the free time and resources to investigate and write on this subject.

5. My immediate colleagues on the board of Business Intelligence Services Limited, managing director Brian Allison, and Colin Walpole, Roger Graham and Philip Marchand, for their foresight and understanding during all the vicissitudes that beset any business from day to day.

6. Mr. Philip Zimmerman, chairman of the Mercury House publishing group, with which I spent $16\frac{2}{3}$ years—or one third of a working life. I deeply appreciate both the personal kindness extended to me during that period of dramatic growth of Mercury House, and the opportunities for new business ventures involving great risk, some of which succeeded and some did not.

7. My founder colleagues in Leviathan House, Dr. C. Northcote Parkinson and Herr Wolfgang Dummer, for their vision in backing this type of international study.

8. Dr. Jack S. Schiff for collecting American research material for me.

9. Herr Erhard Hoppe for collecting German research material for me and arranging German interviews. Also Herr E. Pusch for acting as interpreter in Germany.

10. Mr. David A. Tate, F.C.A., for reading and criticizing the financial chapters.

11. Mrs. Jean Bristor for taking on the major share of correspondence and manuscript typing, etc., in connection with this study.

12. My wife Rita, also Gillian, Brian and Frances for tolerating an absent-minded chap and above all for taking such interest in this work.

FOREWORD

BY DR. C. NORTHCOTE PARKINSON

Books dealing with the technical side of business are many but books on management in the broader sense are relatively few. Bookshelves are crammed with literature about economic theory and accounting practice, to which are added daily the more recent works on cybernetics and systems analysis. Books more obviously helpful to the manager are scarce and open, moreover, to the objection that the author cannot always point to his own success.

Professors at the business school have much relevant information but they are not themselves in business. Their advice is thus less readily acceptable than that of men whose success and prosperity is known.

When we turn, however, to the memoirs of the multi-millionaire, we find that business enterprise is rarely accompanied by literary skill. It is one thing to succeed, quite another to explain. Questioned on the secret of his success, Cornelius Vanderbilt replied in these words, 'Never tell nobody what yer goin' ter do 'til yer do it.' He added, after a pause for thought, 'Don't never buy nothing you don't want or sell nothing you aint got.' These are words of wisdom but they fail to reveal—and were scarcely intended to reveal—how millions are actually made.

There are, nevertheless, a few successful business men who have gone on to achieve success in authorship. To their works our objection must be that men so remarkable are hard to imitate. For the man of ordinary ability, to follow the example of a genius can be disastrous.

Better than books by business men, however distinguished, are works written by consultants. Some of these are excellent but there are still some surprising gaps in our knowledge. How is the normally successful business managed? It is hard to say. How could its management be improved? We do not know.

In an attempt to answer these questions Dr. Copeman has compiled this book. While not without his own experience nor yet devoid of his own ideas, he has chosen to pursue a strictly scientific method. How do managers manage? He decided to ask them. Interviewing over a hundred chief executives (Presidents in U.S.A., Managing Directors in Britain, General Directors in Germany) he analysed their replies and this book is the result.

He does not claim that his findings are so broadly based as to have statistical finality. They are illustrative, however, of contemporary thought and they embody a wealth of recent experience. Where his work is novel is in his refusal to name any one of his informants. It is this circumstance which has allowed each to speak freely. Had the names been given the answers would not have been the same. On this subject Jeremy Bentham wrote that, 'There are two classes of writer to whom the public is very little obliged: those who pretend to say something, and in effect say nothing, and those who say something, but say not what they think.'

Directly challenged and speaking for the record, the business man might choose between these policies or else perhaps combine them. With anonymity guaranteed, he is free to speak his mind, encouraged the more to do so by Dr. Copeman's obvious sincerity. The chapters which follow must speak for themselves, justifying his method and proving his point.

This is a factual book and the author reserves his own opinion to the last. But there is implied from the beginning his belief that power does not corrupt. He believes, as I do, that power is more likely to ennoble and that men grow in stature from being made responsible.

There is much discussion in school or college about the exact scope of the syllabus. Should the student learn this or that? The syllabus matters less, perhaps, than we are apt to suppose. The vital question is whether the teaching has produced people with a thirst for knowledge. If it has, their present level of information is immaterial for they will go on learning for as long as they live. If it has not, their present knowledge is again beside the point for they will soon forget all that they are supposed to know.

This book is written in the belief that there are managers, and people who aspire to managerial office, who have come to realize that a routine performance is not enough. Theirs is a vocation which will demand, they have come to see, a lifetime of action, study and thought. As the starting point for such a truly professional career this book could hardly be bettered.

It includes a great deal of information, derived not from one country but from several, not from one man but from a hundred. With this information, however, comes a new concept of management. Ideas are there but not over-emphasized, the reader being rather encouraged to make further discoveries for himself. I welcome this book as a valuable addition to the literature of business.

I welcome it still more as the first book of a series, one which will help to establish and strengthen the science and art of business administration. If business is to survive in this changing and complex world of the late twentieth century it will owe much to Dr. Copeman and to others who share his idealism and honesty. Where he has shown the way others will follow, bringing order out of chaos and proving that industry can be at least as progressive as government or education.

The work of establishing a philosophy and ethic of management will not be completed within a year or even within a decade. Few of us may live to see this great task finished. It is something, however, to have seen it fairly begun.

C. NORTHCOTE PARKINSON
June 1971

1

WHY AND HOW A SPECIAL INTERNATIONAL STUDY WAS MADE

Do chief executives of business firms behave differently in one country from how they behave in another? And if so, does this help to explain why the rates of economic growth of various countries differ so widely?

Such an explanation seemed to me more likely than any differences in the way ordinary people work—at least for a comparison of industrialized countries. The ordinary worker is supposed to have the advantages of mechanization, training in the job and good management. If the results are low productivity, better to blame the management than the workers.

It was with these thoughts in mind that I set out to do an international study of 'The Chief Executive'—as a natural successor to my earlier British work on 'The Role of the Managing Director'.

Choice of countries

For reasons of cost and time, I had to limit the number of countries visited. But which ones to choose? Britain was a natural choice, for I live there, and the country is of special interest because economic growth has been slow.

The United States was a certainty for inclusion, because of its size, its faster growth rate and its advanced technology. After all, who went to the moon?

Three countries would be enough for a beginning of this study, but which one for third choice? Germany was obvious. Their industrial growth rate has been outstanding. They are near to Britain and of broadly similar size. There could be a language problem interviewing German chief executives, but in fact it proved to be minimal. Interpreter facilities were made available, but were used in only five cases out of 16, and in only two of these was there any extensive amount of interpretation.

Preparation of questionnaire

The questionnaire for the 103 interviews held for this book was based on my own experience as a chief executive—jotting down in daily practice notes on the problems I had to grapple with and wished I could have special guidance on. This was the basis of my first pilot interviews with six British chief executives. Following these I sought academic advice on the re-shaping of the questionnaire and other aspects of my study. This is mentioned in the Acknowledgements.

The next 19 interviews involved some change—though not extensive—in the questionnaire, so that altogether 25 were held before it settled down into unaltered form.

Choice of interviewees

Because the rate of economic growth in Britain has been slower than in Germany and the United States, I decided it would be interesting to compare the chief executives of fast-growing firms in the United States, Germany and Britain, but also compare the fast growers with a sample of slow growers in Britain. Hence my basic choice of interview samples was to be:

15 fast growers in the United States
15 fast growers in Germany
15 fast growers in Britain
15 slow growers in Britain
—
60

Because of continuing inflation, I decided to define growth as follows:

> Any firm growing at less than 10 per cent per annum, in money terms, was a *no grower.*
>
> Any firm growing at 10 per cent and up to 15 per cent per annum was a *grower.*
>
> Any firm growing at more than 15 per cent but up to 50 per cent per annum was a *fast grower.*
>
> Any firm growing at more than 50 per cent per annum was a *super-fast grower.*

Growth had to be measured over a recent period of at least five years, but it need not involve the latest year if there had been a recession in the industry. Growth was measured by either sales revenue or profits, provided that if the one grew, the other did not significantly fail to keep pace.

No particular size of company or type of industry was specified, except that the coverage of both size and industry should be wide and so far as possible without duplication in any one country.

How many interviews?

The total number of interviews held inevitably worked out differently from plan. After the first 25 test interviews in Britain, I did another 31, making 56 in all.

In the United States I was scheduled to do 15, but decided that this did not give me adequate coverage of either the super-large firms or the advanced technology industries, such as aerospace. Nor did it cover the American chief executives of major subsidiaries abroad, who could give me the other end of the picture viewed from head office. Altogether, therefore, I interviewed 31 American chief executives, of whom 24 were stationed in the continental United States, as far apart as New York and Los Angeles, and seven were abroad in charge of subsidiary companies.

In Germany I interviewed 16 chief executives, one more than

the required number because two were in fact at different levels in the same organization.

Thus the total interviews became:

Pilot survey	6
Follow-up test	19
British samples of fast and slow growers	31
American sample of fast growers plus special samples of super-large, advanced technology and overseas subsidiary firms	31
German sample of fast growers	16
	103

Who is a chief executive?

The term 'chief executive' was used because it is coming into increasing general use and it provides a break-through from the confusion between Chairman, President and Managing Director.

Who is the chief? If there is a full-time chairman, he is sometimes but not always named also as 'chief executive officer'. If the chairman is part-time, the president or managing director is almost invariably chief executive.

When approaching selected persons for interview, I used the phrase 'chief executive' sufficiently in my correspondence and phone calls to make it clear as to whom I wished to see. In three cases out of 103 I apparently saw someone who was not strictly the chief executive, but in one case he had recently ceased to hold that office and was now just full-time chairman, in another case he was president and very wide-ranging in his powers but his chairman actually had the title 'chief executive officer', and in the third case (in Germany) it was company policy that there should be no chief executive. I saw the administrative and financial member of the top team of four.

In fact the only problem with interviewing in Germany is that there is a considerable national feeling against the cult of the personality. This makes a chief executive sometimes even unwilling to identify himself apart from his colleagues, and it certainly makes him reluctant to be interviewed. Nevertheless, when the nature and circumstances of my study were explained, I was very generously received and assisted in Germany—as I was in the United States and Britain.

What were the questions?

The final form of the questionnaire is given in Appendix A. As will be seen, it contains basically two different types of questions: (*a*) those on career progress, personal characteristics and attitudes, the answers to which are analysed in Parts I and IV of this book, and (*b*) those on management practice, the answers to which are analysed in Parts II and III.

Who were the interviewees?

An analysis of the characteristics of the interviewees and of their firms is given in Chapter 2. Suffice it to say here that their firms ranged in size from under 200 employees to over 400,000.

A chief executive of a company of any significant size is a public figure. More particularly, his company is of public interest, at least to the employees, the customers, the firm's suppliers, the local community and the relevant government authorities. Even in Britain and America a chief executive is expected to avoid excessive exposure of his own personality, in contrast to obtaining the right kind of publicity for his firm.

Everything he says publicly must be said with very great care, bearing in mind the various 'publics' who may hear it.

In these circumstances I decided that, as with my earlier book, this new study of 'The Chief Executive' would have to carry anonymous quotations. This would be the only way to get to the heart of many management problems and attitudes. Hence every person interviewed has been given a pseudonym.

However, to help the reader see whether a statement made by a particular chief executive is relevant to the experience of his own size and type of firm, Appendix C carries a list of interviewees and against each pseudonym is a broad description of the type of industry and the size of firm (as defined in Chapter

2). For convenience of reference, this list has been designed as a fold-out. There is also, in Appendix B, a very detailed list of more than 200 industries operated in by the 103 interviewees. It is not, of course, possible to put these details against the pseudonyms in Appendix C without risk of having the interviewees identified.

Because readers would naturally be interested in knowing whether a particular quotation came from a German chief executive, a Briton or an American, different styles of pseudonym have been used for the three nationalities.

The Americans all have pseudonyms commencing with A.

The Germans all have pseudonyms commencing with D.

Logically, the British should have pseudonyms commencing with B. The majority do. However, some of the Britons are people who were chosen because they have founded and built up a business very rapidly. They are original capitalists. To distinguish them, and hence to appreciate the significance of this particular kind of chief executive, they have been given pseudonyms commencing with C.

There are seven original capitalists in the American sample and there are two in the German, but these are not significant samples compared with the 23 British original capitalists, so they are not distinguished by a difference in pseudonym.

The majority of chief executives in all samples are not significant share owners, although all the Americans have stock options and over a third of the British have recently installed incentive share schemes. There are only a few inheritors of business wealth amongst the samples, and they are not distinguished by style of pseudonym.

When I speak of a German or American or British chief executive, I do not imply any authenticity as to actual nationality. A 'German' might be of Swiss or Austrian nationality. If so, he was running a business in Germany and his native language was German. Equally a Briton or American might carry a different passport from what he appeared to hold. All that can be said for certain is that there is no obvious 'overlap' of the samples. I would not, for example, have interviewed as an

'American' somebody who admitted he was of British nationality. Again, I would not have interviewed as 'German' somebody from America running a business in Germany.

To sum up on nationality, the pseudonyms used in the book have initial letters as follows:

A = American
B = British
C = British original capitalist
D = Deutsch (German)

When was the interviewing done?

The pilot interviewing was spread out over nearly two years, to ensure that my working experience as a chief executive had maximum impact on the design and evolution of the questionnaire. But when it was completed, the rest of the interviewing was done in a relatively short period—the late summer, autumn and winter of 1970–1. The last interview was held on February 16, 1971, and the significance of this date will become apparent in Chapter 2. In addition to all the travel around Britain, the interviewing involved two long visits to the United States and four shorter visits to Germany.

How authentic are the quotations?

During each interview I made extensive notes, then I dictated the interview notes on to tape within 24 hours. This style of working is habitual for me, and so in the circumstances I can claim that I have a fairly 'photographic' memory. From my point of view, the words quoted are virtually verbatim what the man said, subject of course to editing to fit the context.

However, I cannot prove this, which means that any interviewee who thinks he is identified is free to deny that he actually said the words quoted, and in the literal sense, word for word, he will be speaking the truth. I did not take a tape recorder into any interview. To do so would destroy some of its frankness.

Having used the same system of anonymous reporting in the earlier book 'The Role of the Managing Director' and having received no complaints, I do not expect problems this time. One reason is that I have used a 104th pseudonym, *Mr. Extraman*, for a few risque quotes which I was very keen to use but which were personally dangerous if identified.

What about the fair sex?

I did try to interview two lady executives, but both were unwilling. By contrast, more than two-thirds of the men approached by me actually agreed. So this study has an all-male cast.

Moreover, it contains very little on the private lives of the participants. A few of the self-made businessmen did confide that their devotion to business had disrupted their family life, but the number of these 'confessions' was statistically insignificant. I did not invite them or provoke them. So there appeared to be nothing abnormal about the private lives of the interviewees—whatever 'normal' is these days.

How valid are the conclusions?

It was not my intention to make this a research study in the strict sense of the word 'research', as used by natural scientists. It has not been possible to set up hypotheses, test them exhaustively and reach valid conclusions on them.

The most that can be said is that I have made an enquiry into the career progress, attitudes and management methods of 103 chief executives in the United States, Britain and Germany. Altogether 78 of the interviews were carried out after the questionnaire was finally adapted.

Not all the questions were asked at all interviews. Only those which are answered in Parts I and IV of this book, relating to the career progress, personal characteristics and attitudes of chief executives, were asked persistently. Those questions which are answered in Parts II and III, relating to management practice, were asked when they seemed relevant to the circumstances of the firm and its chief executive.

By the nature of this enquiry into so many aspects of human behaviour in three countries, no claims can be made for having reached scientifically validated conclusions. In business management, however, it is useful to seek out and draw attention to the 'best practice' for dealing with a particular problem. This has been my habit over the years, and this is what I have done in Parts II and III. As for Parts I and IV, I have drawn my own inferences from the evidence presented. The reader is entitled to judge these inferences as well as to judge the evidence.

2

A COMPARATIVE STUDY OF CHIEF EXECUTIVES IN THE UNITED STATES, BRITAIN AND GERMANY

It was hoped and expected that this study would throw some light on why the economic growth rates of the United States and Germany are faster than that of Britain. The greatest number of questions were concentrated on management methods, not only to gather information and report on them, but also to see whether American and German chief executives seemed more efficient, more professionally competent than their British opposite numbers.

My personal judgement after 103 interviews is that marginally this may be so. Computerization has certainly gone further in the United States and Germany than in Britain. The present generation of American chief executives has certainly had more management education and the Germans have learnt more business economics (which is, of course, different from the economics largely taught in Britain). But as the evidence of the book shows, the British participants contributed an enormous amount of management know-how to this study.

Moreover, they included a deliberately chosen sample of chief executives of slow-growing or stagnant firms, almost all of which seemed to have surprisingly good managements. There was a surprising dearth of evidence that the slow-growing and stagnant firms were worse managed than the fast-growing firms, in the professional sense of having less acceptable attitudes and methods. I can say this only on the basis of having had some experience of management myself and of having asked the same set of questions, that seemed to me relevant, of each sample.

It could be that some of those who refused to see me did so because they knew they were bad managers. To this extent my sample could be biased. Nevertheless, I did actually see the chief executives of a sample of slow-growing and stagnant firms, who had all sorts of explanations, given in more detail in Chapter 10, as to why their firms were in the doldrums in spite of all the management efforts made so far. Important among these reasons were: the problems of obtaining planning permission; the slow growth rate of the British economy; the closing of traditional overseas markets; and the cutting off of traditional overseas sources of supply. But the firms themselves did not appear to be significantly lacking in management expertise.

What I did discover was something quite different. It was not something aimed at in the study. The extent and significance of this discovery was not known until February 23, 1971, seven days after the last interview, when at last it was possible to make a full analysis of the basic characteristics of all participants. Meanwhile almost all the chapters of this book had been put into first draft, using the information already to hand, with a view to incorporating the evidence of the last interviews during revision.

This chapter, however, containing the analysis of basic characteristics of participants, had been deliberately left to last. Hence the nature of the discovery came as a considerable surprise.

Overall dimensions of the survey

In order to understand the surprise results of the survey, one must see them in terms of the overall dimensions of the study. Therefore these dimensions are given first.

A total of 103 chief executives were interviewed in firms operating in over 200 product and service areas identified and listed alphabetically in Appendix B and classified by country and basic industry type in Table 2.1

The firms ranged in size from under 200 employees up to over 400,000 employees, the largest firm in size of capital assets having a net equity of over $2,400,000,000 (£1,000,000,000) and over 500,000 stockholders.

Table 2.1

CHIEF EXECUTIVES' MAIN INDUSTRIES CLASSIFIED BY COUNTRY AND BASIC TYPE

	United States	United Kingdom Original capitalist	United Kingdom Non-owning	Germany	Total
Consumer goods	9	4	9	7	29
Extraction and materials	3	1	2	2	8
Capital goods	11	7	13	4	35
Construction	0	3	0	0	3
Wholesale and retail	4	3	6	1	14
Service (incl. financial)	4	5	3	2	14
Total	31	23	33	16	103

The size range of firms, in terms of numbers of employees, is shown in Table 2.2.

Table 2.2

FIRMS CLASSIFIED BY NUMBER OF EMPLOYEES

Small (up to 200 employees)	3
Small to medium (over 200 and up to 1,000 employees)	22
Medium to large (over 1,000 and up to 10,000 employees)	35
Large (over 10,000 and up to 100,000 employees)	39
Super-large (over 100,000 employees)	4
Total	103

Effect of size on growth

It is obvious to every experienced businessman that fast-growing firms are easier to find amongst the small and small-to-medium than amongst the large and super-large. The latter usually have many products, supplied to a number of markets, and hence the odds are that if some of these markets are booming, others are not, with a net result of slow growth. By contrast, a smaller firm which happens to get itself into a growth market is likely to concentrate its resources and attention on this one market.

Table 2.3 compares growth rates with size. It will be recalled that the definition of:

Super grower is growth at more than 50 per cent per annum.
Fast grower is growth at 15 to 50 per cent per annum.
Grower is growth at 10 to 15 per cent per annum.
No grower is growth at less than 10 per cent per annum.

Moreover, it needs to be emphasized here that 'growth' in the tables of this survey means organic growth of a line of business activity, where due to its success in satisfying customers, demand for the firm's products exceeds supply. This sometimes means taking over other firms, though by far the greater part of growth in these tables is not due to takeovers. So far as is known, there is very little conglomerate growth in the firms in these tables. At the pilot stage of the survey, two chief executives were interviewed who could be described as conglomerate financiers, and this is acknowledged in the list shown in Table 2.10. But these financiers do not appear in any of the tables before 2.10.

From Table 2.3 it will be seen that none of the super-large firms is a super grower or even a fast grower. But equally it is clear that super growers and fast growers are not concentrated towards the small size end of the range. They are spread across the small to medium, medium to large and large categories.

Why the surprise at the results?

It must be remembered that this was intended as a study of management methods, not of company size or ownership. If, for example, I had planned a study of the influence of share ownership on business efficiency, I might well have planned it differently. In fact, however, I ignored ownership when choosing my samples.

Table 2.3

COMPARISON OF GROWTH RATES AND SIZE

	Super growers	Fast growers	Growers	No growers	Total
BRITAIN					
Super-large	0	0	0	1	1
Large	2	3	3	12	20
Medium to large	2	7	1	7	17
Small to medium	6	6	1	3	16
Small	1	0	1	0	2
Total	11	16	6	23	56
UNITED STATES					
Super-large	0	0	2	0	2
Large	4	4	5	2	15
Medium to large	2	4	5	0	11
Small to medium	1	1	1	0	3
Small	0	0	0	0	0
Total	7	9	13	2	31
GERMANY					
Super-large	0	0	1	0	1
Large	0	3	3	0	6
Medium to large	0	2	3	0	5
Small to medium	0	3	0	0	3
Small	0	1	0	0	1
Total	0	9	7	0	16

Because I live in Britain, I had long observed that some British businessmen are very successful and their firms have grown by 20, 50 or even 100 per cent or more a year, in trading revenue and profits, even though the country's economy as a whole is growing very slowly. So for my sample of fast-growing firms in Britain I naturally did a hand-picking job on these very fast growers. They seemed to make a fine comparison and contrast with the obvious slow-growers reported in the business and financial press.

My problem, however, was how to pick similar fast growers in the United States and Germany.

At first the United States looked easy. By perusing the 'Fortune' lists and Moody's Handbook of Common Stocks, I could pick the larger fast-growth companies. Through my stockbroker contacts I could find the names of newly listed companies of smaller size which had obviously grown fast. But it proved impossible to find anyone in the United States who would take exactly the same interest in hand-picking growth companies as I took myself in Britain.

At first Germany, too, looked easy. I gave a detailed briefing on my requirements to a business friend in Germany, and a lot of hard work was done on the selection. But the problem of interviewing across a 'language barrier' plus the German antipathy towards personal publicity, made the task rather difficult, and in the end we had to settle for a 'fast-growth' sample whose firm's rate of growth is slower than the American, which in turn is slower than the British. So these fast-growth samples are actually in the reverse order to national economic growth rates.

The problem of getting the right samples, and indeed the problem of getting samples at all, at long distance, plus my deep interest in studying management methods, diverted my attention from the factor of ownership. It is obviously more difficult to know in advance about ownership of firms in other countries than in one's own.

Hence the full significance of how the total interview sample would analyse out did not strike me until February 23, 1971, after the last interview had been held. Fortunately, I had asked mostly the same basic questions all the way through, even though the questionnaire had changed its shape during the first 25 interviews. Hence I was able to go back to the large British sample and to the larger-than-intended American sample, regroup the participants and find even further evidence to support my surprising results.

Who is an original capitalist?

To explain these results, one must take a look at what is meant by an 'original capitalist'.

In this survey I am using the phrase for someone who previously did not have any significant amount of capital, and who then starts a business in which he has a substantial share stake, but more particularly, in which he profoundly believes because he has original ideas on how to supply a particular type of customer with a particular product or service on worthwhile economic terms that will make his business grow rapidly to meet the needs of more customers. Of course there must be plenty of 'original capitalists' who do not succeed in this way, but I am concerned here only with successful original capitalists.

There are also a few cases in the survey which I have described as semi-capitalist because the chief executive concerned, though not a major owner of the business, has been able to acquire or has been helped to acquire a significant share stake because he is the key man in regenerating an existing business. This process of helping a key man become a semi-capitalist is, of course, older than formal stock option schemes or share incentive schemes for company executives in general.

All other chief executives in the survey, that is all except those classified as Original Capitalists or Semi Capitalists, have been classified as Executives. A few of these have inherited some shares, but their behaviour does not appear to be significantly different from that of non-owning chief executives. They happen to be wealthy persons who happen to have executive responsibilities—in contrast to the attitude of an original capitalist who has been through the specific educative experience of acquiring shares for the first time and building up a business, hence understanding how capital is accumulated, its nature and significance when judging the worthwhileness of a new business project.

Table 2.4 gives the surprise results of the survey, for it compares growth rates with ownership status, and it shows that in this survey all 18 of the super-fast growers, that is the firms growing at more than 50 per cent per annum, have as chief executive an original capitalist. And perhaps just as significant, in

Britain, the country with the slowest rate of economic growth and at the time of this survey, the highest personal tax rates, 11 out of the 16 fast growers also have as chief executives an original capitalist. In fact altogether 22 out of 27 fast and super-fast growers in Britain have an original capitalist as chief executive. Four of the others are semi-capitalist, and only one, so far as can be ascertained, comes in the non-owning executive category. It is almost as if there were a law saying that only capitalists can make a firm grow fast in Britain.

Table 2.4

COMPARISON OF GROWTH RATES AND OWNERSHIP STATUS

	Super growers	Fast growers	Growers	No growers	Total
BRITAIN					
Original capitalist	11	11	0	0	22
Semi-capitalist	0	4	0	0	4
Executive	0	1	6	23	30
Total	11	16	6	23	56
UNITED STATES					
Original capitalist	7	0	0	0	7
Semi-capitalist	0	0	0	0	0
Executive	0	9	13	2	24
Total	7	9	13	2	31
GERMANY					
Original capitalist	0	2	0	0	2
Semi-capitalist	0	0	0	0	0
Executive	0	7	7	0	14
Total	0	9	7	0	16

By contrast in the United States and Germany there are nine and seven non-owning executives, respectively, running fast-growing firms. Executives in the United States and Germany have presumably found the rewards of fast growth more worth while.

By the nature of the sampling process, there are no super-fast growth German firms in the survey, but it is significant that even in America, where the tax position has been easier for executives than in Britain, all seven super-fast growth firms are run by original capitalists.

One is led to wondering whether there isn't, perhaps, something in this capitalist business, and whether the way to get more growth is to create more capitalists. Certainly a lot of the growth of west European countries and Japan, rebuilding their economies after 1945, can be explained in terms of original capitalists starting up and building on their own, without the sophisticated executive career structures and financial markets of Britain and the United States. But let us leave such speculation until nearer the end of the book, when we have seen all the evidence.

Meanwhile we should look more closely at the characteristics of chief executives in the various samples.

Table 2.5 compares the age, education and ownership status of the chief executives of the fastest-growing British and American firms and the fast-growing German firms. Readers will appreciate that, because of the smallness of the samples, the average percentage growth rates cannot be considered in any way as accurate measures. Both arithmetic averages and medians are shown.

At first sight this table might suggest that successful British businessmen are under-educated, but that this is no bad thing, because their businesses grow faster than those of their better-educated American and German counterparts.

However, when Table 2.5 is read in conjunction with Table 2.6, it certainly is not true that under-education is good for growth. Of more significance is ownership status. By far the fastest growers in Table 2.5 are the British, who are all original capitalists. Next come the Americans, of whom seven out of 15 are original capitalists.

Table 2.6 splits off the American seven original capitalists from the next 15 fastest growers, in order of growth rate, who are of course all non-owning executives.

These two samples are then compared with the 13 German

non-owning executives, after taking out the two German original capitalists.

Table 2.5

COMPARISON OF AGE, EDUCATION AND OWNERSHIP STATUS WITH GROWTH RATE IN THREE NATIONS

	Rate of growth	Ownership status	Age	Education
British fastest growers	AV = 170%	C = 15	AV = 46	University = $\frac{4}{15}$
	MED = 80%	E = 0	MED = 44	Postgrad = $\frac{0}{15}$
American fastest growers	AV = 34½%	C = 7	AV = 53	University = $\frac{13}{15}$
	MED = 25%	E = 8	MED = 53	Postgrad = $\frac{6}{15}$
German fast growers	AV = 18%	C = 2	AV = 50	University = $\frac{13}{15}$
	MED = 15%	E = 13	MED = 48	Postgrad = $\frac{9}{15}$

Table 2.6

COMPARISON OF AGE, EDUCATION AND OWNERSHIP STATUS WITH GROWTH RATE. AMERICANS AND GERMANS

	Rate of growth	Ownership status	Age	Education
American original capitalists	AV = 46%	C = 7	AV = 52	University = $\frac{6}{7}$
	MED = 20%	E = 0	MED = 49	Postgrad = $\frac{4}{7}$
American executive fast growers	AV = 18%	C = 0	AV = 56	University = $\frac{14}{15}$
	MED = 12%	E = 15	MED = 56	Postgrad = $\frac{7}{15}$
German executive fast growers	AV = 15%	C = 2	AV = 50	University = $\frac{12}{13}$
	MED = 15%	E = 13	MED = 48	Postgrad = $\frac{8}{13}$

Table 2.6 suggests that in America the Ph.D.s and other postgraduates who go into business on their own seem to do all right. These highly educated original capitalists have a growth rate roughly twice that of the also-well-educated non-owning next 15 chief executives in the survey, whose rate of growth is similar to that of their similarly well-educated German counterparts.

A few words about educational qualifications. Most of the postgraduates in this survey have higher degrees, but because this is a survey of businessmen, a professional qualification, such as in law or accountancy, on top of a first degree, is counted as 'postgraduate', whether or not it involved taking a university course. Similarly a full professional qualification counts as equivalent to a first degree when no actual university degree was obtained. Throughout all samples of the survey there are sprinklings of lawyers and accountants, and substantial minorities of engineers.

Amongst the Americans in the survey there is a significant minority of business school graduates. Even amongst the Britons and Germans there are some, and amongst the Germans, seven out of 15 in Table 2.5 studied business economics.

Because there has been a historical trend towards rising standards of education, it might be thought that a comparison of older executives with younger executives would show the latter to have a higher general level of education. Table 2.7 makes such a comparison of the older half of the American, British and German samples with the younger half. It is clear from this that there is no significant relationship between age and education in these samples.

Table 2.8 compares the education of chief executives in the survey with the size of their firms. In the British sample there is a discernible relationship. Almost half the non-graduates are running small-to-medium firms. By contrast the greatest number of graduates are running large firms. This same relationship is suggested, less emphatically, in the combined figures for all three nations in the survey. The American and German samples on their own are not large enough to indicate any significant relationships.

Table 2.7

COMPARISON OF OWNERSHIP STATUS AND EDUCATION WITH AGE. THREE NATIONS

	Average Age	Ownership status	Education
Older Americans	58	C = 2	N = 3
		E = 13	U = 7
			P = 5
Younger Americans	46	C = 5	N = 1
		E = 10	U = 6
			P = 8
Older Britons	61	C = 8	N = 11
		SC = 2	U = 16
		E = 18	P = 1
Younger Britons	42	C = 15	N = 10
		SC = 1	U = 17
		E = 12	P = 1
Older Germans	55	C = 0	N = 0
		E = 8	U = 3
			P = 5
Younger Germans	44	C = 2	N = 3
		E = 6	U = 2
			P = 3

N = non-graduate
U = university graduate or equivalent
P = postgraduate

Table 2.8

COMPARISON OF EDUCATION OF CHIEF EXECUTIVES AGAINST SIZE OF FIRM

		Small	Small-medium	Medium-large	Large	Super-large
American	Postgrad	0	0	4	8	1
	Grad	0	2	6	5	1
	Non-grad	0	1	2	1	0
British	Postgrad	0	1	0	1	0
	Grad	2	5	11	14	1
	Non-grad	0	10	6	5	0
German	Postgrad	0	2	3	3	1
	Grad	0	1	2	1	0
	Non-grad	1	0	0	2	0
Three nations together	Postgrad	0	3	7	12	2
	Grad	2	8	19	20	2
	Non-grad	1	11	8	8	0

However, the survey does not on the whole indicate any tendency for the highly educated to avoid small firms. As we have already seen, some of the American and German original capitalists are postgraduates. Indeed there are altogether 11 graduates and postgraduates running small to medium firms and the two chief executives of British small firms in the survey are both graduates.

Table 2.9 compares the British fastest growers, who are all original capitalists with the next 15 fast growers who are mostly executives, and with the no growers who are all executives.

Table 2.9

COMPARISON OF AGE, EDUCATION AND OWNERSHIP STATUS WITH GROWTH RATE. BRITISH ONLY

	Rate of growth	Ownership status	Age	Education
British fastest growers	AV = 170%	C = 15	AV = 46	University = $\frac{4}{15}$
	MED = 80%	E = 0	MED = 44	Postgrad = $\frac{0}{15}$
British medium-fast growers	AV = 22%	C = 2	AV = 49	University = $\frac{7}{15}$
		SC = 2	MED = 48	
	MED = 20%	E = 11		Postgrad = $\frac{1}{15}$
British no growers	AV = 3·6%	C = 0	AV = 56	University = $\frac{11}{15}$
	MED = 5%	E = 15	MED = 58	Postgrad = $\frac{1}{15}$

Again, at first sight it looks, from Table 2.9, as though the more educated a businessman becomes the slower the growth rate of his firm. But we know from the German and American samples that higher education is not or need not be a brake on economic progress. What is significant about Table 2.9 is again the interrelationship between ownership status and growth rate. The original capitalists have an average growth rate at least 16 times that of the non-owning executives group.

Before leaving this comparative study of the participants in the survey, we should turn again to the thoughts expressed earlier that perhaps there is 'something in this capitalist business', and that maybe 'the way to get more growth is to create more capitalists'.

Are these thoughts putting too much emphasis on the importance of ownership in crystallizing a chief executive's initiative and drive so that his growth rate is above average? Could it be that ownership is not a significant factor, and that perhaps the fast-growth people in this survey, who happen to be original capitalists, are also in the fast-growth industries or the advanced technology industries?

Table 2.10 lists alphabetically the industries of all the original capitalists plus the four semi-capitalists in the survey, whether British, American or German. Where an industry is represented more than once in the list, this is shown by a number in parentheses.

Table 2.10

ALPHABETICAL LIST OF INDUSTRIES OF ORIGINAL CAPITALISTS IN SURVEY—BRITISH, AMERICAN AND GERMAN

Aerospace

Building equipment
Building materials
Building supplies

Chemicals and electronics
Computers
Construction (2)
Construction services
Construction supplies
Construction vehicles

Electronics (2)
Electronics and electrical

Finance (2)
Food Processing
Furniture

Home chemicals
Hotels and restaurants

Industrial machinery

Mining
Motor service

Pharmaceuticals
Plastics
Publishing

Retail (clothes)
Retail (domestic equipment)
Retail (food)
Retail (food, clothing, hardware, furniture)
Retail (jewellery, watches, etc)

Toys (2)
Transport
Travel

Waste disposal

Though the chemical (including pharmaceutical), electronics and aerospace industries are actually represented in Table 2.10, by no stretch of the imagination could it be described as a list of advanced technology industries, or indeed as a list of predominantly fast-growth industries. Moreover, as the reader already knows, the great majority of these capitalists are in Britain, whose economy had been growing slowly compared with those of other major industrial nations, in the years before the survey.*

Though a substantial number of the capitalists in the survey may indulge in patent and design registration in order to protect new products as much as possible, in many fields of business activity and indeed in most of those listed in Table 2.10, such legal protection is of limited value.

As can be seen from the table, a lot of the fast growth occurs in industries where people are providing such everyday necessities as food, clothing and shelter. Having met these capitalists, my abiding impression is that very few owe any significant amount of their success to strong patent or design positions. They are for the most part just good businessmen, in the sense that they have observed closely and thought through thoroughly the actual needs of their customers, and have then gone to endless pains to see that their customers get what they want.

* When the results of this survey were seen to be pointing to the significance of ownership as a factor influencing growth, an attempt was made to find samples of fast-growth companies in the United States and Federal Germany, equivalent to the super fast and fast growth samples in Britain.

However, the new samples chosen in the United States and Germany by local experts did not come anywhere near the average growth rate of the original British samples. The reason seems clearly to be that the British super fast and fast growth samples were chosen by watching the business press with eagle eyes over a period of more than two years. Anybody given a similar brief at short notice could not be nearly so successful, though Germany and America undoubtedly contain many success stories of fast-growth firms.

Federal Germany is a member of the European Common Market and the United States of America is itself a large common market. I believe that this is an important factor accounting for their superior growth rates. But the fact that Britain can produce some super fast and fast growth businesses in spite of a low overall growth rate, suggests that the British economy could grow faster if it were within a large common market, more suited to its degree of industrial sophistication.

PART I

HOW THE CHIEF EXECUTIVE HAS ACQUIRED HIS SKILLS

3

PERSONALITY TYPES IN THE CHIEF EXECUTIVE'S CHAIR

Before looking closely at how chief executives acquired the particular skills that seem necessary in their job, we need to look at what kind of people they are.

Are chief executives mostly extrovert or introvert?

It was not, of course, possible to give a personality test to the chief executives interviewed. But almost all of them were asked their own views on whether they were more inclined to introversion, or more inclined to extroversion.

The popular view of a successful businessman seems to be that of a dashing extrovert. But this is not the general view that chief executives have of themselves. In the first half of the survey, 39 per cent claimed to be introverts, 45 per cent claimed to be extroverts and 16 per cent either didn't know or answered in such a way that they claimed some characteristics of both.

Because the popular view is one of extroversion, any bias in the answers given is likely to be towards emphasizing extroversion factors.

The tendency to bias is well epitomized by the head of an American machinery manufacturing firm:

'People tell me I am an introvert and that is probably true, but all introverts think they are extroverts.'

Because of this, and because of the embarrassment that the question seemed to create, I found myself intent on improving the 'bedside manner' with which it was presented. For the second half of the survey I provided much more reassurance to the participants, along these lines: 'Obviously, to reach the position you have, you need some of the characteristics of both introversion and extroversion. But if a fine line were drawn down between them and you had to say whether you leant ever so slightly towards introversion, or towards extroversion, which way would you say you were inclined to lean—even if ever so slightly?'

This rewording of the question produced a major shift in the answers. Now 63 per cent admitted to being introverts, 29 per cent to being extroverts and only 7 per cent claimed to be both. One of these middle answers was: 'I try to be as extrovert as I can, but my wife says I am more introverted.' So even here there was the possibility of someone being more introverted than he cared to admit.

When both halves of the survey were put together, 51 per cent of the total are admitted introverts, 38 per cent are admitted extroverts and 11 per cent are both, or don't know. These admittedly unreliable figures do seem to suggest that at least half of the chief executives in the survey are inclined towards introversion.

How then does the popular image of extroversion arise? It certainly does not come from the social life lived by company chiefs. In fact, one of the characteristics of many successful businessmen, as was clear from the interviews, is that however extrovert they may appear to be in their business activities, they are extremely shy in social life. Many of them tend to avoid social activities and compensate for this by working extra hard in their business.

Says a titled British head of a major international group: 'My decisions are made with my colleagues, in discussion, and are not made by communing alone. In this sense I am extrovert. But in the sense that I do not go to big dinner parties at the Savoy, I am introvert.'

Rare is that special kind of determination shown by the

hereditary American head of a world-wide business who knows in his heart that he is an introvert, but who is determined to have a more balanced image: 'I do a lot more socializing, both in business and in private life, than I am really comfortable doing. I don't average two nights a week at home.'

The German head of a business with a household name takes a major part in industry affairs on a national scale. He has a similar personality situation: 'To myself I am more inclined to introversion, to others I have been considered as more inclined to extroversion.'

Who, then, manufactures the extrovert image of the typical businessman?

An English vehicle builder who has created his own multi-million-pound business from scratch in the last 25 years, gives one answer: 'I am not as extrovert as public relations and newspaper people are trying to suggest. I am shy and retiring. I have to push myself to be the extrovert public figure because it is good for the company.'

Could it be that different types of industry, and different circumstances, require different types of personality?

There may be something in this. Here are two examples, though it is not suggested that they are of general application.

The head of a retail group: 'I am more extrovert. I do have the ability to select people to fulfil responsibility. An extrovert is better able to gauge abilities and how they rub off and also judge the people with whom we do business, such as our suppliers.'

The chief executive of a mass production engineering firm: 'I am possibly more introverted. I generally like to let people think an idea is theirs. Then they have a lot of interest in carrying out the job. Drop a few hints and let them figure the whole think out my way.'

If one were choosing a new chief executive for a consumer goods firm with big advertising and marketing requirements, one might be inclined to appoint an extrovert. In any case, when an outsider is appointed to be chief executive of an existing company, there may be a tendency to choose an extrovert character who can come in and grapple confidently with the existing situation.

However, the building up of a new business from scratch, or the introduction of new policies to an old business, requires qualities of creative imagination that are likely to be at least as prevalent in the introverts, if not more so than in the extroverts. And when these qualities are present, the introverts find their own way of coping with the situation.

Here is the experience of a highly inventive engineer who has built up a large international trade: 'It's much more difficult to run a static business. You've got to be a strong personality. I am not, so I've had to go all out for expansion and enthusiasm, and with these things they follow your lead.'

Possibly this engineer underrates his ability to adapt his own behaviour to the requirements of running his very successful business.

Is there any evidence, then, that outward behaviour patterns can be changed?

There is no measurable evidence in the survey, but it is significant that over 38 per cent of those who confessed to introversion in the second half of the survey added a comment to the effect that they had had to become more extrovert. Here are typical comments:

'I had to work my way through college and didn't have much time to be very extrovert, so I was rather introverted early and became more extrovert later.'

'In early life I tended to be an introvert. But it soon became clear that for career purposes one should not be an introvert, so I became a converted extrovert. One must get heard, particularly in sales.'

'You can change, and you have to, if you are going to run a business.'

'In business life I am more extroverted, in personal life I am more introverted. I force myself to participate as a matter of business discipline. But I prefer to go fishing or read a book.'

'I am more of an introvert with an appetite to be an extrovert. A lot of people have a bit of the ham in them, they like to be on stage. I guess I have that desire, more perhaps than the ability.'

'I am more introverted. Nevertheless you have to be something of an actor. You must feel the reaction of the public to you. It is corrupting, too. You come to like it.'

Are the psychological concepts of introversion and extroversion of much use, then, in analysing the personalities of chief executives?

However useful they may be in the clinic when treating patients or in the classroom when analysing and educating children, there is a case for saying that they are of limited use in the analysis of mature adults of above-average learning ability and motivation—which is what chief executives surely are. These people, because of their abilities and self-help attitudes, are more than usually capable of adapting themselves to the changing requirements of life. To the extent that outward behaviour patterns are changeable, they have a high capacity for change.

In the world of business management, I have found that a helpful way of analysing managers is in terms of their relative abilities at using two quite distinct types of mental process:

(*a*) the ability to be conceptual and deep-thinking, and
(*b*) the ability to be observant and quickly responsive to the immediate situation.

Moreover, I have noticed that some managers are good at both, some are good at one and not the other. To be good at one often means to overplay it and hence to underdevelop the other. There is an analogy in boxing. Some boxers are good with both right hand and left. But if a boxer is particularly good with one hand, he has to be careful not to neglect the other, or it will, in terms of boxing strength, atrophy.

Because this simple classification of managers can be helpful, I followed up the question on introversion and extroversion in the survey with one on conceptual and responsive skills. The immediate and spontaneous reaction of over a third of participants in the survey was: 'That's a good question', or some similar remark.

I asked initially which of these skills, the conceptual or the responsive, is more important for running a business. Altogether 20 per cent said it was more important to be deep thinking and conceptual, another 20 per cent said it was more important to be observant and quickly responsive, while the remaining 60 per cent said it was important to be both. Wherever possible I then asked them for examples of uses of these respective skills, and obtained a fund of varied experiences, classified as follows:

In which situations is it more important to be observant and quickly responsive?

Those who had built up their own businesses to medium size were inclined to answer, like MR. CHRISTIE who is a manufacturer, that in the early stages 'it is more important to be responsive to market trends and conditions. One must be ultra-fast in one's reactions.'

In the fashion-conscious industries, observation is at least as important as creativity. 'You must go with observed trends rather than create them,' says MR. CHILDS.

'In business generally,' says MR. DACKWEILER, 'quick reaction is particularly important because of the market.'

MR. BELLAMY runs a widely diversified group. 'The quick operator, the observant and quickly responsive person is needed here in the chief executive's chair,' he says. 'I can hire better skills to do the long-range planning, the deep thinking and conceptual stuff.'

A similar outlook is that of MR. BLUNDELL, who is head of a large design-oriented business, and an engineer by background: 'I don't think I can be deep thinking on the details of the company. Rather my assignment is to make sure that those who have the knowledge and position to do the deep thinking and the development have every opportunity to do it and that their views are taken fully into account.'

What are the special situations which require a chief executive to give priority to deep thinking and conceptualization?

There are some industries where quick action does not get you very far. MR. BLOOMFIELD sells fashion-influenced durable goods. He describes this as being 'a bit like driving a motor car without any brakes. If there is a sudden slump, I can only plan what to do in six months. I can do gimmicks like getting my salesmen to stand on their heads or wear top hats, but I cannot alter the product. I have to think in August this year what I am going to be selling in September next year.'

Also there are large unified groups with one product or a group of products, where the firm's commitments would make quick action a disaster. Says MR. BEATTY: 'I have seen too much of people who see a set of figures and who act too quickly. I fall back on trends. Recently it was the longer and total picture which demanded that I close the xyz shop.'

In some of the science-based industries, the thinking has to be way ahead of the customers. 'It is not enough any more to be merely responsive,' says MR. AVERY. 'This is too late. Technology is helping us to anticipate rather than to respond.'

In what circumstances is a change in emphasis needed in a business, from the chief executive being observant and quickly responsive, to his being deep thinking and conceptual?

As a business grows from its early beginnings, a change like this may well take place. MR. CLARK explains: 'When our business was small and very dynamic, growing like topsy, I had to take everything as it came, so to be observant and quickly responsive was most important. Now we have the biggest share of the market and a three year lead in technology over our competitors. I have to spend far more time on organization structure and with big bankers. I need to be more deep thinking and conceptual.'

A similar change may be needed when a new chief executive takes over a failing business. MR. BIGGS had this experience: 'I came in here seven years ago. In the time since, profits have risen threefold. When you take over a firm that is run down, you have to be quick off the mark, and it's easy. You can make a very important contribution very quickly. You cut out this and that which is overstaffed or not selling well. Then you have the problem of formulating a plan and looking into the future.'

MR. ARNOLD: An organization is like a person. While it is on the rise, the responsive skills are needed very greatly, although the cause of the rise may have been the original use of conceptual skills. But once you get past the peak, as the aero-space industry has in California, you need the conceptual skills to point the way to where you should be going now.

MR. BOWLES: It depends on the stage the business is at. All big businesses go through a stage when you need the deep thinking and conceptualization, but the need for observation and quick response is always present. Mind you, this is easier to delegate—discovering what is going wrong. What is normally difficult is to get people to accept what is going wrong and to write off their errors. It is very important to be willing to recognize quickly enough that you have made a flop of something—to have the courage to cut it out. As my predecessor said, you have to go into these markets impulsively on insufficient facts, and therefore you must be willing to pull out quickly. The chief executive's style must suit the state the business is in, whether for example it has lost its way. A lot of businesses have lost their way.

However, the experience of the majority of chief executives in the survey is that there is a continuing need to be both conceptual and responsive. Indeed one might suggest that a person would be handicapped in the chief executive's chair if he could not be both. The following examples illustrate the need for both skills:

MR. ATTWOOD: In a service industry like this our success depends on how well we serve clients and how well we are perceived by the clients, so I suppose responsiveness is in some ways the more important, but the conceptual approach is very important for thinking of new ways to conduct the business and new concepts that may serve the client best. If you are not conceptual, you can not be responsive to the needs of your client.

MR. ATKINS: If you just react to the situations that arise, this precludes any long range planning. Moreover, you've got to let people under you have their freedom and then you react to their actions, so there must be some responsiveness too.

MR. ATTFIELD: I would like to spend all my time at deep thinking and conceptual work, and if you have a good staff you can do more of it, but you cannot divorce yourself from the daily decisions. A most frustrating thing for the staff is not to have decisions from the top.

MR. ANTHONY: In our size of company, a person who can't be both, is going to fall flat. As the business has grown larger I have been able to spend more time on conceptual aspects of the job and less time on day-to-day matters. But if I ever lose consciousness of the day-to-day problems the chaps won't do a proper job.

Each of our 15 operating divisions runs as a profit centre, with its own design, manufacturing and marketing facilities. You might think the head of each division would run it as an independent company, but he won't because he has a group vice-president to whom he reports and the group vice-president won't because he reports to me. They consciously or unconsciously accept that certain things are out of their orbit.

I have continually to fulfil my role with them. I must know what they are doing. They may have a serious problem and not tell me, but it is up to me to know all the same. The solution to their problem may be distasteful in that it is a solution they would take if they were running their own independent business, but they may not even suggest it to me. I have to encourage them to suggest it forthrightly and sometimes I have to suggest the answer myself. I have to use devious ways of filling in all the bits of information.

Where a company has both a full-time chairman and a full-time president or managing director, to some extent the division of duties may be made along conceptual versus responsive lines.

MR. ASKEW: As chairman, I must be deep thinking and conceptual. The man I have as president and his group vice-presidents must be observant and quickly responsive to immediate situations.

MR. BRIDGES: Now that I am at the top I am more inclined to be introverted again. I am required to be more deep thinking and conceptual.

MR. ARROWSMITH, who is a company president: Because we produce very expensive products in small numbers, everybody wants to deal with me. It is top-level people who make the decisions to buy such products. Hence I am continually being pummelled by immediate problems. I have to be observant and quickly responsive, there is not enough time to be deep thinking and conceptual.

How interdependent are the conceptual and responsive skills in most chief executives?

MR. CAMERON considers that they are completely interdependent. He thinks deeply about business problems because he is responsive, and he responds because he thinks deeply: 'Every business is to do with people. If you don't respond to them you think fallaciously.'

MR. DAHLMANN is head of a large international group. Even at his level, he must periodically engage in detailed activities, 'both to get things done and because if you live always with generalities, you get out of touch. You must give a personal impetus to particular projects and make people realize you're not a god but a man who happens to have more responsibility and pays more taxes.'

The interdependence of the two mental processes is explained in system terms by MR. ACLAND: 'You set up alarm mechanisms for being observant and quickly responsive, and when they are triggered you react with diligence to do the deep thinking and conceptualizing. The alarms are not going off all the time, hopefully, so you can do your conceptualization of what you would like the company to be in future years.'

It is important, however, to distinguish between the need for making quick decisions about some immediate situations and the need for allowing longer-term problems time to mature.

MR. CONSTABLE: The role of the decision-maker is today blown up too big. One is assumed to have to make a decision today. But maybe tomorrow would be better. One may have to wait for the last 10 per cent of the information.

MR. DILLMANN: Some questions have to be thought over a long time and must get mature and then suddenly you say, now is the moment. Others come to you for quick decision and it must be made quickly or people get disturbed. Here are examples. Our engineers wanted new offices, but I kept saying there was no money. Then the computer people were needing to expand. Then later I had a deputation from the chemists who wanted more space for the library and the patents department. Then suddenly it came to me that I had the right project—to build that new building over there with the data processing on the ground floor, then four floors for the engineers, then the library and patents department on the top two floors.

Here is another example. Data processing is my responsibility. It must be organized from the top, for it is a new kind of communication. I looked at one of the computers and said immediately that the capacity was too small, they must have more storage. I said this after asking just a few questions. Even the computer experts wondered why I said it. Now they have told me today they wouldn't be able to manage without the extra storage. When you are running a company you must have the right and responsibility at times to make a quick decision.

Some of the apparently quick responses made in business are in fact well-thought-out decisions. MR. ATKINSON puts it this way: 'I can make a decision quickly because of my experience in this business. It is important to know your business very well so that you can shorten the time for decisions.' MR. COLE takes a similar approach: 'First decisions are nearly always right. But you want to be thinking about the business all the time. I have lived for it. I am always ready to take a decision, and it falls into place precisely because I have been thinking about the business.'

4

HIS APPROACH TO KEEPING UP TO DATE AND TRAINING

Because he is the centre to which information must be designed to flow, a chief executive does not usually have a major problem in keeping up to date. There is a fair chance that any new, significant information about his markets or his products will come to him in the course of day-to-day operation of his business.

The internal, company sources of information available to keep the head of a business up to date, range from daily, weekly and monthly reports on current activities up to periodic reports on activities concerned with new ventures.

The internal methods of up-dating specifically mentioned in the survey were the following:

1. *Watching customers.* This ranges all the way from watching the reactions of customers in a retail store, to watching the behaviour of an industrial customer when you present your own product or service. He has probably had a presentation from your closest competitor. A chance remark or attitude will tell you important facts you could never find out directly.
2. *Operating statements.* Following closely the trends of figures is essential to keep the business in the black. But it is also the best memory-jogger for making you ask WHY, when something goes wrong. It starts the curiosity ball rolling.

3. *Reading the mail.* One letter from an irate customer can tell you a lot that may not come any other way.
4. *Checking major purchase orders.* This may be essential for control of credit and expenditure. It is also another way of keeping abreast of what is being wanted today and tomorrow.
5. *Sales staff reports.* The primary purposes of these reports may be to check on the efficiency of salesmen, and to sort out who are the best types of customers for the business. But an extra copy of each report can be used to keep top management up to date. Explains MR. BIGGS: 'We are very interested in what the customer has to say and why, about our products. Our report forms are specially designed for this, and they are discussed at our board meetings.'
6. *Internal technical reports.* Says MR. BLUNDELL: 'I get all the important reports that lead up to a new project.' Fortunately for him, he is an engineer at the head of an engineering business. MR. ACLAND runs a science-based business with a number of product divisions. His background is law and chemical engineering. He is able to cope with technical reports because: 'Firstly, we don't go into areas beyond my span of comprehension. Secondly, I also do a lot of reading. And thirdly, we have the track record of people who have reported to us in the past and how it worked out.'

A contrary view is taken by MR. BELLAMY, who says: 'It is a plus point that I cannot keep up to date on all the various products, their technicalities and markets. I am not going to become product obsessed and want to play with it and know what it is all about. If you are a good manager, you can make ball-bearings just as well as marmalade.'

Whilst it is clearly possible for a 'good manager' to take charge of an ailing business and cut out the dead wood, being more or less right about the main decisions even if he is not steeped in the particular industry, it is more difficult for him to take a positive approach and build up a business unless he knows it thoroughly. Certainly the original capitalists in this survey, whose growth record was so outstanding, seemed to be steeped in the industries that they built up.

7. *Listening and asking questions.* As we shall discuss more fully in Chapter 21, a chief executive must be continually gathering information as he moves about. Perhaps the biggest impression he can make on young managers and staff is to take an interest in what they do. But this also helps to keep him up to date.
8. *Acquisitions.* Even when an acquisition does not come off, the amount of investigation involved and the amount of information it produces can both be phenomenal.
9. *International business ventures.* Here are two quite different examples. MR. BLUNDELL takes the chair at the twice-yearly meetings of his managing directors' committee, where new developments are discussed on an inter-continental basis. MR. DACKWEILER went into partnership with a North American firm in South America. This indirectly brought know-how to the parent company in Germany.
10. *Long-term planning.* In the words of MR. DAUTZENBERG: 'We keep up to date as a result of our long term planning work.' The discipline of planning causes information to be gathered about market and technical trends which might otherwise be neglected. It is just one of the reasons for commissioning market research.

The external sources of information mentioned in the survey and used by chief executives in keeping up to date were the following:

11. *Watching changes in fashion and human taste.* This is fine, but to do it you need a high level of the observation power discussed in Chapter 3. And you also need an analytical approach. As MR. CHISHOLM explains: 'I go around looking at shops, I absorb from the outside and try to analyse why they are a success.'

12. *Travel.* See how they do it in another country, another continent, be it America, Europe or Japan. This means visiting the competition. Often a competitor in another country will be more frank and helpful than in your own country.

13. *Reading domestic publications*, even when your product or service is at one remove from the domestic market. Says MR. BAXTER, who sells directly to the building industry: 'I am very close to the housewife and the man in the street, who are the ultimate buyers.'

14. *General reading of the daily press.* It was through a newspaper report on the development of polypropylene that MR. BOSWORTH came to use this material in his products. But others can do some of the reading for you. MR. AUSTIN has a widely spread business and he sees that local offices clip their local papers and send up relevant items to head office.

15. *Reading of technical, trade and business journals.* To prevent this becoming a burden, MR. CLARK has a system of prescribed reading for every director, to cover all the relevant journals. This in his case includes journals from each of the leading industrial countries.

16. *Use of a clipping service* to provide clippings of every public mention of specified subjects, as well as mentions of your own company. MR. DOEBEL has the clippings provided for him by his secretary to read on planes and in hotels.

17. *Membership of a management association.* In exchanging management know-how, people have to tell you a fair amount about their business. MR. ASKEW, like some other Americans in the survey, belongs to the Presidents' Association.

18. *Membership of trade associations.* A casual word from a competitor about prices, costs or discounts can fill in an incomplete picture for an alert businessman.

19. *Membership of an industry training organization.* Says MR. BEATTY: 'I meet other employers and also trade union leaders and educationalists prominent in my field.'

20. *Membership of an international professional or trade association.* This is where the friendships can go deep, under an overlay of international brotherly love. And this is where people can be frank indeed and helpful to each other, if they do not compete extensively in each other's territories.
21. *Visiting salesmen of computers and management techniques.* Explains MR. BAYLISS: 'Nobody can come into my office and try to sell me something to improve my business without imparting highly relevant know-how. He has probably already been to some of my competitors.'

Training

The chief executive's attitude to training is largely conditioned by the fact that he is doing it to himself all the time, in the course of keeping up to date. In the words of MR. CLEMENTS: 'A man who cannot keep learning isn't mature.' As we shall see in later chapters, there is a case for saying that it is the ability to master certain fundamental skills, in particular the Numerical Skills, the System Skills, the Social Skills and the Policy-forming Skills, which marks out the man of all-round maturity who is capable of successfully leading a business organization. And mastery of a skill does not mean that one knows all there is to know about it. Mastery involves both the ability to use the skill and the ability to go on learning it, adapting it to meet changing circumstances.

However, there is a marked difference in approach to learning between the original capitalists and the executives. MR. CLIFFORD is a self-made multi-millionaire, and his views are typical of the original capitalists when he says: 'I am not a believer in courses for people at my level, though there are successful courses for middle management. They are hopeless for top management for whom an empirical approach is much better than an academic approach.'

Another self-made success is MR. CHESHIRE, who says: 'Ninety-nine per cent of my management training has been self-experience.'

Another original capitalist is MR. CHRISTIE, who believes he has developed a key to self-teaching: 'I have been to almost no courses at all. I learn about management because I keep asking myself a single little word—WHY? It is always visible to me'—and he showed it on the shelf beside his desk. 'It conditions my thinking. I have observed how a child keeps asking its mother why this, why that. Most of us are too conditioned by our surroundings, but I am not as conditioned as most people, because I keep asking why.'

MR. CHRISTIE is a very successful businessman, but the trouble with accepting his advice and making a precept out of using the word WHY, is that it is already at the very foundations of academic training. Students are taught to question, question, but this is not proving an instant success in training skilled and inspired managers.

There are at least two possible explanations. Firstly, in a world which has to produce a lot of material goods before there is even enough food, clothing and shelter for everyone, the skill of able students in asking WHY may be of limited use if they have not first acquired a taste for asking HOW, so that they can get on with doing the world's immediate work.

There is an observable gap between the academic-trained who know how to ask WHY and some of the doers who know only how to ask HOW. When we look at MR. CHRISTIE, we see an outstanding man who was very good in the first place at asking HOW, so that he understood the workings of everything around him and could run it all himself. But in addition he could ask WHY, and hence change and expand his business organization as opportunity allowed.

Secondly, the ability to ask WHY is of limited value if one is not motivated or oriented towards a goal. The successful original capitalists in the survey who scorned management training for themselves actually had an inspired love for producing and/or selling a particular kind of product or service to customers, and their interest in succeeding at this task was reinforced by ownership of shares so that their economic well-being, their personal confidence and to a large extent their standing, as businessmen in their own community, rose or fell with the success of their venture. Analytical skill divorced from these circumstances may be largely directionless.

In contrast to the original capitalists are the non-owning chief executives, who are much stronger believers in management courses and book learning, for themselves as well as for their staff. Here are typical experiences:

MR. DERKUM: I attend seminars and workshops and I have been to the Harvard Advanced Management Programme.

MR. ASKEW: I have been on the management course for presidents, a one week course run by the American Management Association.

MR. BELLAMY: Apart from the staff courses we all go on here, I also read books and magazines on management and also do a lot of speaking at business schools. I find the question sessions give me much guidance. I only agree to speak if I have as long on questions as on speaking. If I speak for 40 minutes, then I want 40 minutes on question and answer.

MR. BELLAMY is clearly using the ability of students to ask WHY, to help him think through his problems.

MR. DEGENHARDT: I read a lot of management books and I always attend one course a year. It could be financial analysis or corporate planning, it is usually about five days.

MR. ACLAND: Peter Drucker comes to our three-day management planning meeting in the winter. The only cure for insularity is a huge exterior exposure. I go back to business school for three weeks a year and I bring down Harvard professors to our internal courses.

MR. BERESFORD: If I want to learn about a subject I ask someone who is an authority on it to recommend the best book on it.

Four non-owning executive members of the survey are part-time or former professors of business administration. Within this foursome, all three countries are represented, with Germany twice.

Who is right, the original capitalists or the non-owning chief executives?

My own reading of the situation is that the non-owning executive approach to management courses must be right—provided they are good courses. To acquire all knowledge empirically is to put the clock back, and in fact to require everybody to re-invent the wheel.

At the same time it must be recognized that because the original capitalists are strongly oriented towards the pursuit of customer satisfaction, reinforced by their experience in becoming a business owner, they are capable of learning very fast and efficiently the essentials of everything that is relevant to the success of their firm.

It is my belief, supported by the evidence of this survey, that at senior levels of management, training courses for people who do not have an element of ownership are to some extent a waste of time. It is like giving someone a ship with a good rudder but no chart or destination. He can steer but will largely waste this skill in going round in circles.

When so many members of senior management are non-owners, is it surprising that the world of management training sees a continuing succession of new-fashioned subjects of study—e.g. Corporate Planning and Management by Objectives? I am not critical of these subjects as such, but they are typical of the new guises for basically the same set of disciplines that original capitalists have always re-invented and taught to themselves—planning and budgeting to win more business, profitably, from customers. The realities of ownership, including its responsibilities, make this process of re-invention and self-teaching automatic within the new business creator.

In doing this survey, it was a strange experience to interview original capitalists and listen to them trotting out all the 'old-fashioned nonsense' about management training being a waste of time for them, then to do my analysis of the results and confirm that these people with the 'old-fashioned' ideas are in fact the most progressive managers with the fastest growth rates, the newest ideas and products, the latest computer systems, and so forth. By contrast the non-owning chief executives who uttered all the right up-to-date jargon about management training couldn't in general come near them in business performance.

It seems to me that we need to take the best of both sides in this argument. Management training is clearly desirable to save people the inefficiency of re-discovering known facts and skills. But at the senior levels its effectiveness can be reinforced by the experience of an element of share ownership. The capital system used by the business world, which involves the commitment of expenditure before the customer pays a single penny, is not easy to understand, in its full implications, by management training alone. No amount of training can be as realistic as the experience of actually laying out one's own money, with all the personal consequences, in the hope that customers will buy.

How an impoverished manager can invest money he hasn't got, is a problem to be looked at in Chapter 20, but we are concerned here only with the reinforcement value of ownership to management training. From time to time one hears someone propound the theory that the well-paid manager in charge of a $50 million business should work just as hard and effectively if he is only a salaried manager as if he owns shares in the business. He may work just as hard, in the sense of doing the hours, but effectiveness is another matter. It is to my mind not realistic to propound a theory that two quite different circumstances have the same effect. Anyone propounding it should be under obligation to prove it.

One might just as well say that a woman should look after all children equally, when we observe every day that she has a special regard for her own. Similarly in my experience a man has a special regard for his own business, or one in which he is at least a part owner.

The difficulty of actually learning management, as opposed to merely knowing the jargon and the theoretical techniques, was emphasized in the survey by MR. DAHLMANN, an outstanding international industrialist and one of the most impressive chief executives interviewed. When I asked him the age at which he became attuned to the numerical skills needed in business, he replied: 'Instinctively at 24, but intellectually at 44.' At first I thought that there was a language problem here, and that he had inadvertently put the words round the wrong way. But he had not. At the age of 24 one instinctively knows some of the more obvious 'common sense' things about profit and loss, if one is at all alert and perhaps educated to the problems of the business world. But it can take another 20 years of experience to grasp the full intellectual significance and all the ramifications of committing capital expenditure and seeing whether it will pay off.

My point is that any speeding up and reinforcement of this process through the experience of share ownership can be of advantage in improving business effectiveness and efficiency.

5

HOW HIS ACCOUNTING AND BUDGETING KNOWLEDGE WERE ACQUIRED

Surely accounting and budgeting are central to the whole business operation, so anyone destined to become a chief executive would make certain he acquired this kind of knowledge while still at college, or very early in his career?
Maybe this is what should happen, but it hasn't worked out like this in the past. Those who began in the accounting profession and those who went to business school before entering the world of commerce or industry did in fact acquire their accounting and budgeting knowledge by their early twenties. But these are comparatively rare cases. In the survey the average age of acquiring accounting knowledge is 28 and for budgeting it is 35. The latter is, of course, a much more recent technique, at least in its widespread use throughout industry.

These averages, however, hide a very wide range of age of learning. The lowest claimed age of acquiring knowledge of historic accounting methods is 16—a very bright boy learning in his father's business. There is another teenager accountant, then there is a wide spread through the twenties, thirties and forties, even into the fifties.

In four cases (two British, one German and one American) it is claimed that they do not yet understand accounting. There is undoubtedly a degree of leg-pull in these latter claims. Hence the hearty laughs. Accounting has been in the past the sort of subject which one might want, half in jest, never to understand. Leave it to the practitioners of the mystery!

There is a similar spread of ages of acquiring budgeting knowledge, ranging from under 20 to over 60, the latter being the American head of a world-wide and successful corporation who introduced the technique to his group only a few years ago. And there are three Britons and two Americans who claim they have not yet got to grips with budgeting.

Table 5.1 shows the distribution of ages of acquiring accounting and budgeting knowledge. As will be seen, the majority of chief executives in the survey acquired accounting knowledge in their twenties, but the greatest number acquired budgeting knowledge in their thirties. We can expect this gap to be closed and perhaps even reversed in studies of future chief executives who will have become accustomed to a budgeting system as soon as or even sooner than they have learnt about accountancy.

Table 5.1

DISTRIBUTION OF AGES OF ACQUIRING ACCOUNTING AND BUDGETING KNOWLEDGE

	Under 20	20–29	30–39	40–49	50 and over
	per cent	per cent	per cent	per cent	per cent
Accounting knowledge	13	56	16	12	3
Budgeting knowledge	1	34	41	18	6

Table 5.2 shows the average age of acquiring accounting and budgeting knowledge amongst different national groups. It will be seen that the Germans have a slight edge for youthfulness over the Americans, who have a somewhat larger edge over the Britons. But when the British sample is broken down, the original capitalists are excluded* and the non-owning executives are

* The original capitalists are excluded because their attitude to formal management training, as reported in Chapter 4, made a significant number of their answers to the questions on accounting and budgeting not specific enough for satisfactory analysis. By contrast, as seen in Chapter 6, they answered quite specifically on numerical skill.

divided into fast growers and slow growers,* it is seen that the fast growers claimed to acquire accounting and budgeting knowledge seven and 10 years respectively younger than the slow growers. But the fast growers have an average age of 49 and the slow growers have an average age of 56, so these differences in age of learning may partly reflect the possibility that in slow growth firms, senior appointments requiring accountancy and budgeting knowledge may come later in life.

Table 5.2

AVERAGE AGE OF ACQUIRING ACCOUNTING AND BUDGETING KNOWLEDGE

	All Americans	All Germans	All Britons	British fast-growth executives	British slow-growth executives
Accounting knowledge	28	27	29	25	32
Budgeting knowledge	33	33	37	27	37

What is the explanation for the great spreads in ages of learning accounting and budgeting techniques? What were the circumstances that caused such wide variation?

It appears to be simply that, though accounting and budgeting are central to business, these are subjects which, unless they have been learnt at school or college or in the profession, are usually left until they are actually needed. So when a man rises in responsibility to the point where he needs historic accounting or budgeting knowledge, he somehow acquires it. Or he may already be in a responsible post and his firm decides to introduce budgeting, so he learns about it there and then.

* In this and subsequent analyses throughout the book, the categories of 'growth' and 'no growth' are combined to form one category called 'slow growth', which includes all whose firms grew by up to 15 per cent per annum. This category is compared with 'fast growth', meaning more than 15 per cent and up to 50 per cent, and in some cases also with 'super fast growth', meaning more than 50 per cent per annum.

Here are some of the circumstances which stimulated such on-the-job learning:

MR. AVERY: When as a result of vision, hard work and the death of my grandfather, I suddenly found I owned a large business, I learnt about balance sheets in a hurry. A lot needed doing. The firm was in a run-down state.

MR. BELLAMY: I went to work in a City (of London) office and analysed my first big company balance sheet when I was 17. I remember being told: 'Don't let it frighten you, it's the same as a smaller company if you just take off the last three 0's.' I always remember this and follow it, that running a big show is the same as a smaller one only you have more 0's on the end.

MR. ATWICK: It was when I was 28 and formed my own business that I got to understand balance sheets and profit and loss accounts. Because of the tightness of money setting up my own business, I gave the balance sheet more attention than the profit and loss account. When starting on your own, making money isn't as important as keeping afloat and growing.

MR DOBLER: At the age of 16 I was trained by my father's book-keeper to understand balance sheets and profit and loss accounts.

MR. ALLEN: I learnt about accounting at Yale and understood enough so that later, when I was out selling, I could sometimes take an order which showed no profit but which absorbed our overheads when business was bad.

MR. ATKINSON: I learnt about balance sheets when I started borrowing lots of money. I couldn't generate it internally to grow fast enough. I had to know about balance sheets and the pro-formas of plans that the bank wanted me to fill in, to show them how I could repay the money.

MR. BOOTH: I knew about balance sheets and profit and loss accounts when I was 18, from working in my father's business during school holidays. I did not bother about them when I was at university in England, but of course I came back to them again at Harvard.

MR. ACLAND: When I was 27 and put in charge of the company's subsidiary in Columbia, I read accounting books and also taught myself how to do budgeting.

MR. BLYTH: At the age of 27, when in charge of a subsidiary, I was looking for a better information system for management control, so I put in costing and budgeting. Up until then we had just the monthly profit and loss account, in traditional accounting style.

MR. ANSELL: When I was 63 I started the company system of budgeting. I was on the board of another company and saw how well they did it and said we must do the same here.

MR. DERKUM: I learnt about historic accounting at the age of 22 when I was doing evening classes and was a merchandising apprentice. Similarly I learnt about budgeting then, but I became really experienced at these things as a result of doing the Harvard A.M.P. at the age of 43.

MR. DODEN: I was 24 when I learnt about balance sheets and audit accounting. I was a financial journalist and the paper for which I was working was going bankrupt, so I jolly well had to know what it was all about.

I learnt about budgeting when I was 35. I taught myself from the frustration of looking at my business not doing too well and not being properly planned. I worked out the budgeting system from first principles.

To run a business successfully you must be in balance, that is you must have this feeling about a balance sheet, that if you deduct something here, it will show up there. One must have this simple understanding of double entry.

MR. ATTERBURY: I was in charge of credit control at the age of 21. When you pass credit for customers, you are always looking at balance sheets and profit and loss statements.

MR. BENHAM: I began to become attuned to balance sheets at the age of 46 when I took over this job as managing director. But I had become attuned to budgeting at the age of 41 when I was sales manager in a big group.

MR. CHRISTIE: I picked up traditional accounting as I went along, but did not pick up budgeting until much later. It was only three years ago that we started having proper budgeting—when I was 50. One lets it go until one gets to a certain size.

MR. ARGENT: I learnt about balance sheets in my training. We have actually had annual budgets for the last 28 years that I have been here, but they were not detailed and they were not broken down by cost centre. Also there were no whys and wherefores on individual items.

MR. CONSTABLE: I don't yet understand traditional balance sheets, but I have been understanding and working budget accounting since the age of 21. This comes naturally to any business leader. He must make plans, set targets and budgets and then compare performance against targets and budgets.

MR. BECKETT: I was 45 when I became attuned to budget accounting and performance comparison. But this was only putting on paper a mental process that always goes through the mind of everybody running a business. When previously we were looking at the weekly figures, we were in fact projecting them forward to the end of the year, though it wasn't translated on to paper to anything like the extent it is now. Incidentally, when I prepared my first budget, I had a lucky fluke, the year's results ended up very close to the budget. It has never happened like that since.

In the light of this last paragraph, is budget accounting a system which really fits the thinking of a businessman, while historic accounting does not?

By and large this is true. Historic accounting is devised from the invention of double-entry book-keeping, described in his writings by Luca Pacioli, a Genoese merchant, in about 1340. The essence of this was the recognition that every transaction should be recorded twice. For every payer of money there is a payee, for every sender of goods there is a receiver, for every creditor there must be someone in debt. By making double entries to recognize both sides of each transaction, and having them recorded, wherever possible, by different members of the staff, one can add up thc various accounts and 'balance' the books, checking that the two sets of entries are equal. This provides protection against simple fraud, though not, of course, against sophisticated crookery involving counterbalancing false entries.

The elaborate systems of auditing practised in business are designed primarily to check the accuracy of a firm's books and certify as to their accuracy. Specifically, the objects of auditing are these:

1. to check against fraud by investigation, for example, whether in fact the monies claimed to be paid and received were in fact paid and received;
2. to ensure that the firm's bills are paid—both the accounts receivable by the company and those payable;
3. to check the balance sheet, showing on a specified date the amount of the firm's net assets and the precise positions of debit and credit that result in the net asset position;

4. to check the income statement or profit and loss accounts showing for a specified period of trading the firm's profit or loss and the precise amounts of various payments in and out that go to make up the resulting profit or loss;
5. to verify or certify the accuracy of the accounts or financial statement to the tax authorities;
6. to verify or certify the accounts or financial statement to the shareholders as being a true and fair view of the company's position, thus meeting the requirements of company law.

How can auditors give a true and fair view of a company's position, when so many take-over battles in recent years have shown how the same company's accounts can be presented in different ways to give a pessimistic or optimistic picture?

Certainly in recent years there has been much controversy over accounting practice. Rightly so, for not every cost incurred by a firm is precise. Overheads, for example, have to be allocated between departments. But how much to each? Also the cost of plant has to be depreciated over the expected life of the machinery. But how long will it 'live'?

Even on the receivables side there are imprecisions. When are goods actually sold—when the order is placed, or when work is accrued against the order that has not yet been completed, or when delivery is made and the goods are invoiced, or when payment is made in cash, or when payment is promised but deferred on credit terms, or when the final total is paid in cash?

The scope for Accountants' Headache is endless, since there is so much scope for presenting the financial statement of a firm in different ways, according to how sales revenue, depreciation, overheads and various other items are treated.

Is there any hope that accountants will ever be able to present just one set of true and accurate accounts that have no alternatives?

Not much hope, really, though some improvement is possible

through closer agreement on accounting principles and the use of supporting schedules. To give a full picture, accountants would have to present a large number of sets of accounts, showing how the firm's position would look if various items were treated in different ways. The biggest trouble is that they are up against the problem of time periods.

When a financial statement has been prepared, the auditors must certify it as being a true and fair view at one particular moment of time. But as we have seen, many of the transactions of a business are capable of being moved forward or backward through time.

A business operates on the trust of its creditors and capital providers. But capital is only a money-storage system which makes it possible to move payments backwards and forward through time, in the same way that a water reservoir can be described as a storage system for moving the water flow forward and backward through time (i.e. before and after the rain falls).

If we are going to have the convenience of such storage devices, so that for example people without enough capital can borrow the use of it and pay for plant and for work to be done before they obtain sales income, then we must put up with the fact that there will be a problem of deciding how to set down the sales income and the expenditure in the accounts, so that they show truly and fairly when the income was received, how and when the capital was spent.

We have a parallel problem with water supplies in a drought. The water engineer can only give a completely 'true and fair' view of the supply position if he gives us a large number of alternative pictures of rainfall and river flow, (i.e. income received), and use of domestic and industrial water (i.e. expenditure). In practice he gives us just one picture, saying: 'There's enough to last six weeks if you go easy.' Behind his simple 'true and fair' view are assumptions about rainfall, river flow, domestic and industrial usage of water which he does not spell out in detail. We trust his professional judgement in using the assumptions that seem most valid in the circumstances. A similar level of trust has to be placed in company accountants and auditors.

Fair enough, but does this mean that the audited accounts relating to the past history of a business are just as inaccurate as the forward budget accounts?
Not quite. Both can be inaccurate, but for different reasons. The historic accounts do contain some unalterable facts. For example, on March 9 the company ordered a $4,800 machine, it was finally installed on July 10 and in operation on September 2. A down payment was made on March 9, the machine was invoiced on August 14, but on October 2 the managing director phoned his supplier and said he would like the payment spread over four months as they were rather tight for money at present. He actually completed payments in 11 months, after much pressure from the supplier.

There is room for variation, but not too much, in how the capital cost of the machine is entered in the accounts, as a purchase. But there is far more room for variation in how the $4,800 is depreciated. Will the machine be worn out in four years or eight, so should the monthly cost be around $200 or $100? And if the machine is used for making five different products, how should the cost of running it be split between them?

In forward budgeting, by contrast, there is even more scope for variation. Plans are made but easily altered. Plans are executed but the customers do not respond at the forecast level. They buy either more or less. MR. BECKETT, it will be recalled, was quoted as saying that when he made his first budget, it was a 'lucky fluke' that 'the year's results ended up very close to the budget. It has never happened like that since.'

Nevertheless, budget accounting is an essential and natural business process which MR. BECKETT described as 'only putting on paper a mental process that always goes through the mind of everybody running a business'. It is more natural than historic accounting, only in the sense that if a businessman has a good professional accountant he will be inclined to say to himself: 'Let the past look after itself. I can rely on my auditor to check that I have not been defrauded, and to confirm to me in due course whether I made £50,000 profit or £70,000. I suspect it was closer to the former.'

What he cannot himself neglect, however, is to be always projecting forward the latest figures, anticipating how his products will sell, comparing the likely costs with the anticipated revenue to see if he is going to be in the black or in the red. Moreover, he must look at the likely cash flow and future balance sheet. Because of extended credit and capital payments, money may be received and paid out on quite different dates from those on which it is recorded as sales and expenditure. If he does not watch the likely cash flow, he can go bankrupt even when he is doing very profitable business.

This type of forward thinking is as old as business enterprise. It not only pre-dates formal budget accounting done on paper, but it may possibly predate the discovery of double-entry book-keeping. The first Merchant Adventurers, whether trading across Asia by caravan or through the Mediterranean by sailing ship, must have thought ahead along these lines.

Is it reasonable, then, for a modern chief executive to concentrate on the natural thinking involved in forward budget accounting, watching how his plans work out against budget, while he leaves historic accounting, with its mysteries of double entry, to the professional accountants?

The detailed accounting practices—for example, why your accountant insists on opening a separate account for this or that—may be left to him. But the principles of double entry must be understood. For example, at the peak of the whole system is the balance sheet, and this must balance. Since there cannot be someone in debt without someone or some others being in credit to the same amount, and this principle applies to firms as well as people, it follows that the total assets of a firm at any period of time, its plant and inventory and work in progress, cash and the money owing to it by debtors, must exactly balance the liabilities—the money owed by the firm to creditors, to the bank and to shareholders as capital. If the two columns do not balance, there must be a missing debit or credit somewhere. Failure to recognize it can lead to bankruptcy.

The balance sheet is a discipline for ensuring that no items of debit or credit are overlooked. And this, mentally, is an attitude which every businessman must have, even if he leaves the actual figure-work to his accountant. Hence the significance of what MR. ATWICK said about starting in business on his own: 'I gave the balance sheet more attention than the profit and loss account. When starting on your own, making money isn't as important as keeping afloat and growing.'

This lesson is not unique to America. MR. DOBLER is a self-made, very successul German businessman whose company has now been sold to a large group. But 'until a year ago I still kept an inside pocket book recording all expenses because I was expanding my business and I wanted to ensure I had sufficient funds'.

MR. CLIFFORD is a self-made British millionaire. 'In the early stages of building my business, every Saturday night I did my own balance sheet. I added up the value of all I possessed, subtracted what I owed. What was left was the value of net assets to start the next week with. I knew exactly what I could afford to spend that week if an opportunity came up.'

6

NUMERICAL SKILLS

How important are numerical skills in business?

Though a loaded question like this could not be asked in the survey, those interviewed were asked at what age-level the Money Game of Business began to fascinate them. From the answers came a substantial volume of evidence on the importance of simple numerical skill—not higher mathematics.

The education system in many countries causes most of the intellectually 'brighter' children to be finished with simple numerical skill around the age of 11, and to turn on to algebra, leading to more advanced forms of abstract mathematics. This not only reduces the amount of subsequent practice they have with the relationships of numbers, it also means that they have stopped doing money sums before they are mature enough to understand business problems, other than the very simplest.

A teacher can set a young class the problem of calculating the amount of change if someone buys two pounds of bananas in a shop and tenders a £5 or $10 note. Both teacher and children have bought bananas in a shop, so they know the problem. But probably neither has had any experience of the business problems of pricing and costing. Still less are they likely to have had much experience involving the spreading of payments over a period of time, e.g. credit and capital expenditure. Ironically, it is the children who are less academically inclined who are likely to continue with money sums at school until they are older, and hence, have a better chance to maintain and develop the numerical skills needed in business.

But to return to the question, how important are these skills? An answer can first be given in the words of those in the survey who feel that they 'suffered' from the higher education system. These examples are particularly prevalent in Britain.

MR. BOOTH is a very successful multiple retailer, but he originally took an engineering degree with first class honours at a famous English university. He says: 'It is ludicrous that in four years, though we did a lot of design work, we never assigned money values to anything.' Is it surprising that MR. BOOTH, with a family business background, gave up engineering in disgust?

Is it surprising, too, that MR. CHAPMAN, another engineer, complains of the problem he had during his early business career 'to get away from the basic engineer's concept that a thing must be designed regardless of cost—engineers are notoriously bad at finance, they tend to feel there is an intrinsic value in a thing, regardless of its market value.'

Yet this situation need not be so, according to MR. BARRETT, who sees a parallel between an engineering drawing and a financial statement: 'Look at a drawing and you see how the thing is being produced, look at a financial statement and you see how a job is running.' Both are symbolic ways of describing an important aspect of an activity.

The necessary change in outlook happened to MR. BASSETT as he rose in managerial responsibility: 'I turned from being the engineer who liked to solve the difficult problems, because they were a challenge, to asking myself: "Is this worth trying to solve?"'

There lies the rub. Is a particular problem worth solving? You don't know until you 'estimate the value of time and effort' (MR. CAIRNS). But to make this estimate 'it is necessary to have some common denominator to measure industrial activity. The only common language is money at some stage of the proceedings' (MR. CLEMENTS). Money is 'just a shorthand for saying what is going on' (MR. BAINBRIDGE). But to use this shorthand you have to learn to 'think money'. That is, it is not just numerical skill which is important but the ability to put money figures, or economic value, on to objects and activities.

How easily is this skill acquired?

A self-made millionaire, MR. CLIFFORD, says that measurement in money terms didn't come easily to him. 'All my mistakes have been made when I have not done my sums, but doing them isn't instinctive, I always have to work at it. Someone once said the only natural instinct in man is the ability to suckle. Everything else has to be learnt. Even if this isn't entirely true, it's a good rule to work by, you must personally develop all the other skills.'

MR. CLIFFORD further asserts that this problem of measurement is by no means unique to the business world: 'In everything you do you have to seek a yardstick to measure yourself by so you know how you are doing compared to the opposition. If you miss this out, then you are an amateur. The professional always measures his success.'

Not all the problems of measurement in business are, of course, expressed in money terms. It depends on the job. MR. CHARLTON says he 'gets very annoyed with the manager who doesn't know his tonnage (of daily output)—he should be living his job like I live mine'.

Nevertheless, for the measurement of business success as a whole, money 'is the name of the game' (ADAM SMITH, nearly 200 years before this survey). For business purposes, money measures worth.

This view comes most easily to those who grew up in business homes. MR. BATCHELOR recalls: 'My father imbued me with the belief that anyone else, that is anyone not in business, could be regarded as a limpet on society.' An extreme view, but those who run a business probably do it all the better if they have an intense attitude towards the importance of their task. Certainly the consequences of their falling down on their task should not be underestimated. The point is emphasized by MR. BOND, who was left in charge of a sugar company at the age of 29: 'I really began to be fascinated by the money game. You can't very well be in charge of a business unless you are very money-minded, otherwise the business will slip, the profits will slide and the people who are dependent on you will be demoralized.'

Necessary though the money game may be, this is not to put it as the ultimate objective of business. The head of a very large, fast-growing and world-wide British business, MR. BAKER, describes the position this way: 'If all we were doing was making profits it would be terribly boring. Profits are only a means of going on serving. The more profit you make the more confidence people have in your ability to carry out your own endeavours.'

And MR. DAHLMANN, the chief executive of a giant German enterprise, says this of the money calculations and measurements needed in business: 'They are the craftsmanship of the job, they are secondary. They are problems of technique, not problems of thinking and policy.'

What is the typical age at which chief executives have developed a fascination for the money game of business, and a facility with the numerical skills involved when thinking in money terms?

The survey shows an average age of 26, but this average masks a wide span from the early teens up into the fifties. The distribution of ages is shown in Table 6.1. It will be seen that two-thirds of chief executives in the survey acquired their numerical skills in their teens or twenties.

The Americans had the lowest average age, 25, the British were next with 26 and the Germans had 29. This relatively high average age of acquiring numerical skills is partly explained by the long German education system.

More significant, however, than differences between national groups are the differences between the three British samples—the original capitalists who are super fast and fast growers, the non-owning chief executives who are fast growers, and the non-owning chief executives with slow growth businesses. The average age of acquiring numerical skills claimed by the original capitalists is 20, the average claimed by the non-owning fast growers is 25, and the average claimed by the non-owning slow growers is 28.

Table 6.1

DISTRIBUTION OF AGES OF ACQUIRING BUSINESS NUMERICAL SKILLS

Under 20	20–29	30–39	40–49	50 and over
22%	44%	24%	9%	1%

Why is the spread of ages of acquiring numerical skill so wide?

It appears to be because, as with other business skills, this skill is likely to develop rapidly only when circumstances encourage it. There may be other, equally capable people in the world who never develop numerical skill with money problems because circumstances do not encourage them.

Here are some of the situations described in the survey:

MR. CAVELL: We were a poor family in the East End (of London) and on Saturday night I went to the market with my mother, waiting to see the left-over meat slashed in price. The attitude built up in me of always looking for a bargain.

MR. CHESHIRE: In my teens I realized that if one wanted things in life, one needed money. I had to work to get my first motor bike and all the parts to pep it up.

MR. ARCHER: By virtue of my original training with General Electric, at an early stage I was alerted to pricing and costing problems. My first design job involved trying to achieve maximum quality at minimum cost.

MR. ATKINSON: I became fascinated by the money game in my last year at college when I was 21. I had a girl and an automobile and I went into business, offering merchandise for sale, to pay for the girl and the car.

MR. CHRISTIE: At the age of 11 or 12 I had a burning desire to have my own business. I didn't know what I wanted to do, but some of my earliest memories are of making a factory at home in the garden. I calculated how much sand and cement and gravel were needed to make it although I had no idea what I was going to produce. I had the strongest motivation to be independent. Of course, if you don't qualify in your exams, possibly the motivation to succeed thereafter is stronger.

MR. DACKWEILER: After leaving university I became the first head of the Economics Department for costing and pricing, efficiency and rationalization, in this business. I did my doctoral thesis on this subject.

MR. ATWICK, a scientist by training, with a doctoral degree: I was just a Western farm boy and I had to teach myself. I became fascinated by the money game when I was 24–25 and decided that if ever I was going to make any money I would either have to get a management job or own my own business. So I set up on my own.

MR. CHILDS: I became interested in the money game when a management trainee with a big steel company. It was too bureaucratic, and making steel was far too removed from the consumer for my interests. I was fascinated by packaging and television advertising. I had to get out of steel and came into toys.

MR. BAXTER: I was 35 and in charge of a branch of a large retail group. They kept sending me too much red knitwear. I realized that their paperwork system couldn't cope. After putting in the figures week by week and getting no response, at last I put no more figures on the order form and wrote across it in large words: 'FOR CHRIST'S SAKE, NO MORE RED.' I was brought up to head office to be fired and I realized then that I was surrounded by idiots who were running a system that was ineffective. In the event, they didn't fire me. But I learnt something about figures, and so did they. We altered the system radically.

MR. BAYLISS: I was a district depot manager in India when around the age of 26, and I began to appreciate that all the various technical and other specialized functions were a means to an end, to making the business viable.

MR. BIGGS: At the age of 22, when I was a planning engineer, I had to take a drawing and estimate what it would cost to make the product, so that a quotation could be submitted. If an order came, I was responsible for getting it into the works, getting it made at that cost. I kept going round the works trying to find what could be made cheaper.

MR. BLOOMFIELD: At the age of 31 I became an advertisement manager, and the managing director said to me: 'You eat with the directors. The more you know what the business is about, the more you can contribute.' I used to join the board for half an hour at the end of their meeting and then stay for lunch. I began to appreciate how crucial advertising was to profitability.

MR. BLUNDELL: At the age of 30 I was given responsibility for undertaking a completely new activity for my company, a contract taken on a low-cost basis, during the Depression. I felt extremely responsible for making it successful within the money available. We needed the contract to keep the men at work, but we couldn't afford to lose money on it.

MR. ANSELL: When I was 40 I was put in charge of a division of the group. This was my first real taste of the money game. Before that I had been responsible only for sales.

MR. BLYTH: When put in charge of a subsidiary company at the age of 28, I got very wound up in wanting to make it go. The business was in a dreadful state. When you're given a job like that, the thing that really hits you every month is your profit and loss account. This forces you to find out how things work. You are continually doing little sums. You are expecting a good result, say, and you know the sales are going O.K., and you feel that the factory is O.K., and then the figures produced are disastrous. The first question is, can it be true? This brings you into contact with the whole system of accounting, of costing and stock records. It encourages you to delve in and find out how it works. Sometimes the figures are wrong and it takes days to get them right. If you push hard enough you get a deep understanding of how profits come, why they come. This teaches you how businesses succeed or fail. Size is terribly important here. If the company is small enough, you can literally get to the grass roots in a way that you can't in a big operation.

This is priceless experience. Subsidiary managing directors who are dependent on central information get caught in a mesh that they cannot investigate properly. They can never really learn in the same way. This is one of the problems with computers. If, by contrast, I had had a problem of excessive stocks, I could actually walk around and see the people concerned, both those in the accounting department and those in charge of the stocks. A big company almost needs to keep a couple of subsidiaries for training its potential general management.

MR. DEDERICHS: From the age of 17 I was interested in the money game because I had to support the family after the war. I was an assistant geologist, responsible for 12 drilling rigs. I was forced to think about what times means, what it costs.

MR. DERKUM: We were a highly educated family, but in prison camp at the end of the war I learnt that an academic background was not everything. In all classes of society there were fine people who kept themselves clean in difficult circumstances and had something to contribute to life. I got tired of those who claimed to be well educated. The most interesting and self-disciplined people were usually those with a business background, and I decided not to have the type of career which was common in my family. When I got out I was exposed to an unfriendly world where everybody was fighting for survival. This was a very hardening period, and looking back I am very pleased that I was exposed to it.

MR. BOWLES: During the war years I was with one of the production ministries and became fascinated with the relationship between engineering and business. For example, the economics of tooling up to make a product, the number of different routes open to you, to make on different scales of activity and consequently to market at different levels.

MR. ATTFIELD: At the age of 21 I became office manager of a family company. Three years later I became a director and secretary. I chose a small company to start in because I felt I could get more all-round experience.

MR. ATTERBURY: At the age of 21 I started my first job as office and credit manager in a retail store belonging to this group. It had its individual profit and loss statement, and it is still true that each store in the group has its own accounts. I got to know every aspect of that little business.

MR. ASHBOURNE: My father said, when I graduated in engineering at the age of 23, 'Now if you want to be successful in business, you must understand money, you must understand balance sheets.' So I studied at night school and part of the day when I was first working in the firm.

MR. ASPINALL: I understood the money game at the age of 25 when I came out of Harvard. But in my experience the top executives in technically oriented businesses are handicapped if they don't have a technical background. I was lucky to have this. For example, in understanding research department budgets, people who can't talk the language find it very difficult.

MR. ASCOT: It was not until I was 33, when I drew my first lease for a store, that as a Scotsman I felt the need to get the best lease for the lowest rent possible.

MR. DILLMANN: It was not until I was 37, when I became managing director of one of the factories in the group, that I really understood money. Earlier I was much more enthusiastic about engineering.

MR. DECKER: Although an engineer, I was never in design. I was always in production and always liked managing people. At the age of 42 I became a professor of industrial organization and management. Then I began to see the whole picture of the business world, not just part of it. I was a professor for five years before coming back into industry.

MR. ASHFIELD: Although I trained as a designer, I realized that I was not too good at it, but felt I would be better at the business end. My family of course wouldn't believe this. When at the age of 40, I decided to go into business on my own, and asked various members of the family to back me, they said, 'But how do you know you will be good at the business side?'

MR. BURKE: Until they do get the responsibility, young people think mainly of themselves. I was 30 when I began to think about the significance of money and business. At that time I was made a sales manager.

MR. ARNOLD: I became fascinated by the money game when I was about 18 at high school. I ran a small business then with two others, supplying flowers to tourists on the ships that passed through the Panama Canal. It taught me a lot about costing and pricing.

MR. DEGENHARDT: At the age of 36 I was assistant to the managing director of a small ice-cream company which lost its capital every year for three years. Then I personally convinced the group that they should let me run the company for another year, and fortunately it succeeded. I came to the conclusion that return on investment is important. When I was arguing with the group management, they kept asking how much capital was involved, and pointed out that they could have at least made 4% in Savings Bonds, instead of losing the money.

What kind of quick numerical calculations does a man become skilled at in the run-up to becoming chief executive?

No doubt there are as many kinds as there are business problems, but here are some examples of the numerical attitudes and thought patterns that were revealed in the survey:

MR. BATCHELOR: What is needed is for figures to mean something to you. One must be able to look at the page and not be bogged down. From an early stage I was disinterested in the shillings and halfpennies. What mattered to me was a close approximation. If I read out figures to you from this balance sheet, I shall read them out in millions, so that you can get the relative relationships.

MR. BLOOMFIELD: I know what percentage profit I need to cover overheads, etc. The price we can sell at is of great importance to me. The cheaper the line of products, the more crucial this is, as to whether we can charge £5 or £6. I do the calculations which tell whether a product is likely to be viable, and how much of the total can be spent on advertising.

MR. CHARLTON: The whole thing stems from sales and the margin you make on sales. We calculate fine margins to beat the others. We know last week's production of each product on Monday and the profit on Thursday night. My family were cornmillers, used to working to low margins. I am quick at calculating how much profit there is in a line. Anybody can make the stuff, anyone can sell it, but working to fine margins is not so easy.

MR. BELLAMY: I can only run such a large business by an enormous amount of travel and plant visiting. Only when I have been to a company and seen the people can I take an interest in the figures and understand them.

MR. DECKER: The financial figures are only symbols for physical activities, and you have to understand these. My staff complain that they cannot act quickly enough if there's a down-turn, because they only get the complete figures every three months. I say: 'Look around you—you can tell by the orders being phoned in and the trucks going out the gate whether there's a down-turn.'

MR. ALLEN: I have always been good with the cost sheet. I can still estimate our earnings on the back of an envelope.

MR. BECKETT: Instinctively when I look at a set of figures, I try to see how the final figure is arrived at. I go through a working. In order to understand figures you have got to put them into your own way of understanding.

MR. CHANDLER: One has to develop a sense of proportion over what the figures should be. This is acquired with practice. It is detail which matters. If you acquire a facility for mastering detail, you can quickly see if anything is amiss and not be caught by surprise on any new trend.

MR. CHISHOLM: I am always doing simple sums when buying for the group. I quickly calculate what I can sell a product for and what I can make on it.

MR. CHATFIELD: I pay my service engineers a hefty percentage of invoices, subject to inspection. Their commission rate is always high enough for them to earn real money. Then I only have to worry about how many hours of their time we have sold.

MR. CAVELL: There is hell to pay at the end of the month if anyone is in trouble on a job. I usually spot it immediately and am on to it. This is the key—plus the drive to complete the task, a sense of knowing dates. A time sense as well as money sense. I can look at a cost and say 'This doesn't make sense to me.' In spite of Critical Path Planning, one has to have a feel for knowing how far a man should be with a construction contract when he has spent a certain amount of money.

MR. BOLTON: For years I have been immersed in the cost implications of investment. The sums I have come to do are concerned with the fact that in this industry there is a temptation to make research the objective. In fact one has to have more immediate pay-offs, otherwise one cannot finance the research effort needed for longer term growth and survival.

MR. AUSTIN: I have always purchased the heavy equipment we lease to customers, figured out myself the costs, and calculated the lease rates. This is too vital a task to delegate.

MR. ANDERSON: In my early days I was concerned with a specific task, not the corporation as a whole. By the time I was 32 I had begun to realize that in addition to specific tasks there was a top management problem, the allocation of resources. You had a number of alternatives.

MR. COLE: When we started planning for growth, I developed a method of simple ratios that has worked very well. Once I have a reasonable estimate of wages and salaries and total on-cost, I can produce an estimated trading account. I have available the hire revenue figures, the sales revenue figures, material consumed, wages and salaries, other miscellaneous on-cost. This leaves a balance of profit before interest. I myself suggest the ratio of profit necessary on turnover. Also I have the production figures and the hire stock, to tell me the capital employed, and the rate at which I am turning over my money.

From the forecast revenue I know the output I must achieve within the expenses laid down. I have always achieved the turnover targets, but not always managed to restrict the costs, so we have never made quite the profit we wanted.

7

SYSTEM SKILLS

System is the result of delegating specific, detailed tasks. Such delegation of specific, detailed tasks must be distinguished from the delegation of departmental or unit responsibilities.

The sort of specific, detailed tasks which are delegated to form a business system are mainly, though not entirely, in the areas of order processing and fulfilment, payment terms, credit and collection terms, accounting and statistics. They involve the precise design of business forms and information flows across the business between such functions as marketing and sales, production, distribution, warehousing, purchasing, research and design, where relevant. They also involve the flow of information up to the chief executive, and to a less extent down from him.

They are an essential means by which departments receive from each other the precision information of business, e.g. precisely how many items of a certain specified kind were ordered by X Y Z company, at what price, on which date and for delivery when, if not immediate. They are also an essential means by which the chief executive keeps in touch with the performance and progress of the business. Most of the report figures he receives are a by-product of the flow of figures between departments, summarizing what actually happened and comparing it with what was either forecast or budgeted to happen.

By contrast with the specific, detailed tasks which are delegated to form a business system, there are departmental and unit responsibilities which cannot be spelt out so precisely. Sometimes the dividing line between the two is narrow. For example, a company which recruits and trains women to sell cosmetics from door to door may find that it is worthwhile to lay down precise sales patters that the women use when they approach a potential customer. To this extent they have systematized selling. But there is a limit to the systematizing of specialist functions. Selling is an important social skill. The saleswoman who approaches a customer's door must exercise her own intelligence and personality. However well she knows the basic sales patter, she must 'play it by ear' according to the reactions obtained. Unless she does so, she is unlikely to achieve many sales.

The chief executive of any established and substantial business is likely to see at his level more problems needing departmental initiative than those which need better systems—as witness these comments.

MR. CAVELL: It's people rather than systems which matter. One sets a policy and the systems follow, sometimes through mistakes corrected. [Yet MR. CAVELL first made his name at a lower level of responsibility when he developed and used a pre-Network Analysis scheduling system for ensuring that an important construction contract was completed on time.]

MR. AYLWARD: Organization charts are suicide for the type of company I want to run. We purposely blur the lines of authority. An organization chart stifles employees.

MR. BASSETT: One can end up spending more time trying to define the job than doing it. What is more, people leave things out of their definitions because they are difficult. So in this company they just receive from me a brief job specification and a talk about it, and they know what their job is.

MR. BOOTH: I have always been highly systems and organization oriented, right from Harvard days. This is a weakness because it tends to disregard the personal relationships that make the system work.

MR. BOWLES: If you have a fine organization, good disciplines and systems, in order to get something running smoothly, without a flaw, than it won't go off course in order to take a short cut and save a lot of money or develop a new product. You can't have it both ways.

Here we see a potential conflict between the need for system and the need for initiative. But from the chief executive's viewpoint the problem of initiative so often appears paramount that there is a danger of neglecting system.

When a man starts his own business, it is important for him to do his own detailed systems design, albeit with advice from specialists. MR. CAIRNS wisely did this, and his manufacturing business has recently been growing by an average of 140 per cent per annum: 'Working out all the system paperwork myself gave me close contact with the staff. In any case it was essential to design the initial business forms myself. No one else could possibly think in detail about what I wanted to do with the whole business. But this meant initially working a 16 to 18 hour day.'

MR. CHISHOLM wisely took the same course and his retail chain has recently been growing by an average of 170 per cent per annum: 'Retail is detail. This means controlling stock. The real problem for any retailer is control of stock. I do all the systems. We use a computer better than any other retailer in the world.'

The man who takes over as chief executive of an existing business has a similar problem. MR. BOOTH says: 'I spent a lot of time initially, a bit in each department, doing a consulting job on each. I even set up the objectives for it and formed the budget, including the detailed costs. This took me nine months but it gave me a fairly clear picture. It meant that initially I worked a 15-hour day.'

He goes on to explain that 'at first of course I under-delegated and under-systematized because I didn't have trusted people and didn't have enough facts. Now I have trusted staff and a good information system.'

Notice how MR. BOOTH sees no real conflict between delegation to trusted functional experts at the same time as he is installing detailed systems which not only make the company perform but also supply him with good information. He has always kept clearly in mind the difference between having flexibility in job definition, once you have good people, and at the same time having precision in systems design.

To keep this distinction clear, as an organization grows, a chief executive should always ensure that he knows the precise detail of any systems used both one and two steps below him in the executive hierarchy. Why two steps? Surely the second step is the responsibility of the people immediately below him, who report to him?

Yes, it is, but unless the chief executive knows in detail how their systems work, he cannot closely question his immediate subordinates about matters that go wrong, he cannot hope to understand fully why they go wrong. He cannot have complete rapport.

The man who starts his own business does not usually have more than one or two steps below him. As the business grows he will hold on as long as possible to every detail of its systems. But in time he will have to delegate systems responsibility as well as other responsibilities, and the only way he can be sure that he and each level below him give due attention to systems, is to require himself and in turn each executive below, to keep closely in touch with the detail of systems design for two steps down from his own particular level.

At what age does the potential chief executive usually feel that he has developed some system skill, and is definitely aware of the importance of having good systems?

This is a particularly important question because it became quite clear from the survey that most of the chief executives were very much individualists and not very system conscious when they were young. The survey showed that the average age at which they became conscious of system skill was 29. This was three years later than for their numerical skill. The American average was 28, the German 29 and the British 30.

Again, however, more significant than the difference between national groups was the difference between the three British samples of original capitalist super fast and fast growers, non-owning chief executives with fast growth firms and non-owning chief executives with slow-growth firms. The average age of acquiring system skills among the original capitalist super fast and fast growers was 27, amongst the non-owning fast growers it was 28 and amongst the non-owning slow growers it was 33.

The distribution of ages of acquiring system skills, in the total sample of the survey, is shown in Table 7.1. It will be seen that more than half the chief executives felt they had this problem under control before they were 30.

Table 7.1

DISTRIBUTION OF AGES OF ACQUIRING SYSTEM SKILLS

Under 20	20–29	30–39	40–49	50 and over
9%	49%	33%	6%	3%

Here are some examples of the circumstances in which those in the survey became conscious of their need for system skill.

MR. DAMM: At the age of 22 I organized a group of 400 students, in 1948 at the time of the currency reform. We sold razor blades made from German steel from door to door. These were scarce at the time. We bought them at a discount and sold them at the full price, so the students got money for their studies.

MR. ASHBOURNE: Having studied industrial engineering, I was very organization and system conscious.

MR. ATTERBURY: At the age of 25, in my second position, I was in charge of several retail units in a large city and had to be dependent on the people at each shop to meet their goals.

MR. BARRATT: When I was 23, a £6 million job was held up for six weeks because I had forgotten a small detail.

MR. BATCHELOR: From the late teens I was very interested in system. A key part of the training of chartered accountants is the importance of systems. They are a key to success for any activity involving a substantial level of employment.

MR. BEST: System skill came to me at the age of 25. I had just been moved from production to sales. When I had been an engineer in the plant, my job was closely defined, but when I went to sales it became apparent to me that I had to have a basic self-discipline. I began asking myself what information do I require, in what form and at what frequency, to enable me to carry out my function?

MR. AUSTIN: I became interested in organization and system at the age of 26 when I was chief dispatcher for a trucking company. The business depended so much on the thoroughness and accuracy of my system.

MR. BLUNDELL: It was at the age of 30 that I developed systems for an important contract for which I was responsible. I had to have a system that would make sure I kept within estimated costs and that the company did not lose money.

MR. DACKWEILER: I came to grips with system skills at the age of 28 when I left the university and entered a tradition-bound company which I tried to reorganize. I endeavoured to put theoretical knowledge into practice.

MR. ALLEN: After the Korean War, for which I was called back into the forces, I returned to the family business when I was about 28, and was able to develop my system skills because I had a great deal to do with the reorganization of the company. I was made assistant to the vice-president for marketing.

MR. ANTHONY: I didn't really appreciate the need for standard procedures written down until I was 40. I had been president of a company for a couple of years before I realized that these things couldn't just be done by word of mouth.

When a man builds up a small business into a larger one, there seems to be a natural tendency for him to do everything himself and to have a minimum of systems, self designed. How can he avoid this?

Anyone developing such a habit, like anyone developing bad health, needs professional help. As the following examples show, some people adapt, quickly or slowly, on their own, but others need outside assistance.

MR. ATWICK: I started developing my system skills at the age of 28 when I went into business. Since I couldn't do everything, I had to ask myself, what sort of a team should we put together to get the best of each skill? I quickly got myself good sales, controller and operations people. Some of the original team are still with me. [MR ATWICK is now in his early fifties.]

MR. DAGENHARDT: When I was about 36 I turned the ice-cream company into a success, and then increased the staff from 85 to 5,000 in four years. I quickly realized that I could not do everything myself, and anyway my subordinates liked operating on their own.

MR. CHILDS: Although I am bored by system, it has to be done. For the first year or so I did everything myself when the business was small. Then I gradually shed the routine. I became systematic around the age of 28.

MR. ATTFIELD: We paid less attention to formal system and organization in the young firm. The larger you are the more you have to have a formal organization, with built-in checks and balances. I hated it when we were taken over, when I was about 30. It was frustrating to have to conform to the slow moving procedures of the big company. That is why the survival rate amongst small company people moving into big firms is not very high. But small companies themselves survive because they are more flexible.

MR. DOBLER: My system skills developed at the age of about 36, at least five years after I went into business on my own. At first I tried to get as big a market share as possible. Later I looked at how I was organizing the business. I feel that this was the right policy, because I started with 25% of the market, even though I was small compared with the giants.

MR. ATKINSON: My system skills developed when I was about 34, when I had been seven years in business on my own. Up till then I thought that I could do it all myself.

MR. COCHRANE: I was 50 before I really put in good systems. A chartered accountant did it for me. But the human touch is important. One must never lose this.

8

SOCIAL SKILLS

What is meant by social skills in this context?

For the purposes of this survey, social skills are the abilities directly used in getting things done through a significant number of other people. The emphasis is on the word 'significant'. When a man sets up in business on his own, he may at first have no employees. He does everything himself. Then he engages an assistant or a secretary. Whilst he has only one employee, he does not require great social skill, he needs rather a compatibility of temperament. The two people work together, though each knows who is the boss.

When a second employee is engaged, close working harmony is still possible, though there is some truth in the saying: 'Two's company, three's a crowd.' There is the possibility that two out of the three people will work closely together, with the other one feeling an outsider.

As soon as there are three or more employees, there is a potential 'trade union' situation, where the employees are close together and the boss is the outsider. Moreover, the nature of work now changes. The boss is now more definitely doing the work of a leader, supervising his subordinates rather than working alongside them, so that their work becomes more distinct from his. And his thought habits must be different, if he is to be successful as a leader. One might even say his shaving habits must be different. When he is shaving in the morning, instead of thinking: 'What will I be doing today?' he needs to be thinking more about: 'What will they be doing today?' Unless he can make this change, he will not be very effective in using their time.

I have described this situation in terms of a man setting up in business, but a similar position occurs when a young person with a specialist qualification or skill is promoted within a firm. Whether he is employed in the works, the laboratory, the accounts department or in sales, the nature of his work and his requirement of social skills do not change dramatically when he takes on one or two assistants. But when he has three or more subordinates, he has a much greater need for social skills and he must think more about working through people, than about his own work.

When are social skills acquired?

The average age at which members of the survey claimed to have achieved some confidence in the exercise of social skills was 24. For the Americans it was 23, for the British and Germans it was 25. These figures therefore reflect the recognized lower degree of diffidence amongst Americans.

In the large British sample, the super fast and fast growing original capitalists showed an average age of 23, the fast growing non-owning chief executives showed an average age of 26 and the slow growing, non-owning chief executives showed an average age of 24.

In so far as these figures can have any significance it appears not to be lack of social skill at the top which contributes to slow growth. As we saw earlier, lack of numerical skill may be partly a factor, in other words the slow growth firm may not have done its sums thoroughly, thought through and evaluated its policies properly. But the man at the top is probably a good talker. He needs to be, for personal survival.

Table 8.1 shows the distribution of ages of achieving confidence in the exercise of social skill. As can be seen, 28 per cent achieved this before they were 20. These were mainly the good sports and social leaders at school. Another 48 per cent achieved it in their twenties. But it is comforting to late developers that amongst this sample of chief executives 22 per cent did not achieve it until their thirties and 2 per cent not until their forties.

Table 8.1

DISTRIBUTION OF AGES OF ACHIEVING CONFIDENCE IN THE EXERCISE OF SOCIAL SKILLS

Under 20	20–29	30–39	40–49	50 and over
28%	48%	22%	2%	

What are the sorts of situations which participants in the survey remember as contributing to the development of their social skills?

Possibly there are as many situations as there are people with developed social skills. Here are examples taken from the survey:

MR. ARMSTRONG: At the Harvard Business School we had a special course on administrative practice. Before that I thought it was a lot of bunkum that you had to be careful how you handled people. The course made me aware of it and I tried to apply it. But you can be too sensitive in business. I don't want to get too aware of the problems and attitudes of people who report to me. I just don't want to know.

MR. ALLEN: I developed my social skills in the navy. I had to get along with all kinds of people and weld them together into a working unit in a short period of time. At the age of 19 I was in charge of 65 people in the engine room. You either learn fast or they throw you overboard one dark night.

MR. DACKWEILER: I developed my social skills at around the age of 15, when I was a youth movement leader, and later in the army. I got the language of the workers in the ranks and got quick promotion.

MR. COLE: I realized I had social skills when I was 33. During the war they wouldn't let me join the forces so I joined the Home Guard and there I met the managing director of a big firm. He noticed that the chaps would do anything for me and he said: 'You've got something very valuable. I don't know what it is but for some reason they like the smell of you. You can do things with them. They will die for you. . .' How do I get across? I don't really know. But if they think that you are trying to do it right, they are prepared to give you all the backing they can. Enthusiasm is infectious.

MR. BLOOMFIELD: I learnt my social skills from school around the age of 17 and from the army. Public schools (in England) give responsibilities to small boys early. But I needed a lot of social skills because later I was a manager with my colleagues, then I was promoted to be their boss.

MR. ARCHER: The development of my social skills started in High School when I was captain of the football team and I also ran the Band. Then, when I was at General Electric, I was engaged in running various activities, both in the firm and outside it, before I got my first promotion.

MR. BLISS: Around the age of 24 I began developing my social skills even though I was very shy. I was made secretary of the pension fund committee and I had to visit factories and tell them about it and answer questions. Also I used to organize company sports days. I enjoyed working with people. As a result of all this activity, I found that I became quite persuasive, even though shy.

MR. DOBLER: I came out of the army and took my doctoral degree. Then I went into consultancy and soon realized that it didn't make any difference whether I turned the door handle of the president of the company or of the toilet, there was nothing to be shy about. My higher degree actually helped me when I was out selling because people would at least receive me in spite of the fact that I came from Bavaria. At that time it was still regarded merely as a holiday area, not a serious place to do business.

MR. BENHAM: I began to get to grips with social skills at the age of 33 when they put me in charge of a unit containing diverse skills. Previously I had been in charge of my own kind, engineers.

MR. CLARK: I joined a trucking business, as a driver, then got into the office and realized what could be developed from it, so started doing management studies at night school. It was during this period that I realized that I could get people to do things for me because I knew where I was going and could feel the potential.

MR. ARROWSMITH: At the age of 29 my company was merged with one of the giants and I was put in charge of the whole budgeting operating. I had a staff of diverse skills and had to negotiate with other heads of departments to get my men in on the job.

MR. DENYER: I learnt my social skills mostly around the age of 26 when I was assistant to our manager in Berlin, and responsible for various special assignments. It was very important, for example, to motivate the chemists in the business, and to do this you had to learn their job, not learn it to the extent of being able to take it over but to be able to discuss the results of their work.

MR. ANTHONY: The development of my social skills was helped by the fact that I went on the road selling, after I graduated. Selling technical equipment is a very good start for the introvert with background qualifications, because he has to get to know the product well and how to apply it to the firm he is selling to. He already has technical skills and if he can learn to sell as well, to be persuasive, he makes a very good salesman. Social skill is largely persuasion.

MR. BLYTH: I became aware of having developed social skills when I was only 20, as an apprentice. I noticed that something went wrong in the rolling mill and the head roller explained to me that it was entirely the fault of the engineers. Half an hour later the chief engineer happened to explain the same event to me and said that it was entirely due to the stupidity of the rollers. Having heard both sides so soon after each other, I could see that this was a matter of misunderstanding and lack of ability to communicate. I went back to see both, and said don't you think so and so, maybe it's this. To my surprise, it worked. Mind you, it required tact. But it gave me confidence. After all I didn't control either of these lots of people. I was only an apprentice. This instance gave me the feeling of ability to understand different points of view, see the way through a problem and get people heading in the right direction.

I have distinct limitations in getting across to a large body of people, but I think I can get a very good understanding from individuals and small groups. The small group is really what matters in a business hierarchy, because it is only small groups at each level all the way up or down.

Can social skills be taught?

This is endlessly debatable, and is too big a subject to do justice to here. The survey gives no direct evidence on this, but it is reasonable to suppose that if participants in the survey had not been able to obtain opportunities for leadership and had not exposed themselves to leadership situations, they might have acquired less social skill. MR. ATWICK gives a fragment of evidence to support this view. He is the 50-plus head of a science-based American business, who holds a doctoral degree and was apparently very introverted and lacking in social skill during his student days. While at college he was given an aptitude test, and in 1966, some 25 years later, he was given the same test again by the same professor. MR. ATWICK was sent the results, and his professor 'pointed out that the changes in aptitude and social outlook had been spectacular.'

What sort of attitudes are conducive to the effective use of social skills, in situations of business leadership? The examples which follow are given without any attempt to indicate which are the right attitudes. The reader will decide for himself:

MR. DAUTZENBERG: Treat everybody as a valuable human being. Stress as much as possible their positive qualities.

MR. CHESHIRE: One gets disappointments. People don't live up to expectations, not so much in pure ability but in moral courage, a sense of honesty, a fair day's work. One can't employ a lot of people without experiencing this. It is never any easier to understand or to accept.

MR. CHAPMAN: I find there are not many bad people, but people who are insufficient. I have a naïve belief in the fundamental goodness of mankind, and would rather feel that a person was mistaken than evil. I am blind to nastiness and find that I am not harmed by it even though ignoring it. I just refuse to accept that a person could have felt that way.

MR. BASSETT: I don't think it's advisable to get too chummy with people. I don't invite them to my home. It would be embarrassing to eat every day with the same people and then have to give them a rollicking.

MR. AYLWARD: I have coffee with my chaps, drink with them, always stay close to them. Three times I have had to fire a best friend. It is harder this way, but in each case we are still friends. Once I make up my mind I cannot wait. I've got to get him in and get it over with. An unexpected bonus from all this is the staff reaction. In one case I found out afterwards that their general attitude was: 'If the son of a bitch can fire his best friend, and his best friend isn't mad about it, he must have something.' Of course they had seen the way the man was performing, they knew long before me. The president is the last to know.'

MR. BECKETT: Quite early I recognized that people have their private feelings, that one cannot just order them about. They work better for you if you can make them want to do it.

MR. CHADWICK: I have had to learn how to delegate. But they never, ever do it as you would like. I try and assist them. But you have to put up with the mess-ups.

MR. BARRATT: You must try to eliminate your preconceived notions of what is the answer, and be flexible. If people willingly take a course of action, even if it is not the best, it is better than imposing it on them. One hundred per cent co-operation in achieving 70 per cent of the objective is better than 30 per cent co-operation in achieving 100 per cent of the objective.

MR BLUNDELL: You get across to people by having trust in them and always approaching them on the positive side, assuming all the time that they are going to perform, that they will measure up to your expectations.

MR. BOYD: How social skills develop depends on the hierarchy. If it is autocratic, as it used to be here, it is very confining to the people below.

MR. CONSTABLE: I know which of my colleagues are leaders simply by the reaction of the people they lead. A real leader is given carte blanche to do what he wishes with people's lives, but he never abuses it. The benefits to himself of what he does are subjugated to the benefits of the people whom he is leading.

MR. DECKER: I developed my social skills around the age of 25 more or less intuitively and with a lot of authority then. But I have since learnt that modern orders are explanations. I have noticed a big change, and I find all this talk of making people have their say and trying to make them understand has resulted in a decrease in efficiency. I don't think anybody is any happier now. In my early days people had a harder struggle and obeyed. But business was more efficient, given the technology of the time.

MR. BANFIELD: There is a tendency for people to demand greater independence now, and you fight it at your peril. People are not as controllable in the traditional way, but they can still be controlled. I am a great believer in the younger generation, but you cannot treat them like a Dickensian clerk on his stool. It is up to the thirties and forties to give a lead and develop new ways of winning their devotion.

In exercising social skills to get things done through people, is it more effective to take a participative approach, expecting people to participate in making the decisions, or is it better to take a directive approach?

It must appear to be, and in fact be a bit of both, as these views show:

MR. BLOOMFIELD: Top management should be seen to work, and by work I mean be effective in making decisions. But I try and encourage my staff to suggest the decision even if I am guiding them towards my own decision. I don't care two damns if they go back and say: 'I told him what I wanted.'

MR. CLARK: Our people work to the pattern of events that is scheduled, and in this sense their work is directive. But they also participate in how it is arranged through their works committees.

They also pull my leg about me being the boss. When I visited one branch which I had not been able to visit for 12 months, they cleared out a large space in the car park, put up a Union Jack and a notice which said: 'For God.'

MR. ANDERSON: The development of my social skills came from observation that using direct orders to accomplish a certain objective, if the person is not committed, is about as useful as trying to push a broom with a piece of spaghetti. Nothing happens. I also realized that there are innumerable opportunities for conflict between individual goals and corporate goals. Hence the need for persuasion. My academic realization of this when I was at Harvard was not nearly so meaningful as watching and being involved in the process.

MR. BEATTY: There are some subjects on which one has to direct people, others in which they can participate. For example the decision to close the xyz works was a matter of direction. I alone could make the decision. But everyone participated on the way in which the job was done. Another example of participation would be on shop layout. Everyone can contribute to getting the best layout, with maximum working convenience.

MR. BAYLISS: The use of directive management is determined by the condition of the business rather than the nature of the business. The more critical the situation, the more direct leadership is needed to get out of the jam. But such direct leadership does not build a foundation underneath the strong man.

MR. DACKWEILER: I have no key to getting across to people other than to try to understand everybody's arguments and opinions, and to lead by conviction, not by order.

MR. ASKEW: We used to have budgeting imposed by the accounts department but now we have learnt to do it properly, starting with the salesmen's forecasts, etc. Participative management is particularly important where you have a budgeting system which is initiated at the extremities. The argument about which type of management is best is largely void if in fact the mechanics of your budgeting system require participation. Anybody responsible for a profit centre must participate heavily in management decisions, for imposing a budget on him will not produce very good results compared with what will happen if you allow him to initiate much out of it, and you discuss it with him.

MR. ARNOLD: I felt fully confident about my use of social skills when I was 19. I was much more confident then than I am now. I now know that however charming I am to people, however much skill I use in dealing with them, I just can't get things done so simply and so effectively as I could when I was running student affairs at university. Everything is now far more complex. I can give a man a budget which he expects to achieve, but so many things can happen both outside and to him personally, that I just don't know whether he will ever achieve it.

In view of the fact that most business firms are of necessity a hierarchy, to what extent is it really possible for a chief executive to exercise social skills two or more steps down the line?

Here are some examples taken from the survey:

MR. BOLTON: I hold an annual group management conference and we even bring some people from overseas to it. Between 120 and 160 senior managers are present, and I have used it as a forum for putting over corporate objectives. There are also a lot of presentations of only half an hour followed by discussion. The whole team perform, where relevant.

MR. BEATTY: I personally take the chair at meetings of the inner council of shop stewards, every second meeting. I tell them the way the company is going, any major contracts secured and the profits achieved in the last quarter. Then I do the same for a meeting of the foreman's association, and also for meetings of the higher executives.

MR. BOOTH: I have a one-day conference in the autumn and 120 branch managers and senior staff attend.

MR. BEST: One has to be an actor, and think out carefully how you are going to play each situation. I occasionally have to address a staff meeting and tell them what a lot of scally-wags they are—I have to work myself up into a controlled fury—though I know that really they are a nice lot of guys. But like Henry II in relation to Becket, I have learnt to be very careful in what I say. If you are not, suddenly you find that someone has gone. A faithful lieutenant has over-interpreted what you intended.

MR. DACKWEILER: I hold assemblies of employees twice a year, as did my father. I give a 15- to 20-minute talk explaining where the firm is going.

MR. BOND: Between October and March I give two dinner parties a week to executives or trainees, usually 30 at a time. This is a dinner-jacket affair by candlelight, using the company's famous silver, in our board room. After dinner I talk to them quite freely, and I get to know them. Sometimes I will arrange these dinner parties on a regional basis, or I will do it on a functional basis, or I will take a group of young trainees.

MR. DILLMAN: One must be interested in the little problems as well as the big. For example, down in the yard the engine driver's problem of exhaust smell in the cab. I can't have contact with 3,000 people but I can with some. No time is actually lost by giving people a certain amount of personal attention. You gain a lot in general morale when ordinary people find that their problems are the concern of top management.

Does a chief executive's mixing with staff further down the line disturb the hierarchical authority?

Not necessarily, if it is done very carefully.

MR. BOWLES: I don't believe in a hierarchical system of seeing only the person immediately below. You can see people further down provided you never give them an order or instruction or put them in the position of being disloyal to their immediate boss.

MR. BOSWORTH: I move around a lot to see people in the firm. A chief executive doesn't know what is going on if he has only seven people reporting to him in the typical span of command. One must get around and talk on the shop floor. As soon as I find myself on the defensive, I know they are right.

MR. BLACK: I have a theory about work people and getting across to them: 'The men are always right.' If you work with that assumption, you will always be delving to the heart of your real management problems.

If the business world today is inclined to use a participative method of decision-making when circumstances allow, how can a chief executive keep his team pulling steadily in the one direction?

Firstly, by sheer powers of persuasion.

MR. BAINBRIDGE: Though I was late developing my social skills, by the mid thirties I had begun to realize that it was not possible for me to stay in the background and pull strings without sitting down and persuading people, in every case. Not only the key man, but all concerned.

MR. BATCHELOR: Persuasiveness as a social skill is particularly important. I know some very able people but they are not persuasive. When you are gathered around the table and come to an impasse, the managing director must persuade people that what he wants to do is right.

MR. CAMERON: I usually see my colleagues from 5 to 7 p.m. They are not yes men. I spend a lot of time convincing them.

MR. ARTHUR: The authority of knowing what you are doing is a prime motivator. People follow you because your policy has logic and it's what they would do themselves in that position.

MR. ATTERBURY: You must follow a very definite pattern in communication. You can be so familiar with a subject and take things for granted that the other man is not aware of. You must deliberately stop and see he understands what you said, even get him to repeat it without being juvenile about it.

Secondly, by careful tutoring of new staff on current policies, and tutoring of current staff on new policies:

MR. BRADLEY: The university word 'tutoring' is the best word to describe one of the most important social skills of a manager. He has to teach people on a close-up, man to man basis. I have seen it done superbly by one of my area managers, whenever he takes on a new branch manager. He sits in with him and goes around with him for hours at the beginning, talking over every aspect of the job and working alongside. Then he gradually lets go and the nature of the things referred to the area manager changes as the new man picks up the reins, making his own decisions on many things within the limits of the policies he has absorbed.

MR. BARRATT: As you get to know people you understand their weaknesses and good points, and you try to get them to understand things for themselves rather than having to tell them what to do.

Thirdly, by steady probing, continually getting at the facts as to what is going on:

MR. CHAMBERS: I look for straightforward people. I hate people who don't answer the question but try to guess what answer I want.

MR. BLACK: I will tell you my special trick. If I go about and see something wrong or if somebody writes in with a complaint or if there is a threatened strike or a mishap occurs, I fasten on to it, however small, and I never leave it until it has been followed right the way through. It is astounding what this method will reveal. For example, there was a small fire, and when I heard of it, it had already been put out. I was very insistent on knowing precisely how it occurred. A machine had given off sparks which had run along a dust extractor which caught fire. The extractor should have been cleaned every day, but this was 9 a.m. You can bet your bottom dollar that now there is no extractor in any plant in the group which is not cleaned thoroughly every day.

Fourthly, by persistent corrective action:

MR. CHAMBERS: Regular inspection of their work is an important key to handling people.

MR. CLIFFORD: I have found in practice that as soon as I got a sense of shame operating in an individual, then I got results. For example, I had a youth of 16 working for me, cleaning the windows and doing other jobs. He didn't do the windows very well, so one morning I got in half an hour earlier and cleaned them extremely well and showed him how to do it. I said: 'Aren't you ashamed that you can't clean a window as good as me? I'm not asking you to repair a radio set, just to clean the window.'

But you've got to get a sense of shame in the thing that a man knows he has a sporting chance to compete with you at. I once heard a salesman losing a sale, through not handling the customer right. I followed the customer out and said: 'Excuse me, aren't you Mr. Jones?' and he said 'No.' I said: 'Don't you live in such and such a suburb?' and he said 'No.' I was only guessing, of course, I had never met the man in my life, but it was an excuse to get talking and get friendly with him. I managed to get him back into the shop and sold him a set. The salesman who had lost the sale was so ashamed of himself he never forgot this and he went on to become one of my best men. The lesson was effective because I had engendered a sense of shame in the man's own subject, selling. It doesn't work in a region where the man hasn't got the competence.

MR. ANSELL: When at the age of 40 I was put in charge of a major division of the company I quickly realized that I could only be successful because of the people I put into the jobs. I began to keep a journal of new appointments, in which I kept a box office score on how these people made out. It taught me that if I got the right people and watched them while they were getting under way and changed them quickly if it didn't work out, then we could grow quickly.

MR. BOOTH: My training has been highly analytical, so I have a particular skill in unearthing the performance behind figures. I spend a lot of time setting up corporate budgets with each director responsible, and a lot of time in reviewing them. It means that people are under pressure all the time.

Must a person who sets up in business on his own start with a very high level of social skill?

Not necessarily. He can build from small beginnings.

MR. CAVELL: Success breeds success and respect. People will go along with you when you are being successful.

MR. CHAPMAN: Motivation is not mainly financial. Your aura of success is infectious with people. They decide to submerge their personalities slightly into working together for a successful organization. If you face people with a challenge they usually respond very well. Someone joining us said he thought there were a lot of clever people in the company, but he has since found that there are a lot of ordinary people who can work as a team.

MR. CHADWICK: I have become more confident with success. It goes ahead of you. People's attitude to me has altered. They believe you are more than you are, more successful, richer. They believe your publicity.

What are some of the specific approaches that have been developed, to make it easier to get things done through other people?

The following were described in the survey:

ATTENTION

MR. DOBLER: This sounds obvious, but it is very important to listen to what the other man has to say so that you know what he wants.

MEMORY FOR NAMES

MR. CHARLTON: When our works was smaller I knew the names of every man I ever employed. He thought a lot more of you if you could call him by his name.

MR. BAMBER: We have over 20,000 employees. I like to go round the stores. Names are difficult at our size, but the general manager reminds me of the name when I approach someone.

SINCERITY

MR. AUSTIN: The keys to good communication are sincerity and the fact that when I say something it can be depended upon.

HUMILITY

MR. BOND: In being a leader amongst a lot of powerful colleagues you have to have a capacity for being wrong every now and again. Nothing is more boring than to have a leader who is always right. To get a proposal through a board, if you put everything forward as if it is perfect and cut and dried, they are likely to oppose it and find fault in it. If on the other hand you take a more humble approach, 'I've been into this, there may be something about it I haven't seen', they will probably agree it's all right. It's about the age of 40 that you learn this. By then you have more appreciation of the other people around you. Up to that time you are pushing yourself forward all the time to get established, but when you have arrived, you can afford to be more humble.

MR. ATTWATER: It's a strength, not a weakness to rely on others.

FRANKNESS

MR. AYLWARD: When it comes to trouble, I meet it head on, quickly. If two people are at loggerheads I have the two of them up. These problems are hard to resolve if you let them go on.

CALMNESS

MR. BAMFIELD: If there is a crisis and you panic, you don't get help or respect.

TOGETHERNESS

MR. CHISHOLM: I had previously always been in a small office, and thought it would be more difficult to run a big organization, but I do not find it so, maybe because of the open plan layout. I enjoy the human relations here. The staff don't work for me, they think it their own business. They are very keen.

KNOWING THE JOB

MR. CHANDLER: There is no mystique about social skills, it is a matter of knowing the job and getting people's confidence. In one hotel I managed, I even showed the butcher how by using a wire he could cut the time he took to make up a certain joint. He took it without resentment because I knew what I was talking about.

KNOWING THE PEOPLE

MR. CHAPMAN: You recognize people's strengths and weaknesses, extend them to exploit their capability but not put them at risk where their weaknesses are exposed.

MR. ATTWATER: Leadership involves a special sensitivity, a power of observation but with all your senses, not just your eyes. You never handle two people the same way.

GIVING CREDIT

MR. AVERY: The greatest and easiest way to motivate is to be very certain that the credit is given fairly and liberally where it is deserved. Credit is the easiest thing in the world to give away. By contrast you stifle a business if the top people take the credit.

ADAPTING YOURSELF TO FIT

MR. BAXTER: It was at the age of eight that I realized that I had social skills. This was in 1932 when the *Wizard* boy's paper ran a series of cards for boys to collect and I found I was able to persuade boys to swap the difficult ones for the easy ones. I said to myself at the time, 'Boy, you've got skills here.' It seems odd that though I had the skills so early and knew it, I was 35 before I was able to exercise my full leadership potential. But then I was a rough Scot with a very broad accent and this acted against me in certain circles. I was determined to neutralize my accent. The class status system meant that I couldn't get across in things that mattered. I was not credible. So I had lessons, not in order to develop a posh English accent but in order to make myself difficult to define. Then I found that I could get my message over. People listened to what I said rather than just judging me by my background.

Author's Note: For Scot read Irishman, Welshman, Englishman, American, German, Australian or anyone who has emigrated away from where he is readily accepted.

RESPONSIVENESS TO OTHERS

MR. ASPINALL: If you want people to get along with you, you must be considerate and helpful without going so far as to let them take advantage of this. What is important is the ability to be tough and maintain tight control without being nasty. Some people confuse toughness with nastiness.

RESILIENCE IN ADVERSITY

MR. COCHRANE: I began learning my social skills when I joined the Royal Flying Corps in the First World War. Being Jewish, I was pushed around a bit, there was so much prejudice. I learnt then about life and how to hold my own. I became a judge of human nature.

Author's Note: For Jewish read Catholic, Negro, Puerto Rican or any other group which happens to be minority in any area. As a 'compensation' for being pushed around, the talented individual sometimes becomes more socially skilled than his 'oppressors'.

9

NEGOTIATING SKILLS

Is not negotiating skill part of the social skill discussed in Chapter 8?

Partly it is, because of the human contact involved and persuasiveness required. But in Chapter 8 we concentrated on that part of social skill which is involved in getting work done through subordinates. In this chapter we concentrate on the skills required to make a successful agreement with a free and independent person not in a subordinate role.

Because some of the chief executives in the survey had had considerable experience of negotiating major trading contracts and takeover deals, the opportunity was taken to ask them what they considered to be the major factors in concluding a successful negotiation.

The following answers give the total of survey experience on this subject:

MR. DODEN: In making a successful negotiation, you have to be capable of shifting your position. Once you notice that you won't get where you want to in one particular way, you must try from another direction. Also you must never try to negotiate any unfair terms, because in the end they work against you. If you freely make a fair offer, you can be very convincing.

MR BLACK: The secret of negotiation is the ability to get up and say: 'That's all I'm going to offer', and to say it as if you mean it even if you don't; also be able to advance arguments so that you appear as if you mean it even if you don't.

MR. AUSTIN: Negotiating varies with the circumstances. When I am negotiating with a manufacturer to purchase equipment, primarily I have to know at that time how hungry he is for the business, whether he has got a lot of orders and is working overtime or whether he has got a lot of idle capacity and really needs the job.

By contrast when I am negotiating with a customer, particularly a railroad or a motor carrier, I am concerned with first of all our past relationship with the customer, particularly with any personal relationship of a member of the staff who may have been particularly helpful to them—and we go out of our way to be helpful. Then we work out the best price we want to live with, a firm price, and stick to that. We know that they want to deal with a responsible company.

MR. ASHBOURNE: In negotiating a sales contract you must have a clear conception of the job to be done and how you are going to do it, and be able to present it well to the purchaser. Yesterday I was in Washington presenting a proposal. After the moon programme, we set up a study team on this with members of a university faculty.

MR. ASCOT: To negotiate well you must first of all know your strengths and weaknesses, and secondly have an objective and ask for more than you expect to end up with. Thirdly, give and take and know the limit to what you can cede. Fourthly, appreciate the strength of the organization you represent. Fifthly, have a readiness to concede and conciliate, and sixthly, look ahead to the long range benefit when you are giving a little—for example, a high rent will be beaten by inflation and your growing volume of business.

MR. ARROWSMITH: Anyone put in charge of negotiations must of course be intelligent and willing to work long hours, but in addition he must have judgement. He must be able to answer the question; should I check with my superior or shouldn't I—have I the latitude to work on my own? If he has to check everything he is no good, and if he runs off without ever checking back, he is going to get you into trouble. Numerical skill is important for the kind of judgement needed. A man must be able to say to himself; if I agree to that, it would put us five million below, or alternatively it doesn't really amount to anything but it will please him.

MR. DAMM: For a negotiation to be successful, both parties should be satisfied and the contract must always be based on mutual trust. Especially in business, the contract must be based more on mutual trust than on the strict clauses in the agreement.

MR. ARNOLD: Negotiation in the Orient is different from in England, from in Latin America and in North America. For example, in North America they like to get together early in the day and stay together until they complete a deal by midnight or later. In England, of course, this is no good. You have to meet and then go away and meet again and so on. The skill is to recognize the differences and not to typecast the situation.

MR. DEGENHARDT: You must talk him into it, not try any dirty tricks. Tell him what you want, be quite frank with him, leave him time, be patient. Don't leave something to be mentioned at the last minute, oh just one little thing, and it turns out to be a big thing.

MR. CONSTABLE: The implication of dealing is usually that one is screwing someone, but this is not in fact the case. One must leave the other man satisfied with his deal. If I wanted to buy a block of flats, there is a price which is perfectly satisfactory to the owner, but because of my particular skill in developing the site, it is worth more to me. The estate agency training I had is very good for business leadership.

MR. AVERY: If it is a free-standing company, and one of our subsidiaries wants to buy it, we give them guide lines and let them go ahead with negotiations. Our guide lines are: first, there must be excellent management. We have no pool of spare management to put in a company. Secondly, it must be profitable. Thirdly, it must have a profit history. Fourthly, it must have growth potential equal to that of our own business, otherwise there would be dilution, and fifthly, its earnings per share must be greater than our own so that when we add the two together there is an increase in earnings per share.

If on the other hand there is an integrating acquisition, for example a box company wants to buy a cardboard company, then we do not insist on their being excellent managers if the acquiring company can provide management. Also our profit constraints may differ. But unless there is overriding evidence that it is going to enhance the profits, we will not buy. Moreover, it must not increase our long-term debt ratio to more than 30 per cent of our assets. We won't buy if it dilutes our balance sheet.

MR. ATWICK: I was lucky when we made our acquisitions because two of our directors are very experienced in every type of negotiating —labour, contract, company and so forth. They taught me the patience needed, how far you can go, when you have hit a dead end, and so on. But my contribution was the enthusiasm and ability to sell, which added to their negotiating abilities. When you are negotiating with someone to buy his business, he must be made to want to sell it badly, he must like the taste of the money, or he won't do a deal. I did quite a lot of selling in the early days, even as a research man. Fifty per cent of my time was spent selling, and after six to eight months of selling, you get to the position where you can size people up more quickly. You can go in on a potential customer and you can tell quickly whether you are going to sell anything to him or not, and if not, whether just to leave the literature and give him a greeting and be on your way. By contrast someone you are pretty sure you will sell and who will buy regularly from you may be worth spending the whole day with, however tough he seems. I found this experience very important. A lot of your ability in management is your ability to sell properly—particularly to sell people on the decisions you have made.

MR. ASKEW: In a negotiation I look for involvement of my own people. I do nothing single-handed. If the right people are involved, it will be successful.

MR. EXTRAMAN: In every deal where you are acquiring a family owned business, you are up against family problems and you don't know how to get at this one. More deals have probably been killed by the wife and family than anything else. If you could be there when the man first goes home and tells his wife, you could make a deal with anybody because you would have all the answers.

In one case I was buying a chain of stores from a family, and the key people were the old man who was near retirement and his son who wasn't terribly wrapped up in the business. My financial adviser said that I couldn't make a deal because the family would want the son to stay on as president. I said that I wanted them both out, and I would have a go at persuading them.

I went to see the old man and I persuaded him that it was time he took it easy, and that if we did a deal I would want him to remain as consultant and give us the benefit of his advice, but not come into the office regularly, and indeed not to have an office. Then I saw the son. I pointed out to him that he never visited his stores, he was always in his office when he was working at all, and he didn't work very hard. He would be better off out of the business, and if we did a deal I would want him out. To my surprise, he agreed and said he would like to be a stockbroker. I said: 'You can be my stockbroker.' He was delighted, and he confided then that the reason why he didn't visit the stores was that his wife didn't like him going away at nights.

I thought I had the deal all set up, and the date was fixed for the announcement. When it came, the old man got up and said he wasn't selling. I was stoned. There seemed to be nothing I could do, so I just left it there and went and had a game of golf.

In the clubhouse I happened to overhear someone say that the old man's wife had killed the deal because she didn't want him at home. She didn't like the idea of him being without an office to go to every day. So I rang her and fixed a lunch. I didn't of course admit that I had overheard anything, I just said that I had got it all wrong, I wanted her husband to be a consultant but I really wanted him in my office, not in the offices of the company which I wanted to acquire. She was delighted. . . .

10

POLICY-FORMING SKILLS

What is policy-forming skill and how does it differ from decision-making skill?

It is common to include in a management course some training in decision-making. This subject of decision-making has been very acceptable in recent years, and it may well be right for most levels of management training. But in this study of chief executive practice we deliberately talk of policy-forming skill because it gives a greater sense of concern for knowing where the business is going, as distinct from the 'how to get there' decisions of every day.

The work of a chief executive in forming business policy, with the help of his colleagues and staff, may be likened to the position of a man in a well-lit room peering out into the darkness of night. Everything in the room is visible and real and can be trusted. The inside of the well-lit room is analogous to the inside of his firm. He has buildings and employees and equipment, stocks and accounts, etc. These are real enough, even if occasionally some of the people seem enigmatic in their behaviour. But they at least have definable roles.

By contrast, as a business policy-maker he has to peer into the outer darkness. Somewhere out there are his customers. They are never so real, however much market research he does to help him understand them. He can up to a point measure their spending power, their needs and attitudes and various other characteristics, but when it comes to launching a new product or service, or opening a new branch, he doesn't really know in advance whether and how much they are going to buy. Yet he has to form his policies in advance. He cannot usually serve customers any other way.

If he is successful, he can rationalize on his success, telling himself just why he succeeded. If he fails, he can rationalize on his failure. But he never really knows for sure, and always he lives on tenterhooks, uncertain whether tomorrow will bring along a new competitor, a new type of product or source of supply, a change in taste or habit which will cause a rapid drop-away in sales and turn an economic business into a losing one.

Business policy-forming is one of the greatest challenges available to creative and leadership-minded individuals. This is in no way to belittle the importance of other forms of social endeavour, such as bringing up a family, holding a position of public responsibility, or caring for the poor, the sick or invalid. But business activity, because it caters for the everyday economic needs of the vast majority of people who are law-abiding, productive and healthy, is in sheer volume the greatest form of human endeavour. Therefore in quantitative terms it can make the greatest contribution to the workings of a free democracy.

It is worth stopping a moment, however, to note how different are the policy-forming processes of various types of activity in a free democracy.

The public official forms his policies by consultation with the various interested bodies, representing different points of view, but ultimately he is answerable to a parliamentary system dependent on the free voting of the electorate.

The charity worker usually belongs to a voluntary society which in framework copies the parliamentary system, with a council and office-bearers elected by the members. But elections and voting are very much a last-resort affair in the policy-forming of such bodies. There is only occasionally a policy clash at election time. There is more often a personality clash. The real determinant of policy in a voluntary body is membership support (or in some cases non-member support). Those who run a voluntary body that has been set up to further a particular cause are rarely concerned with fighting an election over the cause, but they are concerned all the time on whether members (and non-member contributors) will support their cause, by donations and in other ways.

By contrast, a business firm's policy is not determined by either the parliamentary system that backs up the public official, or by a direct appeal to 'membership support'. Indeed, the members of a company, in the legal sense, are its shareholders, who may or may not buy its products. Business policy is directly concerned with what customers are willing to buy. Its contribution to free democracy lies not in giving anyone a choice of candidates to vote for, nor in giving people a choice of good causes to support, but in giving them a choice of good products or services to buy.

The customers are exercising their democratic choice every day when they spend their earnings. There is no question of waiting for a general election or a by-election. Business is the most subtle and continuing aspect of democracy.

Moreover, business leaders have in a sense a more difficult task than leaders of a government or a voluntary society. Government leaders can very often wait and obtain the views of the electorate before they adopt a policy, and so can the leaders of a voluntary society in most cases. But businessmen cannot. They must spend money, create the product or service, perhaps build a vast production plant, then wait to see the verdict of potential customers. It may be YES, it may be NO, or it may be MAYBE—in which latter case the businessman is left in uncertainty as to whether to spend more money getting the product right, and its advertising and distribution, or whether to write-off the whole venture as a failure.

The customers themselves may not know why they are not buying the new product in sufficient quantities to make it economic. Those who buy it may actually like it. Market research can be done on the other potential buyers, and at this stage it may give evidence of why they are not buying it, though this is not a certainty since the reasons for not doing something can be very complex indeed. But the most difficult research of all is before the product exists.

In spite of all the professional skill that has been put into developing market research techniques, nobody has been able to develop a way of obtaining from a potential customer reliable evidence on whether or not he would buy some non-existent product which is described to him, in circumstances that do not exist yet and at a price which is unreal because no money is actually being paid.

So business policy-forming must always involve great risk. Selling is a great social skill because it helps people make choices —though it can be abused. But business policy-forming is a greater social skill because it has to be ahead of selling. It has to probe, to decide and to risk what the salesmen will be able to sell, way ahead of when they have the product or service to sell.

It involves continuous measurement. In the words of MR. BELLAMY: 'You cannot run a major corporation these days unless you are numerate.' But this is not all. As MR. ARMSTRONG explains: 'One should quantify everything you can, but in decision making that is only a starter. The figures don't decide the issue. The motivation of people and how they react finally decides what you can do. Many of the facts in a decision are really judgements. For example, if you charge more, will you make more money or will you make less?

'We were lucky to be in the right technology and to apply it to the right industry at the right time. Since I have been here our revenue has grown sixtyfold, well into the billion dollar a year class.'

MR. ARMSTRONG is one of the fortunate few who peered out into the darkness and saw a flood of customers coming for what he had to offer. But as MR. CHAPMAN points out, most businessmen do not have it like this, however hard they try: 'When you arrive at success it's usually a lot later than you expected to reach it.'

This is not just because time is required for the average businessman to make mistakes and then achieve a lucky break. Time is required for experience in handling the figures of a business situation, as well as in handling all the various imponderables.

Says MR. BAXTER: 'I did not develop my policy-forming skills until I was 35 and had been with a large retail chain for 10 years. Now I can look at a sheet of figures and say: "That product is no good." But I couldn't do this for about 10 years; I didn't have the breadth of understanding of all the factors that had to be weighed. It is surprising how few people can spot the difference between a good and a bad seller by looking at the figures. If they are looked at without taking all the various factors into account, the figures can be very deceptive.'

The never-ending and elusive hunt for successful business policies—that is, for successful ways of serving customers—is certainly one of the greatest challenges that faces man. It can bring the greatest rewards of income and capital gain (both usually subject to tax), but it can also bring great rewards in the other senses—in job satisfaction for the chief executive and all his employees, in their prospects of continuing employment and prospects of advancement and self-fulfilment. It seems clear from this survey and from other general evidence that the most exciting and rewarding firms to work for are those which are growing at an above-average rate, due to meeting a rising customer demand for their products.

Though these firms involve a lot of hard and challenging work, in some ways life is simpler for their employees than for those of static or declining firms, who face frustration, lack of fulfilment and job insecurity. Even some of the organizational problems of growth are more straight-forward than those of being static or in decline. MR. CHRISTIE's experience is an example. His firm has trebled in trading revenue in five years, by internal growth. Because their production has grown so fast, the average age of the machines in their workshops and assembly lines is 3½ years. This makes it relatively easy to be efficient. Moreover, they can re-layout the whole plant in stages when they expand, without interfering too much with existing production lines. Their planning has to be very good indeed, but the effort is more rewarding in every sense than stagnation or decline.

At what age have those who rise to become chief executives, developed their policy-forming skills?
The survey shows an average of 32 for all participants. There is virtually no difference between national groups, the average for Americans and Germans being 32 and for Britons 33 to the nearest unit, but in fact this figure is just over 32½.

However, this British overall average masks a significant difference between the three British samples. The original capitalists, who are super fast or fast growers, have an average age of 28, the non-owning fast growing chief executives have an average of 32, and the non-owning slow growing chief executives have an average of 36. These differences are surely as one would expect.

The average figures quoted in the above two paragraphs mask a wide range of individual ages. Table 10.1 shows the distribution of ages of developing policy-forming skills for all groups of participants in the survey.

Table 10.1

DISTRIBUTION OF AGES CLAIMED AT WHICH POLICY-FORMING SKILL WAS CONSCIOUSLY DEVELOPED

Under 20	20–29	30–39	40–49	50 and over
6%	37%	38%	16%	3%

As might be expected, the majority of participants were 30 or over when they felt they had developed policy-forming skill, and 19 per cent were 40 or over. There were even 3 per cent who were 50 or over.

The average age of achieving confidence in having developed policy-forming skills is six years above the average age of developing numerical skill, eight years above the average for social skill and three years above the average for system skill. These differences in average ages are what might logically be expected. That is, a person steadily gaining in experience and rising in responsibility might be expected first to develop the ability to get things done through other people. Without this he cannot be a successful leader of even a small unit of the business. Secondly he must develop the numerical skill to make plans, measure results and compare performance with expectations. Thirdly, he must develop a sense of organization and system if his own unit is to be tidy, but more particularly if it is going to fit into the total business. Finally, he is not going to be of much use at or near the top of any viable business unit that is directly serving its own customers unless he develops policy-forming skill.

What are the typical circumstances in which policy-forming skills are developed, and do some jobs provide better opportunity for this than others?

The following examples do suggest that some jobs provide better opportunity than others, but on the whole the range of background experience from which those in the survey claimed to have developed their policy-forming skills is very wide. Indeed there is no particular pattern to it, and so the width of background experience is illustrated by placing the examples in order of age at which policy-forming skill was consciously developed.

MR. DANNEWALD: My father was a banker and chairman of this insurance group. I was educated to have a feel for business policy-forming right from when I was a boy.

MR. CHRISTIE: I was 15 when I developed my first policy-forming skills. I discovered that one could make stuff at one price and sell it at another. I was swopping things at school, and then buying and selling.

MR. COCHRANE: I developed my commercial skills at the age of 19 when I had my first market stall. I knew how to buy and sell. I knew the value of goods, what price each article could sell for and hence what I could pay for it. This is a kind of instinct, but it comes mainly from observing the reactions of your customer.

MR. ATTFIELD: I was 22 when I started in a small company and was immediately exposed to the whole organization. I worked with a 70-year-old chairman who was really a research and production man and he needed me for my knowledge of marketing and finance. I didn't just get chosen for the job, I chose the company.

MR. ASPINALL: I was able to develop my policy-forming skills from the age of 27 when I was in charge in Brazil. It was then a small branch of the business. What is important is to have in a group a small enough package where a man can bungle it and not wreck the system. Also overseas experience is valuable. We are fortunate in having subsidiaries all the way from very small to very large. If a man shows ability, we put him in charge of one of the smaller companies.

MR. CLARK: I felt I was first getting to grips with commercial skills at about the age of 28 when I had been in the office for three years and decided that we should take over our nearest rival. We had to hock everything we owned and take a mortgage. My two colleagues were against it, but I said: 'Either you do it, or I'm going.' So we did it.

MR. ACKLAND: I developed my policy-forming skills around the age of 28. After Harvard I spent three years in specialist financial work for my first employer, and then was made assistant to the president. I saw at close hand all that was going on.

MR. BIGGS: I became interested in policy-forming at the age of 28 when I became works manager. At that time I got experience of all facets of running the company. I had a reputation for always taking on the problem children.

MR. DEDERICHS: I developed my policy-forming skills at around the age of 28 when I was sent abroad in charge of a branch. To do this job I had to understand the business as a whole.

MR. BOSWORTH: My skills developed suddenly at about the age of 28 when I joined the firm after the war. I went to the States on a sales visit and came back with quite a big order. But I didn't like their views of the U.K. I was in Manhattan talking to a businessman and the *Queen Mary* sailed past, and he said: 'You couldn't build a ship like that.' This was the end for me. I came back and hired the most outstanding designers who had just won a world competition for furniture design at low cost. We quickly became the number one influence on furniture design in our range.

MR. BLACK: My skills developed around the age of 29 when I had to take over the buying. I am a natural buyer and negotiator. My father died before I was born, I had no family connections and had to find my own way in an industry of small firms full of family connections.

MR. CHILDS: I became conscious of having developed my policy-forming skills at the age of 29 when I had my first product success. I repackaged an existing toy and put it on T.V. It became No. 1 in the top 20. Then the next year I had three in the top 20, and the year after I had four. But God, have we made some mistakes! The best combination in business is experience and youth. Experience saves younger men from making expensive blunders and younger men force the older ones to try new things. Unfortunately we were all young together.

MR. CLEMENTS: I developed my commercial skills at about the age of 30. I was then with an electronics business. You can acquire a flair for any product business if you are interested in it, have insight and inspiration. Acquisition of this flair, if you move from one industry to another, is almost immediate. You start watching the ads., you watch the prices, you watch the shops. You immediately acquire a feel for the product, its usefulness to people and their reactions to it.

MR. ARCHER: I developed my policy-forming skills when I was about 32 and was sales manager of a product line, and had responsibility for setting prices. I had to get approval for these prices. The products were electrical engineering equipment. In my price assessments, I had to take into account the competition for these products as well as their costs, and what I felt the market could bear in the way of price.

MR. BENHAM: My commercial skills really began to develop at the age of 33 when I started a new division for the group. But I had always had commercial sense, buying and selling motor cars and houses and making a profit as I went along.

MR. CHISHOLM: It was not until I was 36, when I formed this new type of retail chain, that I started to develop my policy-forming skills. As the losses of the first couple of years show, I made many mistakes in the beginning. But I learn not only from mistakes but also from conversations with other business people and from seeing what is happening around me, why people are successful and what they are doing. Marks & Spencer, for example in Britain, and Sears Roebuck in America. I try to analyse the logic of what they are doing and apply it in my own field. Very often I am looking at another industry and trying to apply what they do in my own.

MR. DOBLER: Although I had started my own business and been lucky the first time, I did not really feel that I had developed policy-forming skill until I was about 36, and felt strong enough to make judgments on this business from the monthly reporting system I had set up. At this stage I dared to risk my money in other new ventures while I kept an eye on this one.

MR. DENVER: My skills developed about the age of 37 after I had become a plant manager.

MR. ARGENT: My policy-forming skills developed when I became controller at the age of about 38. As controller you dig into a lot of reasons for costs being out of line, and so on. You have to have a lot of contact with sales, manufacturing and engineering. But the one thing I didn't get into far enough was research and development. In our business it is a big item, in our future planning. But it is difficult to budget for and control because you have to wait years before you see any results.

MR. CLIFFORD: It was when I formed my own business at around the age of 40 that I began very quietly and steadily to develop policy-forming skills. What is important is a sense of alertness—to take an empirical approach, suck it and see, hammer out what works as you go along. If you make a mistake, you've got to cut your losses and try again.

MR. ATKINS: I was 41. You don't get the opportunity to understand the full facts of the situation until you get the responsibility for it.

MR. EXTRAMAN: I was about 45 when I had my first policy-forming experience, for I had a lot of engineering and works experience before getting on to the commercial side.

MR. BLYTH: Though I first became a managing director at 38 I didn't really develop my policy-forming skills until I was about 45. When I was appointed, I believed that the basic problem was to get a better management organization. Only when I felt that this was done, could I think of the longer range strategy—where we should be going. Of course, this situation is the opposite to that of the inventor of a product who sets up in business. He is at first mainly concerned with strategy and whether the product will go well. Only when he has built up a very considerable business does he usually start getting concerned with the management organization.

MR. ASCOT: My policy-forming developed at the age of 50 when I became vice-president on the West Coast. A person of 50 of good ability is able to learn very fast—much faster than younger people, because emotions and inhibitions do not get in the way.

What types of experience and thinking typically go into the development of policy-forming skills?

The types of experience and thinking will depend on whether a person has a junior position in a substantial organization, or whether he is starting up in business on his own, or whether he is responsible for running a substantial business organization.

Firstly, the junior position:

MR. DAMM: My policy-forming skills developed when I was about 22. I believe that a man must be an entrepreneur in outlook, right from the beginning. One sign is that you identify with the top of the firm even if you are an apprentice.

MR. ANTHONY: My commercial skills developed by the age of 25. I was in a machinery manufacturing business in 1938. I had to understand the machines in order to sell them, and moreover I had to understand my product as a commercial aid to my customer in his business. So I had to understand his business as a commercial entity. This put all the arguments about commerce on a real basis. I had to understand whether our product should be dearer or cheaper and what would be the advantages. For example, at one time I wanted the rollers made $1\frac{1}{2}$ inches wider to suit certain customers. My boss pointed out that this would make the machine considerably dearer, and at that time, prewar, if we had made the machine dearer it would not have stood up to price competition from another machine. So one had to learn to compromise and do the best possible job in the circumstances. I also learnt that sometimes you cannot sell at all because the economic situation is against you and sometimes you can sell very well because it is in your favour. And there are other occasions when even if business is fairly lousy, if you can provide a product which enables two machines to do the work formerly done by three, there are some firms who happen to have the finance available who will buy because it is good business for them, however badly they are doing at the time. They will be able to cut their costs. I had commercial experience very early merely by selling to industry a complex product which I had to understand in relation to their need for it and how it could help them in their business.

Secondly, starting up in business:

MR. CAIRNS: I learned quickly that people don't want to be told what they should use. One must find out what they want deep down and aim for it, even if this means producing a half-way product meanwhile until they are ready to take what you would really like them to have.

MR. CHESHIRE: In my mid-twenties I developed the ability to commercialize a technically good product. I realized that there were other people with equal or better mechanical skills, also there were other people with equal or better business skills. What was lacking was the ability to match the two together. In fact in business one needs both the ability and the money to match the two together. But this doesn't necessarily mean having big finance to start with. One has to be able to negotiate credit for purchasing, as distinct from straight borrowing.

MR. ATKINSON: My policy-forming skills developed when I was about 36. I got the people first and then the policies. We grew from one retail unit to 168 units in seven years. When I found that the formula worked, I repeated it and repeated it. It is important to keep up the momentum, but do it with moderation. I had very little trouble with selecting trustworthy people. Ninety-nine per cent of the people are honest. I used a checking agency to check their entire background.

MR. DODEN: My policy-forming skills began to develop when I was 28, when I set up in business on my own. But they go up and down, or so it seems. I become overconfident if I make good decisions that turn out well, and I lose confidence if I make mistakes.

MR. CHARLTON: Fortunately we had an expanding market. Because we were an efficient, low-cost producer we could out-sell the older, less efficient firms. We bought them up one at a time to get a large-volume market and lay down new, more efficient production lines.

MR. CARLISLE: I do an initial costing on new products myself, then this is checked out by the costing department. We keep re-designing until we get down to the agreed price level, which may be say 12p. If a new one works out at 40p we ask ourselves: 'Does it look 40p?'

MR. CHAPMAN: Our latest product was designed by development engineers, salesmen, service engineers and customers, not by me. We asked the sales people to crystallize all their recommendations. Then when we had finished designing we had a week-end conference and unveiled the new machine. I was able to say to them: 'You thought we were not listening. But this is your machine.' It meant that a salesman could say to a customer: 'I was responsible for having that built into the machine', and he could explain to the customer why he couldn't have in a £5,000 machine the £50,000 facilities. The following week-end we had a similar conference for the service men.

MR. CLEMENTS: I don't regard policy analysis as a special problem. For instance, when I was with my last firm, we made television sets. I was not a television expert, but I analysed the situation pretty closely. I knew what things cost the most, what needed special testing for reliability, what parts of the production could be mechanized, and so on. I got to know every aspect of producing and using every part of the product. One doesn't have to be a technician to make this kind of analysis. This is commercial sense.

Thirdly, when responsible for running a substantial business organization:

MR. DAUTZENBERG: By the time I became general manager I was ready with my own strategy for a product range and price and quality.

MR. BOYD: For years I was nagging away in the boardroom without too much success. I had three ideas I was keen on. There was a new line of products I thought we should take on. Also we should have more self-selection in the branches. And there was a new system for measuring branch productivity which I thought we should adopt.

MR. BOWLES: I was certain I had a clearer notion of the business than the rest of the board. I explained to them that they would always produce too much capacity if they based their calculations on such a low rate of return on capital. Seven years later my policy was actually accepted.

MR. BOLTON: After I became chief executive I realized how disastrously dependent we were on the one product for which the typical rate of return on capital employed is 10 per cent. There is a basic profitability for an activity. By contrast in a related but faster changing industry you could get 30 per cent to 40 per cent—if you were successful, of course. Hence if I was planning to increase earnings per share I must be continuously moving from the fundamentally low profitability activities to those which were higher. So I developed a plan for steadily moving our investment across.

MR. BIGGS: We concentrated on one sector of the industry, and have gone for the world market. Eighty-five per cent of our products sold are manufactured by us but we also merchant the most sophisticated items from other suppliers. This gives us colossal feed-back in technical know-how.

MR. DAHLMANN: Profit centre thinking is rather new in this group. The emphasis has been much more on the perfect functioning of our apparatus. We produce to world class technology, in a style which would be a compliment to our forefathers.

MR. AUSTIN: Previously in the trucking business you just went with the economy. If there was a lot of business about you just worked very hard, if there wasn't because of a sudden recession there was nothing you could do about it except fire people and lay up the trucks. But now we can't cut corners on our employees; what we have to do is look for other ways to put our equipment to work.

MR. ACKLAND: We have just had a policy meeting on where we are going in the next few years, analysing which products are most successful and which are not, and analysing each product group in terms of its impact on the company in four ways—(*a*) on the image of the company, (*b*) on the future of that particular product class, (*c*) on our marketing skills, and (*d*) on our technological involvement.

Research and development and acquisition suggestions for new products come from the divisions. If we have a good product in a particular field we decide whether to extend into that market properly, and perhaps get out of another one where we are not doing so well. We make decisions in terms of desirable expansion, desirable disposal, the need for immediate disposal, and so on.

MR. ATWICK: About one-third of my time is spent on acquisition work. Why? Because it is easier to acquire a technology than to build it. We usually find when we are developing a new area that something else is needed to round out the position. Each unit can only tackle one, two or at the most three projects at the same time. The amount of study and research necessary before deciding which way to go is enormous in any new field. We try to hire the very top man in each field, and this may mean buying his company and in effect taking on his whole team.

MR. AYLWARD: My policy on acquisitions now is that I want the damn thing to fit. It may be a wholesale distribution company which fits in with certain stores. My jigsaw requires a lot of pieces and you just fill them in one at a time. There is nothing complicated about it. For example when you have got several dozen stores selling many millions of quarts of milk a week, it is pretty obvious that you ought to buy a dairy. But any support facilities that I buy must be competitive. My warehouse, for example, sells to other stores as well as to my own. And under the anti-trust laws there can only be one price for an article to both markets. So there is no risk of the warehouse competing favourably outside and subsidizing this activity at the expense of our own stores.

The real secret of competing favourably in consumer markets lies in below the line activity—in saving money on trucking, on distribution, on buying and warehousing. Our stores are allowed to buy outside our own warehouses if they can get a cheaper buy, but this rarely happens.

MR. ALLEN: We cover the full range of textiles from lingerie to dress fabrics to carpeting. But I'm now very interested in the multinational company. If we could form a group which had strong bases in say the United States, Europe and the Far East, then these companies could buy and sell to each other and do a lot more than if they were separate national companies.

MR. BOND: Commercial sense is born in you but experience sharpens it. Experience is very sobering when you make mistakes. Each succeeding challenge makes you more confident of your judgement. I encourage people to give me their opinions of how a particular thing should be played. You've got to make yourself a good listener. Having listened, you must comment on the logic that has led the man to what he has said. If you disagree, you must give reasons. It is not sufficient to say: 'It's a lot of rot.' You can of course say that it will come up at the next management committee meeting and we will give the matter a better airing. If the man is right, you must tell him you agree and why.

Bearing in mind that successful chief executives usually aim for growth of the business, what in general are the types of policy which lead to growth, and what are the obstacles which stand in the way of growth even when it is eagerly sought?

Here are firstly some examples from the survey of general policies leading to growth:

1. Marketing flair plus solid homework

MR. CHILDS has tremendous marketing flair, so he has been able to enter a long-established industry, children's toys, and make his products more exciting to buy. In five years his sales revenue has grown sixty-fold. Not all his products have been new. Quite frequently he has been able to take an existing product that someone has failed with, perhaps re-design it slightly, re-package it and promote it in a more exciting way so that it becomes an instant success. But in spite of his marketing flair, he recognizes the need for running through a 'cockpit drill' to cut down the number of mistakes:

I am preconditioned to be on the lookout but I also have a methodical checklist. I ask myself will the product be inexpensive, will it suit both the boys and the girls, because that way you double the market, can it be packaged attractively, can it be advertised on television, is it of interest to the whole family, does it appeal to a wide age group, and does it involve replacement parts, because better still if it doesn't as you don't then have a parts problem? Flair without having done your homework is bad, but equally, solid homework without flair is bad.

2. Production economies

MR. CHARLTON is selling some products at lower prices than

12 years ago in spite of the general inflation of costs during that time. There is nothing very exciting about his products, drainage pipes. And they are mainly sold to public authorities who are not likely to be impressed by attractive promotion and publicity. But his early skill as a salesman showed him the prospects of getting together much larger batches of orders than usual in his industry, and hence having longer production runs, using more efficient plant and machinery and scheduling a more economic distribution system. His family background in corn-milling made him accustomed to 'working to fine margins'.

3. *Product perfectionism*

MR. CHRISTIE has achieved a threefold growth in sales revenue in five years, making earth moving equipment against competition from world-wide giants. Perfectionism and hence reliability certainly pays when serving an industry in which time costs a lot of money and a breakdown could mean hold-up on a contract, idle workmen and possibly penalties due to late completion.

I enjoy [he says] the sheer delight of making good machines and being number one. We are conscious of an inferiority complex if we don't sell 100 per cent of the market. We must go on to at least 80 per cent anyway.

4. *Meticulous service*

MR. CAVELL's construction business has grown sixfold in six years. He made a name for himself when, over 20 years ago, he proved that he was absolutely reliable. He won a contract to put a new roof on an important public building in 11 months, that is in less than the year that elapses between two major public functions held in the building. He developed his own pre-network-analysis system of scheduling which broke the total task down into small tasks that were easy for participants to understand. He finished the job 10 days ahead of schedule.

MR. CLARK has achieved a tenfold growth in trading revenue in the last five years by performing for industry and public authorities the seemingly unexciting service of waste product disposal. Again, it is the sheer reliability of his service, plus its efficient organization and hence very competitive costing and pricing, which have made such growth possible. In a world full of unreliable people there is money to be made even out of moving muck.

5. *Repeating the instant-success formula*

Everyone in business is looking for a 'magic formula' that just happens to have the right appeal to customers at the right time and the right price. Few people are astute enough or lucky enough to find such a formula to put them way ahead of the competition. But some of the fastest growth records are achieved by those who do, and who go on to repeat their formula again and again. Mass production is essentially this, when it is successful—the mass repetition of a successful formula for winning customers. But some of the more spectacular examples of repeated instant success are found in retailing and in service industries.

MR. CHANDLER runs a chain of hotels and restaurants. In 13 years the chain grew from 6 to over 130 units. He had had many years of hotel experience before he took on the present business. It was actually in the second hotel of this group, not the first, where he found the right conditions to test out certain special theories that brought together architectural and decorative appeal with certain types of food and drink service. When he got the formula right, as evidenced by the spectacular growth in business, he repeated it again and again in further hotels and restaurants.

MR. ATKINSON, as already reported, has a chain of watch and jewellery shops, backed by wholesaling and some manufacturing. When he got his formula right he grew from one retail unit to 168 in seven years.

MR. CHISHOLM has built up a chain of specialized clothing shops appealing to one overlooked but vital section of the community. His successful formula has resulted in an average annual growth of revenue in the last five years of 170 per cent. In his case, profits have grown even faster than revenue, though in most cases of fast revenue growth, profits rise more slowly because of the costs of growth.

So much for the methods of achieving fast growth. Here are now examples of the obstacles to growth which frustrate the attempts of people who may in a professional sense be equally good managers.

1. *Shortage of capital*

MR. BACON is fortunate in that he has achieved a fourfold growth in the trading revenue of his domestic appliance manufacturing business in the last dozen years without needing any outside capital. He has financed a growth rate averaging over 30 per cent a year entirely by ploughing back the profits of the business. But the business was actually started at the end of the last century by MR. BACON's father, who began with a unique invention. Though the original patents have expired and there are now competitors, MR. BACON has a substantial share of his market, his rate of return on capital has been good and his requirements of additional permanent capital have not been high in relation to turnover. His seasonal stock position is financed mainly by bank overdraft, the bank receiving a copy of his forward budget programme for three months ahead, showing his expected revenue and expenditure and cash requirements.

There are not many industries where a fast rate of growth can be financed out of retained earnings. The amount of extra capital required for a given increase in trading revenue varies greatly from industry to industry. It is usually very large in process industries like chemicals, oil refining, steel and cement, and low in craft industries. It can even be negative in those rare cases where someone with an established business or professional reputation starts out on his own with a client list, advance deposits on orders and credit from his suppliers.

It is essential for anyone with a growth business to know the rate at which his capital requirements expand in relation to the volume of business done. MR. DODEN keeps watch on this every month by plotting himself a graph which he keeps in the drawer of his desk.

In cases where outside finance is needed for expansion, the first essential is to persuade the bank or other provider that the business has prospects. This is not too hard if there is an actual backlog of unfulfilled orders. But the other essential is more easily overlooked. This is to persuade the bank that they will not lose their money through overtrading. MR. CAIRNS developed a new product which had a run-away order book. He obtained a bank loan by proving that he had a good control system and was capable of restricting growth in line with the money available, in his case to less than one-third of the orders available. This still meant a growth rate of 140 per cent per annum.

Anyone choosing between growth out of retained earnings and growth financed from outside does, however, face this dilemma. If you choose outside finance because it provides for faster growth, then in the words of MR. CHADWICK, 'you must be prepared to pay your taxes. Unless you have a good record of taxable profits, you won't be able to borrow much money.'

So here lies the dilemma of business in highly-taxed industrial countries. Any businessman concentrating on growth out of retained earnings will try to write off as many of the costs of growth as quickly as possible and show little in the way of taxable profits. But this reduces his performance record, for borrowing purposes.

A change occurs, however, when a private company goes public and obtains a stock market listing. If the chief executive is the former owner and he is not himself trying to retain a majority of the shares, then his attitude to growth and his methods of financing can alter drastically. In the words of MR. CHESHIRE, who has been through this experience and whose growth rate has been 50 per cent per annum, 'as a private company one is concentrating on the growth of the single company, as a public company one is concentrating on growth by acquisition, involving mainly an exchange of shares'.

2. *Shortage of capable managers*

MR. COLE's light engineering machinery business has been growing at the rate of 30 per cent per annum, and it has recently reached the stage of having 1,000 employees and being too big for his personal management style. He admits that it now needs more professional management and he has recently chosen a successor, who is under training.

However, even where a chief executive feels that he can adapt his style and delegate adequately to fully experienced functional heads, there may be a limit to the rate of growth. In the words of MR. BLYTH, who has 11,000 employees throughout the world and makes industrial products, 'we are never limited by ideas or money but by the ability to develop strong management. If we grow beyond a certain rate we have a rocky time.'

MR. BEST has 14,000 employees throughout the world and makes mainly consumer products, but he too feels limited by the people problem. His firm has recently been growing at 25 per cent per annum but he feels that the ideal annual long-term rate of growth is 10–12½ per cent.

MR. CHATFIELD has been successfully growing at 25 per cent per annum, but has still only 300 employees. He is in a service industry and he has been helped in his growth by a staff bonus system which involves paying to service men a substantial percentage of individually invoiced jobs, subject to inspection.

MR. CALDER's financial empire is outstanding for its growth record, having grown eighty-eightfold, from a substantial base, in five years. This is mostly takeover growth. He does not believe that it is necessarily more difficult to grow with increasing size. But there is a management problem. After a while 'the drop-outs will slow you down'. Some of the very capable and ambitious people, selected and trained to make fast growth possible, will want to go off and establish their own businesses.

So much for the underlying obstacles to the general growth of firms. What about the temporary, structural factors which inhibit the growth of particular companies at particular times?

1. *Delays in receiving planning permission*

MR. COCHRANE's grocery chain has already over 25,000 employees and it is still growing by 100 per cent per annum in both trading revenue and net earnings. Their main obstacle to growth is that they cannot get planning permission to build new stores fast enough.

However desirable location planning may be, if it slows down the growth rate of some of the fast-growing firms it almost inevitably slows down the average rate of growth of the economy.

2. *Image requirements*

MR. BOOTH also runs a grocery chain almost as large as MR. COCHRANE'S, though its growth rate is slower. It has doubled in trading revenue in the last five years, but has grown faster in net earnings. MR. BOOTH believes one of the factors inhibiting faster growth is the 'need to develop a clear and identifiable corporate image giving the company a plus over its competition in the eyes of the shopping public'. There is a break-through point where a company name becomes a household name. Until this is achieved, the promotion of growth is much more of an uphill struggle.

3. *Market conservatism*

MR. DOBLER makes plastic pipes and fittings. Trading revenue has doubled in the last five years and he expects it to double again in the next five years. The main obstacle to faster growth is the conservatism of municipal water boards concerning the rates of substitution of plastic for cast-iron.

4. *The need for rationalization to meet technical and market changes*

MR. CLEMENTS produces electrical and electronic goods, both industrial and domestic. His rate of real growth has been very slow in recent years due to the takeover of other firms and the closing down of their unsuccessful parts.

MR. BOLTON makes chemicals. His net rate of growth recently has been virtually nil. His group is moving away from its former dependence on one branch of the industry. This has meant selling a lot of companies which were producing goods that did not fit in with the three chosen areas of research, and which therefore dissipated research effort.

MR. BLACK makes leather goods, travel goods, and now

chemicals. Profits grew very slowly until a finance house took an interest in the firm. They have risen astronomically in the last two years. Previously the main obstacle to growth, when the firm was based primarily in the tanning industry, was that this was a contracting industry due to the impact of synthetics. They have since worked on two problems: first, how to secure a good return on the capital invested in the tanning industry and second, how to diversify into new and more profitable industries.

5. *Limited national market growth*

MR. BLISS makes tin cans, paper and cardboard cartons and plastic containers. Trading revenue has been growing about 10 per cent per year. So long as the company stays in packaging, it is dependent on growth of the total packaging business, unless it increases still further its market share. The company has broadened the base of its packaging business but stayed within it. They have not only moved from metal to plastics and paper, but have developed the use of their types of containers for things not previously put into them—for example beverages, new potatoes, aerosol products.

MR. DACKWEILER makes optical lenses and spectacle frames. Trading revenue has risen by 60 per cent in the past four years, and his business is growing faster than the average in his industry. But the main obstacle to faster growth is the limited growth in the total market. As people become more prosperous, they do not necessarily want to wear more pairs of glasses.

MR. BOND has tens of thousands of employees. His main product is beer, and the company owns hundreds of millions of pounds worth of public houses. Since their last takeover they are not growing very fast. The main barrier to further growth is that they are already so big in an industry which is not growing significantly.

6. *Limited international market growth*

MR. BISSETT also has tens of thousands of employees. His main products are steel and a wide range of engineering and metal goods. When a firm is in so many different businesses, the rate of growth will vary greatly from one business to another, so the overall rate of growth is likely to be near the average for the main country where it operates. Hence the chief obstacle to growth is the limited rate of growth of its main country. In one division the company has such a large share of the total market that it can only grow at the rate that the economy grows, without inviting trouble from the monopolies commission. In another division, the company has a high percentage of the U.K. market and also a substantial share of world exports. More than half the total output is exported. Hence the rate of growth depends upon unpredictable overseas factors such as whether there will be political troubles in Africa, the Middle East or Asia, or whether some major importing country will impose a quota.

MR. BERESFORD's company has several thousand employees. His main products are made from an imported raw material, the supply of which is now limited due to political troubles in the main supplying country.

MR. BLUNDELL's firm has tens of thousands of employees. They make plant used in electricity generation. The main obstacle to growth of the business is the slow growth rate of the electricity supply industry.

MR. BLOOMFIELD has now only a few hundred employees. His main merchandise is watches. Turnover in the last five years has decreased. The chief cause of decline is the removal of the EFTA trade barriers. There are nearly three million extra watches coming into Britain now. The firm has diversified by buying a business making products which sell through some of the same outlets as watches, so that the sales force is now better used. But further diversification is restricted by a shortage of cash, which of course is due to the decline in sales. So they are caught in a vicious circle.

Summing up the last three sections of this chapter, it will be noticed that the policies which led to fast rates of growth were all obvious things, easy to say but difficult to do:

1. Marketing flair plus solid homework
2. Production economies
3. Product perfectionism

4. Meticulous service
5. Repeating the instant-success formula

Moreover, it is worth noting that all the examples are of original capitalists who founded their own businesses. I naturally selected the best examples, and at the time of drafting this chapter I had no way of knowing that in the analysis of growth rates original capitalists would prove to be so very different from non-owning chief executives.

The notes for each chapter are contained in an envelope on which is marked the date when the chapter was drafted. Hence I know that I completed drafting this chapter on policy-forming skills on December 29, 1970, yet it was not until February 23, 1971, that I made the analysis which showed such a marked contrast between the growth rates of original capitalists and those of non-owning chief executives.

In the section of this chapter on the two major obstacles to growth—shortage of capital and shortage of capable managers—the original capitalists (including MR. DODEN) dominate the provision of information on how to overcome these obstacles. Moreover, in the earlier section of this chapter describing the types of experience which led to the development of policy-forming skills, it is two American original capitalists, MR. ATWICK and MR. AYLWARD, who are found to have made perhaps the most significant contributions.

By contrast with this hopeful evidence on successful policies, at the end of the chapter we have a catalogue of woes concerning structural factors which inhibit the growth of particular companies at particular times. Any very capable businessman, whether he be a non-owning chief executive or an original capitalist, can find himself caught up by one of these structural factors. He is in effect knocking his head against a brick wall. It may take him years to break through with a new line of policy, either for the same industry or for another one, which will permit expansion again.

Is there an ideal rate of growth?

The answer will vary with the circumstances of the business. As

MR. BOWLES said earlier, 'a lot of businesses have lost their way'. If a business has lost its way, mere planning for a certain rate of growth may lead only to frustration and failure to achieve the plan. And the business will almost certainly face 'a shortage of capable managers'.

If on the other hand the chief executive has discovered an 'instant-success formula', as did some of those quoted earlier in this chapter, and if he has a share stake in the business so that he feels personally committed to the financial consequences of fast growth, then it may be possible for him to achieve a very high rate of growth indeed. The problems of selection and training of capable managers will be considerable, but they will be simplified by the clarity of the instant-success formula, which will enable him to have very precisely defined requirements and disciplines for staff.

In other words, the key to fast growth lies in Mrs. Beeton's recipe for jugged hare: 'First catch your hare.' The chief executive who wants fast growth must first analyse and master-mind the problems of his business in detail, in the hope that he will find a business policy which really pays off, which causes customers to flock towards his goods or services. Only then are the other problems of fast growth likely to be clearly definable and simple enough to be manageable.

PART II

A DETAILED ACCOUNT OF HIS METHODS OF PLANNING, ORGANIZATION, MOTIVATION AND CONTROL

11

CHOOSING AN ORGANIZATION STRUCTURE

Is it possible to establish any general principles of organization?

Some members of the survey suggested that it was not. For example:

MR. ASPINALL: Designing an organization structure is a fluid thing, one cannot lay down precise rules. Sometimes you base your organization on the market, sometimes on the product category and sometimes on the function. Business is always changing. There was a time when it was fashionable to split up according to function, then according to products, but now nobody lays down precise rules. Here are two examples. We used to let all the different manufacturing companies run their own subsidiaries abroad, but we found that these subsidiaries became step-children in which nobody took much interest, and the man sent abroad, for example to a particular country for our electronic products business, found that he was left out there and rather divorced from the whole organization. So we have reorganized all these into a group international company.

This has transformed all the overseas operations. Now the chaps abroad feel that they are really going somewhere, and indeed they are making great progress.

A second example can be seen in a part of the group where there are eight basic product divisions, and a number of these divisions have done development work on information systems. We have now brought them all together in a new division concerned solely with information systems, taking all the various elements out of these other divisions. We have concentrated interest, and more particularly we have avoided the problem of distraction. For an organization to succeed, its shape must be based somewhat on the motivation of the executives, on their being able to be interested in and see a viable area of attack. The unit must be of a size so that it can really perform, but its activities must not be so diverse that managers are distracted from chasing specific goals.

Typical of some of the most successful businessmen, MR. ASPINALL began by denying that there could be any rules, then after quoting a couple of cases he ended by pointing to one or two decidedly interesting principles.

To build up a set of principles, however, we really need to start with the problem of the small businessman who has grown to the point where he needs to take on or promote his first manager with defined responsibilities.

What basically decides the head of a small firm to delegate a particular activity, and hence to begin shaping his future organization?

In many cases, when the work load becomes too great, what decides him is that certain skills can be bought or taught, that they must be performed well if the firm is to succeed but that they are not so crucial as the tasks he intends to retain.

If, for example, he is a retailer and he opens a second shop, he will put in a manager for the second shop but he will retain control of the buying. Shop managers can be hired and trained, but good buying is absolutely crucial to retail success and is not so easily taught or delegated as a responsibility. This was the case with MR. CHISHOLM and MR. CLIFFORD, whose success stems substantially from their skill as buyers.

Equally, a small manufacturer who gets tired of keeping his own books will hire a bookkeeper, then later an accountant. He knows that good accounting is essential to his business, but it doesn't have to be done by him.

If the unique feature of the business is the chief executive's technical inventiveness, he may proclaim that marketing isn't really his line, and he may hire an experienced marketing man.

Examples of chief executives who started with technical flair are MR. CHESHIRE and MR. COLE.

Again equally, a small manufacturer whose real flair is marketing may appoint a technical or production manager on the plea that his own flair is not technical. Examples of chief executives who started with marketing flair are MR. CASEY and MR. CHILDS.

Does each type of business, then, have a centre of gravity, a special core of responsibility that the chief executive takes a personal interest in?

This at least is the experience of MR. DECKER:

My last firm produced consumer goods and was very much a sales oriented business. Production was less of a problem. But here each division must find the right product and do their own research, and they all have entirely different markets. In each field the centre of gravity is different.

You don't sell heavy machinery because of the wrapping around the parcel, you sell it because you have the image of being technically competent and reliable and because you are permanently on very good relations with your customers; for the point is, to sell a long-term and high-value technical investment like for instance a turbine you have to have strong mutual trust at the top level.

Household appliances again are different, you have to do the publicity and you have to have retailers and wholesalers and appoint stockists, etc.

Again, selling equipment to the railways means producing it to the specification of someone who thinks he knows all about what he wants.

Again, putting transmission lines across Malaysia means having a kind of John Wayne character who knows how to handle a thousand local people and cut through the forest, come what may.

Again, producing transistors and selling them means having some very clever laboratory boffins. The centre of gravity varies from one kind of business to another.

What is the difference between centre of gravity and centre of motivation?

None really, in this context. Here are two Americans talking along the same lines as MR. DECKER but referring to motivation.

MR. ACLAND: At the age of 27 I was put in charge of a Columbian biscuit plant where everything seemed to be wrong. I completely reorganized on the basis of worker motivation—all organization is essentially based on this.

MR. ARMSTRONG: The company's divisions are based on geography. We don't worry about overlap in our sales forces for the different products within a particular territory. When you reach a certain size, it is far more important to involve people in one particular product group. The training costs are so great if you try to involve them in more than one. Also there is the motivation problem. And we need not only salesmen but servicemen. They must all concentrate their attention. There is a breadth of product line that can be handled, and beyond that it is unsafe to go even if the product range is homogeneous.

Here is a Briton talking along similar lines.

MR. BOWLES: In its home market the company is divided into ethical pharmaceuticals on the one hand and advertised products on the other hand. It would be easy and perhaps logical to join these divisions up, but the advertised products have a much harder, more competitive position. So long as pharmaceuticals are kept apart from the advertised products, the temptation is resisted to make easy money on pharmaceuticals at the expense of neglecting advertised products.

What is the difference between organization based on motivation and organization based on markets?

Very often none, since a businessman's motivation is closely tied up with serving his markets.

MR. ARTHUR: The company has been broken down into manageable parts which have logical input and output boundaries. The natural boundaries are the markets, both buying and selling. We have an oil and gas division, domestic, and another one for overseas. We have a refining and marketing division, also there is a chemical and carbon division and a fertilizer division.

MR. BERESFORD: Two companies in the group have recently been joined together because they are both serving the building industry.

MR. ALLEN: The logic of our organization structure is division by market. There is no way for me to make meaningful day-to-day decisions on products with such different markets as hosiery and carpets.

MR. BOND: We have concentrated very much on modern production facilities, but we have also had to concentrate equally on local marketing facilities. There is a managing director in every region of the country, in charge of marketing in that region. Note that he is a managing director, not a marketing director. He is fully profit responsible, buying in his beer and other supplies from our breweries and elsewhere.

Surely motivation in businessmen is associated with profit? Why not therefore base an organization structure on profit centres rather than on markets?

This amounts to much the same thing, since one cannot have a real profit centre without definable markets that pay real prices.

MR. ATTERBURY: Every type of product in our business is a profit centre, as well as each distribution outlet. For example, moulded goods are a profit centre and so are aircraft tyres, though these things may be sold through our normal distribution channels.

MR. AVERY: It creates much greater motivation on the part of the managers of the business if the companies retain their separate identity yet are part of a federal system.

MR. CLARK: I re-designed the whole company on the long journeys to Australia. We set up a system by which each unit produced its own trial balance and therefore had its own accounting capability.

MR. DODEN: One must have departments that are profit centres, enabling people to work full out on their goals. For a good man, I form a separate department, but I won't form a department unless I have a good man for it.

I have my administrative services now in a separate company, doing service work for other companies to spread the cost of the most up-to-date administration system.

MR. BIGGS: We like to make a company as self-supporting as possible. But some things can be shared in common, in our case purchasing, public relations, forms of accounting and computers.

We believe in keeping the names of companies when we take them over. Ours is definitely a federal structure. You mustn't take away from an individual his title, his power. They help to bring the best out of people. Our machine-tool business has grown from fortieth in the industry to third place in seven years. By contrast, one of our competitors abolished the names of all their subsidiaries and this has knocked the staff who ceased to be directors of companies and are mere managers. By our system we get the best of both worlds, a certain amount of centralization where it pays, but individual operation under their own name in the subsidiaries.

MR. ANDERSON: When the firm was smaller it was in ethical pharmaceuticals only, and it had a functional structure. The international division was viewed as part of the marketing arm and it reported direct to the president. When it grew, it needed a general manager as opposed to a functional manager.

In different industries there is clearly a different size level at which a firm can afford a general manager for a division. In our electronics division, for example, we can afford one at a smaller size than in pharmaceuticals. We are trying to vest general management responsibility further down into smaller units.

Two of our major competitors are pharmaceutical firms which could save some overheads by bringing together some of their business, but they are deliberately not doing so because they get better concentrated general management responsibility, and therefore better profits out of keeping the units smaller.

What about the companies which claim to be based on product divisions? Are they different from those which claim to have their organization based on markets or on profit centres?

Not necessarily so. As we can see from the examples given below, sometimes the boundaries between products also denote the boundaries between markets. In other cases they do not. In deciding between product and market boundaries, one must bear in mind a distinction between different types of technologist pointed out by MR. DILLMANN: 'There is a big difference between the outlooks of chemists and engineers. A chemist makes a product and then looks around to find uses for it. An engineer first asks for the task and then he looks around to see how he can do it.'

Using this very rough generalization as a rule-of-thumb, if one happens to have technologists who think and behave like

MR. DILLMANN's typical chemist, then a product basis of division of responsibility may well be appropriate. The staff will get their motivation from concentrating on a product area of research and development, then pursuing all possible markets for their resulting product. By contrast, if one happens to have technologists who think and behave like MR. DILLMANN's typical engineer, then a market basis of division is more important.

MR. BLYTH: Half our operation is overseas. In the U.K. we have two principal divisions, one for metal products and the other for non-metal. Overseas each territory has one company.

MR. ARCHER: We are in three different machinery businesses. Our divisions are product-oriented rather than customer-oriented. In the construction equipment division, there are five separate companies with the same sales force because the products are related. By contrast in the machine tool division, which goes all the way from half million dollar numerically controlled machine tools down to small cutters, we have all kinds of distribution—direct, through dealers, and agents.

MR. DILLMANN: We are organized into product divisions, but we have too many fields of activity, with no relation to each other. This is our strength when one activity goes down and one up, but it is also our weakness. It is dangerous to scatter your attention.

MR. ANSELL: The company is being reorganized now into a new set of product divisions concerned with different aspects of communication—data writing, printing, and telecommunication. All divisions have their own sales services.

What about the companies that cannot adopt one of the simple bases of organization already described?

As the following examples show, there are many special cases:

MR. ASHBOURNE: We don't try to mix the staffs for aerospace and commercial divisions. There are legal, personnel and accounting reasons why we should not, except at the treasury level where the finances are consolidated. Our commercial divisions are basically divided by market.

MR. DITTMER: We have four subsidiaries which are 100 per cent owned and four which are 50 per cent jointly owned with other companies.

MR. BLUNDELL: Our subsidiaries are substantially dependent on us for research and development aid, but with our associate companies in Europe we have a combined R. & D. operation to ensure that there is no unnecessary duplication of work, and we join with them on a contract where this is advantageous.

MR. ATWICK: We have the firm divided into two main operating groups—firstly, the commodity side in which there are various conversion type businesses that take a raw material and put it through a process. Secondly, there are the manufacturing businesses that fabricate, make and assemble parts.

MR. BURKE: We are very centralized. We do have profit centres but it is difficult for them because the people in charge are not really responsible for all the costs of the building materials they sell. We have the biggest linear programming scheme in Europe to run the most economic distribution system and to determine the optimum positions for siting new capacity. If an area cannot supply all they are asked to, the central computer determines where the additional supplies should come from. Thus, although the head of one area may promote hard and sell more, he can't determine his own costs, as to where some of his supplies come from. We may not want him to sell more in a particular area if it costs us too much to deliver. We have our own centralized transport fleet, so this too limits the area man's independence.

MR. AUSTIN: Because of the service we give right across America and on the Continent of Europe and in the Far East, we are organized on an area basis. Each area is self-contained in its management.

MR. DOEBEL: We work on the team principle, not the heirarchical principle. Each team is composed of people with different functions and is therefore complete in itself to handle client business. We find this suits the advertising industry.

MR. DAUTZENBERG: The company is logically divided according to functions—marketing, production, administration. But I stress the importance of team work. I bring together people of various ranks and functions in teams to solve production problems, work on new products, investigate organization problems, do the tobacco buying, and work on personnel relations. There is no clash with the line functions because the teams have to work out and recommend decisions which are then implemented throughout the organization.

MR. DEMMLER: The organization is divided geographically, except that marketing is centralized in headquarters. Two years ago it was different. We had local marketing people. Now there is a concentrated market drive from the centre, for all our brewery products.

MR. DEGENHARDT: Two of my colleagues are in charge of buying—one for textiles and the other for non-textiles. Another colleague is sales director and is in charge of marketing, sales and advertising, operation and control of all the stores. He works closely with the two buying directors and he has under him four store directors who are each running about 15 shops.

MR. BRIDGES: We have a classical line and staff structure within each of the three major product groups. This suits the motor industry.

MR. DANNEWALD: We have a separate company for each type of insurance, and each of these is represented on the executive board by one director.

MR. ASCOT: Our stores are controlled by area heads. Each territorial officer has the same functional staff as headquarters—a personnel man, a controller, a lawyer, an operations manager, a property and real estate man, a construction manager, a display manager, a credit manager, a retail merchandise manager, a catalogue merchandise manager. The equivalent people at head office develop the major promotion programmes, the compensation programmes, the fringe benefits, training, and printed materials. They do research into the best display methods and they even make contracts for these. They prepare and print the catalogues. The buying is primarily done at head office or by overseas buyers who work under head office. The logic of mass merchandising is mass buying.

Whatever system of organization is chosen, there will probably be line and staff officers at the different levels. This means, for example, that a staff specialist at one level reports to his line chief executive and also to his opposite number at the higher level. In these circumstances, how is conflict avoided?

The first task in avoiding conflict is for the group chief executive to make clear the relative roles of line and staff at each level. These can be illustrated by examples taken from the survey:

MR. ANTHONY: We have 15 operating divisions, grouped under three vice-presidents. Also we have at head office vice-presidents for engineering and research, marketing, manufacturing, personnel, corporate development and finance. Under these head-office vice-presidents are corporate specialists in particular facilities such as work measurement, market research, market analysis, the co-ordination of advertising and sales promotion, labour relations, etc.

The individual divisions and operating companies do not and cannot afford to have such specialist services. We have for example a construction specialist who is available to help with any factory extension or rebuilding. A particular company in the group is not doing this all the time and therefore they could not afford to have such a specialist.

The way the system of communication between these various executives works is as follows: The head of manufacturing, for example, in a particular company, is functionally responsible for his manufacturing programme to the vice-president of manufacturing at head office. This vice-president has to see that the manufacturing function is performed at a high level of quality throughout, that it has a high grade of people and it is utilizing the most modern and effective techniques.

If he recommends certain courses of action to the head of manufacturing in a particular company who does not adopt them either because he does not agree with them or because the president of his company disagrees with them, then the vice-president of manufacturing has recourse to the vice-president of the group in which this company is, and to the president of the whole corporation, that is to me.

If it comes to me, I will arrange a get-together of the vice-president of manufacturing, the vice-president of the particular group and the president of the company concerned. We might call in the manufacturing head of that company, we might not, according to the details we wanted. In fact, the head of manufacturing in the particular company, when he is preparing his operating plan for the next year, works very closely with the vice-president of manufacturing of the whole group.

Because they work closely together on future plans, major problems are likely to come up, if they do, at the planning stage rather than at an operation stage. The operating plan prepared by the head of manufacturing of a particular company has to be approved by the vice-president manufacturing for the group and by the man's own company president and by his group vice-president. All have to initial it before it comes up to me as part of the total planning for the year ahead. This means that all these executives concerned have to get together and try and iron out their differences.

The lines of communication are clear on our organization chart which is on the wall in the room of the personnel man responsible for organization. He has to keep it up to date and periodically have it set up in type. We always put the date on the organization chart to make it clear to everybody when it was last up-dated.

MR. DECKER: We have four divisions working in different product areas, and also four functions—finance and accounting, personnel, production and technical including research, and marketing. Here is an example of how the system works.

The entire sales force reports for disciplinary purposes to the marketing director. In a local sales office there is a head of the office who reports to the marketing function, and all the local sales staff report to this local head. But the various salesmen work for the different divisions and specialize in their work. So far as their particular technology is concerned, they report to the appropriate division. It is rather like in a bank where all the staff in a particular branch report to the branch manager, but the foreign exchange man will deal directly with the foreign exchange department at head office.

MR. BATCHELOR: There are no problems of relationship of line and staff at the lower levels, or of line executives and head-office staff, because they all have the right to go to each other's budget meetings. A man can go along to a budget meeting of a colleague and argue the figure relating to his function.

MR. BRADLEY: The success of our company depends on the dynamic being local rather than central. There is always a danger of headquarters staff getting remote from the branches. Good staff men should be prepared to try a branch job, but unfortunately the opposite is rarely possible, a good branch man cannot really come into head office and do a staff job. So moving staff around is rather difficult.

Because we are not large we must double up on line and staff jobs at the top level. There are six members of the family on the board. They all specialize except me. One is responsible for premises and the architects and mechanical handling equipment, one is responsible for buying, one for selling, one for accounting and finance, one for training and education. In addition each is an area director for a group of branches.

MR. ATTWOOD: We have the usual administrative functions such as finance, but we also have a horizontal system of authority, each creative function having a head of department who is responsible for recruitment and training and discipline and the quality of work of all the people in his function with the same specialized skill. Then we have a vertical form of authority from the client whose contact is with the account director for that particular account, who then organizes with the connivance of the heads of functions, a product group containing members from each function who are going to work part of their time on that particular client's account. The account director has an operational responsibility to the client, he works with his team and if necessary he goes to the head of a particular function to argue over a particular point where he does not see eye to eye with a member of the team. If they cannot settle their differences, then they come to me for a decision.

The system has what I call in-built tensions that tend to stimulate rather than agitate or frighten people. I have had to arbitrate only on three occasions in the six years I have been here. People can come to see me without their superior being exercised about it. The system makes people like to work here because there is always a different channel you can go through, always a safety valve.

Although MR. ATTWOOD talks of horizontal and vertical forms of authority, this is really the advertising industry's equivalent of the traditional line and staff system. Each account executive is a line manager responsible for actual results, and he forms around him a group of staff who answer to him for work on a particular client's account, but also report to their heads of their own particular specialist functions. If a line and staff system has advantages for employees by providing them with 'a safety valve', it has also advantages for the chief executive of a parent company. It gives him multi-channels of communication. He receives reports from the line managers in charge of each division, subsidiary or other unit enterprise. In addition, each of his staff men in charge of a specialist function receives reports direct from the equivalent staff men at the next level down. Hence a line manager at a subordinate level cannot hide anything unless he carries all his specialist staff 100 per cent with him. It needs only one of them, perhaps slightly resentful, to get on the phone to his specialist superior at head office, and any secret is out. Even the smallest thing he says about some difficulty they are having at the lower level may cause the chief executive at head office to be indirectly alerted so that he then gets on the phone and starts asking questions. This is certainly a system of 'in-built tensions'. Some important aspects of its working are described by MR. AUBREY:

We have manufacturing, marketing and research facilities which are line functions and then we have a very strong staff organization—finance, personnel, legal, purchasing and engineering, which are common to them all. We have 20 major product groups and some of them have three or four different markets. The division manager for a product group or group of products has manufacturing and marketing managers reporting to him, but the staff who serve them on finance, personnel, legal, purchasing and engineering matters will be assigned to them part-time, probably handling the work of one or two other divisions as well.

These divisional staff men have a functional responsibility to the chief of their function, but they have a direct responsibility to service the division. They get their promotion and merit ratings from the chief of their function and they devote their time and energy to servicing the division, which is their customer.

We keep them belonging to the centre of expertise and they are continually recharged with their own discipline rather than left to their own devices. It is important to have common standards. Also this gives us an element of control. The financial people, for example, should be independent so that nobody can tell them how to keep the score.

In the age of computers, does not a system of headquarters staffing seriously limit the scope for proper functioning by local management?

It can do, and a general warning on the pitfalls of overcentralized accounting is contained in these words from MR. ATTWATER.

We have a central system for laying down how the accounts should be, but each division is allowed to develop its own cost accounting system. What is important for one is not for another. Labour is critical in glass, material is critical in plastics. Some divisions need a further breakdown than others. But we do have a standard system of general financial reporting.

It is worth also repeating here the warning of MR. BLYTH:

Subsidiary managing directors who are dependent on central information get caught in a mesh that they cannot investigate properly. They can never really learn in the same way. This is one of the problems with computers. If I had a problem of stocks, for example (when I first ran a subsidiary), I could actually walk round and see the people concerned, both those in the accounting department who were looking after the figures and those in charge of the stocks.

One can equally, however, give the opposite case of the subsidiary companies which become so independent and remote from head office that the group chief executive does not have an adequate picture of their real situation. A classic case is that of the Penn Central bankruptcy, reported on by the U.S. Interstate Commerce Commission, April 1971.* In such cases there is clearly a lack of rapport between the chief executives of the group and the subsidiaries, and also between the group staff officers and their opposite numbers in the subsidiaries. Expressing this in system terms, as in Chapter 7, there is a lack of master-minding of the detailed systems both one and two steps down the hierarchy. Such master-minding is essential to good organization, but as we have seen in Chapter 7, it is not in conflict with the rightful freedom of the individual manager to act within his own specialist sphere.

To what extent should the detailed organization structure and systems of a business be written down in readily available reference manuals?

Eighty per cent of those asked in the survey whether they had organization and procedures manuals, said they did. But the extent of the detail they record varies greatly. Relatively few have any clear appreciation of what to write down, and what not.

The wrong and the right ways, respectively, can be illustrated by these examples:

MR. EXTRAMAN: We have no procedures manual but we do have job specifications. If we had a manual nobody would read it. If they did, they would take no notice, and if they did take notice, it would be out of date.

MR. BENHAM: We have a procedures manual only for accounting

* London report, *Sunday Times*, April 25, 1971.

processes and for the flow processes of documents. The computer side is, of course, fully documented. We do not have much in the way of terms of reference for jobs. We have become a little disenchanted with these.

If the terms of reference for a job have to be written down in detail, this is a sign of lack of trust and lack of rapport between chief and subordinate. On the other hand, systems do have to be written down in detail. They determine the flow of precision information within a business, the actual quantities and specifications of orders, etc., and the money involved.

A general principle of organization

Up to this point, the chapter had been drafted before the total analysis of participants in the survey had highlighted the remarkable growth records of the original capitalists. It is now proposed to sift from the evidence presented those elements which together make up a general principle of organization based on the outstanding performance of these original capitalists but bearing in mind that a lot of the organization in a fast-growing business run by an original capitalist is in his mind only. He tends to be overcentralized, to delegate too little, and this is often his ultimate undoing. We must now try to make full reality out of his half-real, half-phantom organization structure. We must also ponder on how such a go-getting person can ever hand over to a successor.

It should first be pointed out that business firms suffer from problems of inherited management as well as from inherited ownership. Let me compare these two. Inherited ownership is well enough understood, in particular that the second generation owner of a family business may not have the same qualities as his father. In some things he may be better, in others worse, but almost certainly he will be different. Therefore it can be a major problem for him to inherit and run the organization created by his father, producing the same products or services for the same markets.

Some family businesses get over the problems of hereditary

ownership by having the whole family, sometimes the women as well as the men, so steeped in the firm's technology and markets and management methods, indeed its whole philosophy, that by the time the next generation takes over, any weaknesses in one member of the family are partly made up for by the inspiration and guidance of family 'folklore' about the business, and also partly by fraternal assistance from other members of the family. There may be plenty of arguments, but in some cases the system works.

Even in a public company, with its shares listed and widely held, where no problems of hereditary ownership arise and where the most capable man is carefully chosen for succession to the post of chief executive, it may still be a major problem for him to take over and run an organization with a set of products and markets all uniquely master-minded by his predecessor.

The public company sometimes gets over the problems of inherited management by carefully grooming a successor to the chief executive, a 'crown prince' whose name is usually known to members of the Board (see Chapter 13). It is this man's task to become steeped in both the philosophy and the workings of the business, so that if and when he takes over, he can carry on as if nothing had changed, though logically, being a different personality, he will in due time cause the organization to be different from what it might have been if his predecessor had continued in office. Sometimes jealousy or fear in the top management team prevents a crown prince from being chosen or prevents him from taking over effectively, but there have been cases where the succession was arranged satisfactorily.

We are not, of course, concerned in this chapter with problems of succession, but rather with pondering on what a successor has to know and be capable of doing in order to take over an organization. If we understand this, we are in a position to determine the boundaries of the organization he is capable of taking over.

When I first began studying management in the late 1940s, the Principle of the Span of Control was considered an important principle of management. Briefly it said that a manager could not effectively control more than a certain number of subordinates—generally then considered to be from four to six.

Subsequent management research showed that different industries had such different technical requirements, (e.g. unit production, batch production, mass production and continuous process production), and they had such different marketing and distribution problems (e.g. large scale contract tendering, ordering from a catalogue, over-the-counter sales), that clearly there could be no simple span of control principle to suit all needs. In one case, by the nature of the work, it might be sensible to have 20 managers reporting to the one boss, in another case three might be the right number. Moreover, in counting heads, how can one ever equate staff specialists with line managers? If a chief executive needs seven staff specialists to provide him with certain types of information and services, he has already used up a fair 'ration' of people reporting to him. Does this then mean drastic curtailment of the number of line executives reporting to him?

Clearly, the Principle of the Span of Control no longer stands up. And yet it contains an important germ of truth, for any general Principle of Organization must be concerned with the boundaries beyond which a man cannot effectively run the organization. Once boundaries can be defined according to some principle, we have a concept of a unit organization. We can then put units together to form larger and different units, just as the cells of the human body form organs and the organs together make up the whole body.

I am replacing the Principle of the Span of Control with a principle based on observation of how the successful original capitalists grow their businesses so fast, and I am going to support this principle with relevant quotations from the 103 chief executives interviewed for this study.

This principle is not concerned with the Span of Control, but with the Span of Effective Rapport. I am going to explain this first by giving a brief anonymous case example.

At the time I was preparing to write these words, I happened to spend a weekend in the Cotswolds, and one evening we went to dinner at an Upper Thames Valley restaurant, newly mentioned in a good food guide. The points that I was able to observe about this excellent eating place show that all its concepts and practices had been carefully master-minded by someone, to make up a complete 'package' which exactly fitted its market.

I say 'someone' did the master-minding, though it could have been more than one person, provided that these two or three were in close rapport with each other. My point is that there was not a single jarring note such as could easily arise if the business had been thought of as an organization with several different departments—kitchen, promotion, reception, bar, building, etc., all vaguely and loosely held together in a management committee but all substantially going their own way.

Here are a few of the master-minded points observed about this restaurant:

Firstly, its market. Though there are plenty of well-to-do people in the area, could they and would they permanently support the restaurant? Its creation had been inspired by the building of the Anglo-French Concorde at Filton, a convenient motoring distance away. The British executives and engineers would need to entertain their visiting French colleagues at a standard of hospitality equivalent to what they received on the other side of the Channel. Some challenge, but well met!

Secondly, its architecture. A brilliant blending of modern Scandinavian-type wood with the local Cotswold stone, thus bringing the past right up to date, and very O.K. for either County or Concorde set.

Thirdly, the reception. To avoid the sort of embarrassment when more than one party arrives at the same time, the traditional role of head waiter was fulfilled by two or three young hostesses in long frocks, carefully selected because they sounded as though they came from expensive schools. By contrast those who waited on table were equally charming, but they did not have to sound the same. A small point of snobbery, but it had been thoroughly thought through.

Fourthly, the seating for drinks. Careful extension of the fire-place stonework, and along the opposite wall an equivalent wooden bench, meant that in spite of the intimate size of the reception area, people having a drink could never be short of seats. If a big party arrived suddenly and there were not enough chairs, cushions could be scattered along the benches.

Fifthly, the food. A well chosen mixture of special dishes on which the restaurant made its name and perhaps its profit, together with a selection of the more conventional.

These are just five out of 21 points I counted which had been skilfully master-minded to give the right touch, the right atmosphere—even down to the book left casually on the stone-work by the fire, a copy of Sir Kenneth Clark's *Civilisation.*

Surely this example with its emphasis on master-minding denies the importance of delegation?

On the contrary, delegation is only effective and consistent with a thoroughly master-minded product or set of products and a thoroughly master-minded marketing and distribution system, when there is real rapport between the chief executive and each manager reporting to him. In the words of MR. BANFIELD, rapport in these circumstances 'means that if someone has a problem, by and large if left on his own he will tackle it your way'.

Only if there is rapport between the chief executive and the whole team is it possible to master-mind, yet delegate every aspect of a business operation so that it has special appeal to its customers and has prospects of being a run-away success.

Do not these concepts of master-minding and of close rapport conflict with Mr. Decker's idea that each business has a centre of gravity?

Not at all. Each business is unique, and part of this uniqueness is the stamp of the chief executive's personality. But because there may be a centre of gravity—a particular emphasis given to one aspect of policy—this does not mean that others can be neglected. The whole business must be master-minded.

What exactly do you mean by master-minding in everyday work, and how does it affect organization structure?

A good example of lack of master-minding was given when MR. CHARLTON said that he got annoyed with the manager who didn't know his (daily) tonnage: 'He should be living his job like I live mine.'

One of the best examples of the need for master-minding was given by MR. ASPINALL at the beginning of this chapter when he described how his group's foreign-based subsidiaries 'became stepchildren in which nobody took much interest'. How can a man 'live his job' in these circumstances? But the situation changed when MR. ASPINALL formed a separate international company. Here was something that could be truly master-minded as an entity, and at each territorial level. Here was something in which the managers could have rapport with one another, for they had this in common, that they were all abroad from the headquarters country. Equally, at a more junior level, they were all serving in a particular country trying to adapt or make the best of a range of products and services stemming mainly, but not entirely from H.Q. So again they could have rapport with one another.

A good example of contrast between successful master-minding and close rapport, on the one hand, and on the other hand unsuccessful master-minding and lack of rapport, was provided for me when I let the contract for the first U.K. printing of this book. Because it was to be published internationally, there were several important requirements of facilities for special types of printing and binding, warehousing and despatch, which I wanted from any contenders for the contract. So I listed these in a letter to the chief executive by name of three well known printing firms. We will call these companies A, B and C.

In company A, the chief executive clearly knew the facilities of his own business very well, for he replied immediately. Moreover, his letter named his sales director and indicated that either of them would be happy to provide further information. I phoned his sales director, who was out, but a copy of the correspondence had been passed on, his secretary had read it, she knew who I was and made an early appointment for me to meet the sales director together with a typographic designer. Company A finally won the contract. They were marginally better on price, but I might not have decided the contract on price, if another contender had improved on their very good sales performance. Clearly in Company A there was close rapport between the chief executive and his key staff. This was obvious in my dealings with the estimator and production controller, as well as with the sales and design staff.

The chief executive of Company B did not reply to my letter, but after a week went by the sales director phoned to apologize for the delay. A week later he replied in detail. Except for the delay, this was fair enough, for in my original letters I had asked that the chief executive or his sales director should reply. But the delay meant that, in spite of good performances from then on, Company B were lagging. Their price was marginally higher than that of Company A, but more important, I had less confidence in their performance.

Company C received my letter when the chief executive was on holiday, and the works director acknowledged it on his behalf, but unfortunately it was over four weeks before he wrote again sending the information I wanted. There was no mention of having a sales organization, so I phoned and was told the name of the sales director. He was out. I left my name and was never phoned back. Possibly the sales director never received a copy of my original enquiry, but who cares? I, for one, do not want to do business with Company C until the chief executive gets into close rapport with his key staff and until he has master-minded every conceivable possible event that could happen when he is absent, so that he has complete confidence in how his staff will react.

But why do you keep stressing the importance of rapport and of having an organization that is psychologically compact enough for every function of it to be master-minded by the chief executive? Surely

a business can have a sound organization which is more dispersed and in which the personalities are less intimate?

A lot of businesses do, but as MR. BOWLES said, 'a lot of businesses have lost their way'. What they do for their customers doesn't really add up to a well thought out and well executed service, and consequently it isn't very worthwhile for the firm either.

My contention, from observing the successful original capitalists, is that they know where they are going, they have rapport with their people, they have a psychologically compact organization (up to the time when they may overreach themselves), and they have thoroughly master-minded what they are offering their customers. I am saying that a first essential step for a business which has lost its way is to copy these people and create an organization which is psychologically compact, etc. In other words, it must be a business which follows The Principle of the Span of Effective Rapport.

All right, let us assume that this is correct as a beginning. But what guarantee is there that the system will work, that the compact team will come up with some winning numbers?

None at all, but it will be in better shape to work on the problems and the odds can become increasingly in favour if the chief executive uses some fairly obvious and simple mental drills to stimulate enquiry and constructive discussion.

MR. CLEMENTS referred to this problem when he described an earlier experience of coming into a new industry and acquiring product flair: 'You start watching the ads., you watch the prices, you watch the shops. You immediately acquire a feel for the product, its usefulness to people and their reactions to it.' Again, when he spoke of experience in television manufacture: 'I knew which things cost the most, what needed special testing for reliability, what parts of the production could be mechanized and so on. I got to know every aspect of producing and using every part of the product—one doesn't have to be a technician to make this kind of analysis. This is commercial sense.'

MR. CHADWICK reminded us of another aspect when he said: 'You've got to do your sums correctly.' Building a new product policy inevitably involves a lot of experimental costing and pricing, etc.

MR. CHILDS referred to another aspect when he talked of experience in the toy industry, and said: 'I am preconditioned to be on the lookout but I also have a methodical check-list. I ask myself will the product be inexpensive, will it suit both boys and girls, because that way you double the market, can it be packaged attractively, can it be advertised on television, is it of interest to the whole family, does it appeal to a wide age group, and does it involve replacement parts, because better still if it doesn't as you don't then have a parts problem.'

These sorts of mental drills, adapted to suit a particular industry, are one way of ensuring that every member of a compact management team is well steeped in what the business is trying to do, and that the chief executive is well steeped in what each function is trying to do.

But surely this is amateurism and the real answer is to commission professional market research and technical research?

The answers to some problems may only be obtained by commissioning professional research. But a chief executive must be wary of the subordinate who takes the easy way out of any problem by proposing to commission some expensive research. The mental drills and discussions must be done thoroughly or you won't know whether useful research should be commissioned, and if so, what sort of questions are worth asking.

But some of the key functions of a business are likely to be headed by people with whom it is impossible to have rapport, and more particularly, beyond whom it is very difficult to get, to see what is going on underneath?

Yes, this is true, and time may show that some people have to be moved. But one way of distinguishing those who need to be taken out of the team is to exercise the drills and see who responds. Moreover, the chief executive is aided by the multichannelled information network of a line and staff organization.

The contribution of business to a free democracy lies in giving the customer a choice of product or service and in giving the employees a choice of employment, it does not lie in giving the staff a choice of going off in their own directions, out of harmony. In some ways the analogy of a ship's crew is a good one. For the ship to be well run, the crew must feel a sense of freedom in how they fulfill their role, and they must participate in settling this, but fundamentally they must contribute towards getting the ship to one specific destination.

A ship can be small or large, so how useful can such an analogy be? The captain of a large liner would have to be a genius to master-mind every function in his ship, but the captain of a small tug could do this easily

The chief executive of a large business or of a large ship can only master-mind the functions of those who report to him and of their immediate subordinates, at a level of depth that they individually deal with. They in turn master-mind the functions of the people who report to them and one step below that, and so on down. But in the tug-boat, or for that matter the Cotswold restaurant, the scale of activity is small enough for one person to master-mind the lot.

A ship has a definable boundary, where the hull meets the water. Inside, it is all ship, outside it is not ship. By contrast a large group of companies does not have such easily definable boundaries within its organization to distinguish one viable business from another

Certainly this makes the problem of business organization structure more difficult. But I believe it must begin with the Principle of the Span of Effective Rapport. Any business in which the chief executive cannot have effective rapport with the people who report to him is too big. Provided we stick to this principle, we at least know how to define boundaries. The internal problems of deciding which way to organize marketing and production, for example, and which job functions to have, are so tied up with the actual technologies and territories and types of customer and staff personalities involved, that as MR. ASPINALL said at the beginning of this chapter, there cannot be any general rules. The circumstances will half-dictate what to do and the other half must be common sense.

But how about these boundaries? Has not the business world anything equivalent to the steel hull of a ship, to tell a chief executive where one business should start and another stop?

Yes, it has the profit centre. Any part of a group which can be treated as a genuine profit centre with a chief executive who is answerable for serving a genuine market at real prices and costs, and accountable for profit, can be treated as an operating company, regardless of its actual name. The man in charge must have rapport with his subordinates, but it is a different kind of rapport from that which he has with his superior. The superior is really chief executive of a holding company, regardless of what it may be called.

Because of this distinction, in Chapter 12 where we are discussing top management meeting systems we divide each part of the discussion into (*a*) holding company and (*b*) operating company. The type of rapport, the type of master-minding for each is different.

Few businesses divide neatly into operating and holding companies. Real life is rarely so clear cut. But in each chief executive's mind the distinction in principle needs to be clear. And in the next chapter, what we say about meeting systems will indicate the different types of rapport needed in holding companies and operating companies. Always in both, however, the boundary of the business should be decided primarily by reference to the Principle of the Span of Effective Rapport.

12

TOP MANAGEMENT MEETING SYSTEMS

How often should the top management of a company—meaning the chief executive and his immediate colleagues—meet in order to exchange information, review progress and make decisions for carrying on the business?

The survey shows that in the United States and Britain there are formal board meetings in most companies of medium or large size once a month. Some companies miss out the holiday months, and a few have just four or six fixed board meetings a year, with further meetings called to agree acquisitions or take other urgent decisions. In Germany the typical arrangement is that the supervisory board meets quarterly and the executive board monthly or more frequently—in the majority of cases more frequently.

The survey was not, however, solely concerned with formal board meetings. In fact it was rather more concerned with regular meetings of the top management team around the chief executive, whether or not they constituted a board. These meetings are classified in Table 12.1 under those which occur more than once a week, those which are weekly, fortnightly and monthly.

Table 12.1

FREQUENCY OF TOP MANAGEMENT MEETINGS

More than weekly	Weekly	Fortnightly	Monthly
5%	28%	17%	50%

It will be seen that half the chief executives in the survey have regular top management meetings on a monthly basis, whilst a third have them weekly or more frequently. However, when the figures are weighted to allow for the different numbers of Americans, Germans and British in the survey, a very different picture is obtained, as witness Table 12.2.

Table 12.2

FREQUENCY OF TOP MANAGEMENT MEETINGS ANALYSED BY NATION

	More than weekly	Weekly	Fortnightly	Monthly	Total
	%	%	%	%	%
Germany	11	41	24	24	100
United States	5	32	3	60	100
Britain	4	18	21	57	100

Over half the Germans meet weekly or more frequently, as against over a third of the Americans and just over a fifth of the British.

Of course it may be argued that frequency of top management meeting is no criterion of the efficiency of business management. There is no available evidence, for example, of any correlation between the less frequent meetings of British top managements in this survey and the lower productivity growth record of British industry.

Indeed, some members of the survey came out strongly against the timewasting nature of meetings. One of the most successful businessmen in the survey, MR. CLIFFORD, who became a multi-millionaire in a short period of years, starting from scratch, had this to say:

I am not a believer in anything growing at speed having meetings. When a business is growing fast, the man leading it should be so involved with it that there is no need for meetings. He is there, he is seeing people every day. I couldn't hold a meeting next Monday if I could see someone on Saturday night and fix up the point that needed discussing. I'm not prepared to wait for Christmas to give my wife a present. This underlines the fault of meetings. Once a business is running well, meetings are all right, but not when it is growing. I am always saving facts in my mind, like a computer. I am making comparisons, keeping this and throwing away that. It is better to have a form of mind like this than to have meetings—a mind that stores neatly and gives ready access for the information to come out.

In other words, MR. CLIFFORD was good at master-minding his business.

Here is another self-made millionaire, MR. CHRISTIE:

We have a management meeting once a month but I rarely attend it. People who tighten their belts the quickest, put the others out of business. Our market share is up 10 per cent this year in spite of the hard times.

Here is another, MR. CHISHOLM:

Twice a year we have catalogue meetings with all our branch managers, to introduce the new lines. We also have quarterly meetings for area managers. There are no other formal meetings. The directors are in constant discussion. This is easy with open plan. We can see each other and we just get together at the board table over there.

Here is another, MR. CHESHIRE:

My meeting system is not too rigid. Meetings must never dictate your action. I always make provision for them to go on without me, so long as the minutes are circulated. The working day is too valuable to be tied up in long meetings. Lots of my meetings are informal in the evenings with my executives—perhaps 80 per cent of them are.

If the self-made millionaires can manage without regular meetings, is there perhaps a lesson in this for lesser mortals? Yet the Germans have frequent meetings, and they are on the whole so successful.

The survey reveals no uniform pattern of meeting systems in any of the three countries or in any industry. So we will try to pick our way through the mass of evidence on frequency and type of meeting held, to reach some general conclusions.

Firstly, who meets at the top level more than once a week, and why?

MR. ARTHUR: I have an executive committee of five members, all directors of the company, and this meets twice a week. It covers investment decisions and matters like labour relations policy.

MR. BISSETT: I have a five-man executive committee which meets twice a week. Once a week we meet on our own, and sit informally around my desk, to discuss any problems that have arisen. The other weekly meeting is a formal one in the board room with a secretary and with minutes. This is a meeting at which heads of divisions and units can make presentations on specific projects for discussion and decision. All capital expenditure projects are based on budgets previously submitted. They have to be within the budget as already agreed but they have to come up as separate, detailed submissions for approval. We meet weekly so that there is no delay in getting projects approved.

MR. COOPER: There is a meeting of executive directors and the company secretary and any departmental manager required, daily at 10 a.m.

MR. ATWELL: We have an executive dining room and meet each other every day. We also have daily meetings on production planning.

The other members of the survey who meet more than once a week, MR. DAMM and MR. DERKUM, run daily lunch table meetings for their top executives.

Secondly, who meets weekly?

MR. ATKINS: We have a senior staff meeting every Monday morning to review sales figures and discuss any problems. Ten departmental heads attend.

MR. DACKWEILER: There is a weekly board meeting attended by the chief executive, the two technical directors, the home market sales director, the export director, the finance and legal director, and on an *ad hoc* basis by others, such as the purchasing manager. It is also attended by two assistants to the chief executive who make reports and surveys and prepare figures, and check on the execution of decisions. These assistants are young men of under 30 with a degree in economics or business administration. After working for two or three years as assistants to the chief executive, they are likely to be given a line position. The key to the success of using these personal assistants lies in the work they do in preparing for board meetings.

MR. DITTMER: I have a weekly meeting of the main directors in the holding company, attended also by the specialist staff members who are in continuous contact with the subsidiaries. This keeps us in touch.

MR. ATKINSON: Our weekly meetings are mainly for buying purposes. Good buying is most important to our business. Acceptance of the product by the customer is what makes a profit.

MR. CLARK: We have a staff meeting every Friday from 8 to 9.30, attended by the director and general manager of the holding company, also a director of the waste disposal team, a representative of the sales team, the chief accountant, and a young man from transport. They deal with day-to-day matters and produce an action set of minutes with the name of the person to act, or rather his initials, in the margin. The minutes are done immediately so that by Monday morning when the directors meet from 8 to 9.30, all we have to do is make decisions on about four major points that have been recommended to us by the staff meeting. The directors' minutes are produced the same day and attached to them is a time-table of directors' movements during the week. The director and general manager is at both meetings. Everybody concerned gets the directors' minutes by Monday afternoon, and if there is anything he hasn't completed by the following Monday, as requested, we need an explanation from him.

MR. DECKER: The board meets every Friday and it consists of nine people, myself and the four divisional heads plus the four functional heads. These are all full-time executives and they spend almost a whole day in their weekly meeting.

MR. DEMMLER: The Executive Board meets every Monday at 10 o'clock.

MR. DOEBEL: The partners in each advertising team meet every Monday. Every team has two managers, the creative man and the marketing consultant. The finance and personnel staff are common to all team meetings in the company and so form a link between the teams.

MR. CARLISLE: Our design committee meets once a week. My partner and I both attend. Design is crucial to our business. Others attending are our chief designer, the chief draughtsman and our publicity man.

MR. ARROWSMITH: I have a weekly meeting of corporate vice-presidents—a general staff meeting, to which they all come or send a substitute. Most matters that arise during the week for decision are wherever possible deferred to this meeting, so that the group can participate.

MR. ANDERSON: Our operations committee meets theoretically once a week but in fact it is more like three times a month due to travel taking some of us away. All the major general managers of operating divisions are on this committee, plus the heads of the major staff activities. It brings together input of information from all areas so that all those responsible are fully informed of the group's problems of resource allocation. This committee reviews the five-year plans and the annual profit plan. The input of information consists not only of figures but of reports from members and exchange of views on such subjects as the national health programme. But it is not a voting body. The ultimate decisions must be mine and other members of the family. As chief executive I set up a schedule of reports required from different divisions, and also members request periodically that they may make a report to the operations committee on a particular subject or activity that they are developing.

MR. ANTHONY: We always meet on a Monday so that the rest of the week is free for executives to travel to the different plants.

We have a president's administrative meeting every six weeks, and this includes the three group vice-presidents and all the heads of staff departments at head office.

Every six weeks we have a chairman's finance meeting attended by the chairman who is my top level colleague and primarily responsible for finance, also attended by myself as president, the vice-president for finance, the controller and the treasurer.

Every six weeks we have the administrative meetings for the three different groups—two of them being product groups and the third international. Thus there are five regular meetings in every six weeks. We keep the sixth Monday for odd meetings that may be needed.

Who meets fortnightly?

MR. DEDERICHS: Twice a month there is a board meeting. One is a monthly review, and it deals only with the budget and actual figures. Line members of the board must comment on the reasons for any differences between budget and actual. The other meeting in the month deals mainly with company policy problems, planning, etc.

MR. BURKE: We have an executive committee of eight which meets fortnightly. Apart from myself its members are the directors responsible for the various functions—sales, works, administration and so forth.

MR. DEGENHARDT: The top group of five meet fortnightly for a day.

MR. BOWLES: Our board meets monthly, but we also have a Chairman's Committee Meeting every fortnight on Wednesday, between board meetings. It is not an executive body, it is advisory to me. I make the decisions. This committee consists of the chairman and the three heads of Home divisions and the head of the European division who is also the vice-chairman, also a non-executive vice-chairman and the finance director. We bring in as wanted the director of personnel, the two research directors and the other non-executive directors.

MR. CHATFIELD: We have fortnightly board meetings, which are absolutely essential in the motor trade.

MR. ARCHER: Our board meets monthly and has 13 members of whom five are outsiders, but every two weeks I have on Monday morning a meeting of the 15 to 20 top executives, and they report around the table. It is an informal meeting.

MR. BEATTY: There are fortnightly meetings of the executive, which consists of the managing directors of all the companies and the heads of group services. Each managing director has his own marketing meetings because their markets are so different.

MR. BOOTH: Our marketing strategy policy committee meets fortnightly.

Who meets monthly?

MR. ASHBOURNE: We have a management committee consisting of group chairman and president, the presidents of the aerospace and commercial divisions, the finance vice-president, the international vice-president and the corporate development vice-president responsible for acquisitions and strategic planning at the staff level. This management committee meets for a day a month for general planning and decision making and exchange of information. We also have a financial review each month, attended by the chairman and president and financial vice-president and the heads of the different divisions. The financial vice-president does the chart presentations at these meetings.

MR. ATTERBURY: We have a monthly product review meeting and

a monthly real estate meeting—the latter because of our expanding distribution system.

MR. ASCOT: After each monthly board meeting there is a parent and field meeting, attended by the five headquarters officers and five field vice-presidents. The headquarters men are the chairman, president, controller, operations officer and senior merchandising officer. Other functions are called in when necessary, and include transportation, customer service and installation, physical distribution, warehousing, computing and security.

MR. ANSELL: Very important in this company is the monthly product policy committee which includes the four top officers of the company. The chairman of this committee is the research and development vice-president, the secretary is the director of corporate and product planning. The vice-president of each product division is called to it when it is his turn to have his products discussed.

MR. DODEN: I have a monthly budget meeting, really a motivation meeting, covering both sales and expenses. I plan ahead for half a year in detail and on an overall basis for one year ahead. My monthly motivation meeting is concerned with why aren't sales targets being met, if they aren't, and why are expenses over their budgets, if they are. I don't worry about the figures that are on target.

MR. BRIDGES: Our main executive meetings are as follows: Firstly, the operating policy committee which meets monthly. It considers sales, the market pattern, exports, costs, warranties, anything that comes up, in fact how we are doing. It goes through the monthly results. Secondly, the product committee which meets twice a month and is concerned with what we want to make and what needs to be made. Thirdly, the programming committee which meets monthly and is concerned with how many we need to make and where do we make them. We are prepared to amend a production schedule once a month in total, but only once, otherwise we create great uncertainty both for the labour force and for the buying departments and our suppliers.

MR. AUBREY: I have an operations management committee which meets a minimum of once a month to review the operations of the previous month and the year to date. It is timed for meeting when the figures come out.

MR. BOOTH: We have seven regional companies which are profit and cost centres. They have monthly board meetings at which the head office specialists for the different services and functions are present.

MR. CHILDS: I hold a monthly development meeting for new products, both those coming fairly soon on to the market and long-term developments.

MR. CAVELL: I have monthly board meetings. Tight financial control is the key to business success, but it only tells you the facts. You still need people for the answers. Sometimes a set of figures can be very misleading. One must get behind them by talking to the people who come to the meetings.

Who meets quarterly or less?

MR. ARROWSMITH: There are four company wide staff meetings a year, to which the head of each organization and his top financial man come. One of them in December reviews the current year and produces the budget for the next year and a review of the next ten years. One in July lasts three days and is a review of the first six months of the year, a revision of the last six months' plans and an up-dating of the next ten years. In April we have a meeting on long-range goals in advertising and public relations. The various companies in the group are encouraged to put up some of their younger people to make presentations on long-term objectives and how the company can achieve them.

In October there is a meeting on personnel and industrial relations. It includes such subjects as personnel development, the problems of succession, the training of younger staff and how to turn engineers into general managers.

MR. DEGENHARDT: We have two meetings a year, for two or three days at a time, when we go away together to do our planning and budget preparation. The total group of 220 people, consisting of the five top people, the 20 directors under them and the store managers, buyers and equivalent staff levels, attend. We start with a series of lectures lasting a day, when we talk to them about our plans.

MR. ASCOT: Each functional officer has at least one meeting a year of all the equivalent functional people. But the merchandising men have at least four meetings a year, one per season.

MR. ASHBOURNE: We sit down with the top personnel staff twice a year and review each division president and the three levels below him, for management evaluation.

MR. ANTHONY: Twice a year each staff department head holds a two-day seminar for his counterparts in the different companies. They exchange and teach know-how in their particular fields.

MR. CHILDS: We have quarterly sales meetings for area managers and an annual sales meeting for all representatives.

MR. ARCHER: There is a quarterly research and development meeting for each group, so that in fact we have one of these per month.

MR. ATTFIELD: About three times a year I have brain-storming sessions where we isolate ourselves for a day and a half and deal with a particular problem.

MR. AYLWARD: We have two informal meetings a year of all 32 presidents from the companies, plus our headquarters people. One meeting is in January and it reviews the previous year and discusses and approves projections for the current year and the following year. It also discusses and approves capital expenditure requirements for the current year and the following year. The second year is an exercise in semantics. Retailing does not permit long-term forecasts.

In August we go through the same exercise again, reviewing the first six months of the current year and changing our forecasts for the second half of the year. At the first meeting in late January, we have it in Florida and take our wives and the chaps can either go out with their wives or play golf in the afternoon, we only work in the mornings. This is a special company treat. The August meeting is a stag meeting, we just do the work.

At each of these meetings each person running a unit of the business has to stand up and say: 'I projected a profit of X,000 dollars and I am pleased to be able to say I have made more' or alternatively 'I am sorry to say I have made less', and he will receive applause or boos as the case may be. He has to go right through his last year's performance at the January meeting and answer questions from the others as well as from myself.

This is deadly serious. I use a blackboard and put down the results, both the projections and the actual results, as they are given out by each man who stands up. Then I add up the total at the bottom. Everybody can see who has contributed and how much to the total results of the group.

Who meets annually?

MR. DENYER: We have a special Harvard Seminar every year lasting four weeks for companies holding our franchise. There are two or three Harvard professors and also some German professors who have been to Harvard.

MR. BOWLES: We hold seminars on research, advertising and new products. We may for example have a toothpaste seminar, to discuss how our toothpaste brands are going against the competition, and what we should do about them. These seminars take in 20 to 30 people. We talk through a problem for two days. There is an agenda, but few papers are presented.

MR. ANDERSON: Once a year I sit down with each general management and together with the corporate personnel staff we do manpower planning and review. We have a session in which we go over the organization structure and over each person, their performance and potential, their development and replacement. We also identify high potential among those under 35 whom I would not normally contact. I then plan lunch meetings and assignments for these young men. Sometimes these assignments are internal, such as a special project, sometimes they are external, such as acting as councellor in raising money for a charity.

MR. ASPINALL: I have a president's annual conference when I call in the presidents and have a five-day meeting with them and with the staffs of the parent company on major problems and opportunities and areas of mutual interest. The specialist functions have their meetings too. For example, there is a controllers' conference and a public relations directors' conference.

MR. ARROWSMITH: I take the corporate vice-presidents once a year to the operating companies for a special presentation on each company's progress.

Where do they meet?

MR. BACON: I hold board and management meetings alternately at the two factories and at headquarters, so that the directors can walk around, see and be seen.

MR. ACLAND: I visit the divisions for quarterly review meetings, but alternate quarters they come to head office.

MR. DOBLER: We have a fortnightly marketing half-day meeting, attended by the technical people as well. These meetings are held alternately at head office and at the various works, and when they are held at the works they are called production meetings, but in fact the marketing people attend and the primary aim of the meeting is better marketing, hence better co-ordination between production and marketing.

Who makes the decisions?

MR. ASPINALL: We avoid managing by committee. You can get a

committee to single out problems and get thought done on them, but then somebody has to make the decisions.

MR. BANFIELD: Meetings cannot replace proper line management on a day-to-day basis, if they mean you discuss in two weeks' time what should have been solved today.

MR. DENYER: When I have a special group working on a problem, I expect them to bring me alternative possibilities, so that I can make a decision.

What conclusions can be reached about top management meeting systems?

They seem largely unnecessary in a fast growing business which has been built from scratch by one man who works very long hours keeping in touch with every aspect of the business and co-ordinating it inside his own mind. But the business must suffer some day the loss of this man.

If on the other hand the chief executive believes in open and collective participation by the whole management team, then committees have certain vital roles to play.

1. They act as disciplines for ensuring that operating results are properly reviewed. Indeed an actual presentation to a top management committee of highlights from the operating results can bring a powerful form of group pressure to bear on anyone whose results are bad.

2. They provide a time-saving means of interchange of information wherever two or more functions must agree to co-ordinate their efforts, for example in production and marketing.

3. They are essential for putting the finishing touches to plans and budgets, to ensure that what is agreed is realistic in terms of the experience of every relevant function.

4. They provide a means of participation and a training for members of staff who might not otherwise hear the other man's point of view.

5. They enable all relevant minds to concentrate on one problem at one time and hence to contribute to its solution more effectively than they could separately.

6. Finally, they provide a disciplined forum at which plans and projects may be presented and discussed by all relevant functions before the chief executive makes a decision.

An analysis of meeting systems

Up to this point the chapter had been drafted before the total analysis of participants in the survey had highlighted the remarkable growth records of the original capitalists. It is now proposed to follow through from the Principle of the Span of Effective Rapport and assume that we are setting up a committee structure for a chief executive who co-ordinates and thinks through every aspect of the business in his own mind, as the original capitalists appear to have done, and who therefore would be capable of running the business for some time virtually without committees, but who believes in participation and wants a committee structure which enables him to think out loud his business problems with his key executives and staff.

Table 12.3 sets out nine major activities for which he needs committee work, and it discusses each of these as relevant to the needs of both a holding company and an operating company, in terms of who should be present at each type of committee meeting, how often it ought to meet, and in some cases where it should meet.

Anyone planning his own committee system may in practice find that he can conduct two or more of these activities in the same committee, but it is important to identify them separately in the first instance, so that if he does bring them together, he is at least aware of what he has done to the committee, some of whose members may no longer be needed for the whole of a meeting.

Table 12.3

MAJOR COMMITTEE ACTIVITIES AT THE CHIEF EXECUTIVE LEVEL.

WHO NEEDS TO ATTEND, HOW OFTEN THEY SHOULD MEET, AND WHERE

ACTIVITY 1. Hear presentations on proposed operating and capital expenditure budgets, and approve, modify or reject them. (The full process of preparing budgets is described in Chapter 17.)

(*a*) *Holding company.* The chief executive plus his staff specialists (plus in a large group his operations vice president or equivalent) will usually hold the first of these annual budget meetings at headquarters, but will preferably hear the final presentations on them at a special conference venue or at the offices of the relevant subsidiary company or division, with local attendance by the subsidary chief and by his appropriate staff.

(*b*) *Operating company.* The chief executive will call on functional heads to submit draft budgets at an appropriate interval in advance, and will hold individual meetings to discuss them. Every functional head should have opportunity to participate in the individual discussion of any budget for a service facility (e.g. transport or publicity) which spends money on his behalf.

Final presentation of the whole budget programme should be made by a financial officer or by the chief executive himself, and it should include some motivational material on the plan and its objectives as a whole. This presentation should be attended by all relevant functional heads. In some cases a conference venue away from the bustle of day-to-day operations will be desirable.

ACTIVITY 2. Review performance against operating and capital expenditure budgets, and motivate. (Details of procedures for the measurement of operating performance are given in Chapter 14.)

(*a*) *Holding company.* The chief executive plus a relevant financial officer will want a monthly review

(*b*) *Operating company.* The chief executive will usually review monthly, with his main staff with the chief executive of each subsidiary. They will concentrate their attention on profitability and sales and, where relevant, the time schedules for contracts in progress, also capital expenditure plans in progress. A detailed review of operating expenditure is likely to be less frequent (e.g. quarterly or in some cases not at all, unless profits fall below budgets due to rising costs). The holding company's own monthly review of its total operations, bringing in all the subsidiaries or divisions, will in effect be the chief executive's report to the board. Their meeting will be the review meeting to which he is accountable.

functional heads present, the progress of the business against budget, and where relevant against time schedules. The monthly meeting will include a review of sales, expenditure and profit figures, but in some types of business where profitability is quickly affected by a change in the level of sales or in the level of capacity used, these latter figures may be reviewed weekly in a meeting or daily by the chief executive himself. Monthly expenditure figures which are significantly out of line will be investigated immediately, but in some companies a detailed analysis of expenditure, including overheads, will not be worthwhile more frequently than quarterly.

ACTIVITY 3. Hear presentations on specific new projects or products, and decide on them. (Details of procedure are given in Chapter 17. A distinction is carefully drawn there between the need to have new projects included in overall budgets, and therefore approved on a financial level, and the additional need to go back for approval of each specific project when it is ready, even though it had been previously included in the operating and capital expenditure budgets.)

(*a*) *Holding company.* The chief executive and just a very few senior colleagues will be prepared to meet regularly and frequently, even weekly in a large group, to hear at first hand well-prepared presentations by those executives of the subsidiary companies or divisions who are actually expected to be in charge of a new project or product. Every relevant line executive or staff man will be invited to participate in a presentation before the chief exe-

(*b*) *Operating company.* There are likely to be far less projects to decide on at the operating level, and the chief executive is likely to be already very intimately involved with them, indeed many if not all of them may have been initiated by him. Nevertheless, it will be advisable for him to hold a formal presentation on any new project before it is started, so that all the key people concerned are well informed and motivated towards it. The presentation

cutive makes a decision, advised by his immediate colleagues. The presentation will include financial figures checked and agreed in advance with H.Q. financial staff. Typically, the procedure for deciding on new projects will include an initial presentation when it may be agreed to work on the project, and a follow-up procedure of discussions and reports, so that the homework is done thoroughly and the chief executive is very much in the picture before the final presentation.

should be led by the initiator of the project, who in some cases will be himself.

ACTIVITY 4. Review performance of specific projects or products, and motivate. (Details of procedure are given in Chapter 17.)

(*a*) *Holding company.* Because a holding company is very much concerned with new projects and capital expenditure plans initiated by the subsidiaries or divisions but requiring approval and finance from the centre, the chief executive of a holding company will ensure that he has a follow-up system for checking on all projects and plans approved. Actual expenditure will be monitored in figures presented to a monthly meeting attended by the holding company's chief executive, his chief financial officer and the relevant subsidiary chief. Comparisons will be drawn between budget plans and actual expenditure to date, also between time schedules and actual progress to date.

In monitoring the worthwhileness of a project, the group chief executive will ensure that

(*b*) *Operating company.* The chief executive's monthly operating review should to some extent include the reviewing of specific projects or products, but to ensure that each is given a periodic thorough review, the chief should have a regular programme for the review of each in turn, either at the same meeting system or separately. This may involve preparation of special papers on market prospects, incorporating special market research. If detailed sales analyses or detailed expenditure analyses are only available periodically, such as quarterly, this will influence the pattern of special product review meetings.

his controller or chief accountant brings it back on to the agenda six months or a year or some relevant period after the start-up of operations, to compare its actual pay-off with the expectations held out when it was planned.

Thorough review meetings of subsidiary operations, on a product by product basis, are not likely to be needed more often than quarterly, and preferably they should be held alternately at H.Q. and at the subsidiary site. These four reviews a year will be additional to the annual budget preparation meetings involving the same people.

ACTIVITY 5. Coordinate and control specific operations.

(*a*) *Holding company.* This is not typically a holding company activity. Those operations which need close coordination and control should be integrated in an operating company.

(*b*) *Operating company.* The chief executive will be mainly concerned with bringing together the various functions which have to schedule and dovetail their work together, whether it be: (a) research, design or development with production; (b) marketing with production; (c) buying with marketing and stock control; (d) buying with production and stock control; (e) distribution with production; (f) marketing with production; (g) advertising with distribution; and so on.

Once he has set up the right committees and has got reasonably compatible people working on them, who can concentrate their attention on producing work schedules that they then respect and adhere to, the chief executive need not attend all these meetings. He can leave them to be chaired by a general manager or operations president or vice president, content to receive the minutes and schedules they produce, and then to use his review meeting, as already described, to sort out why the results did not come out as scheduled, if they did not. In some industries, coordinating committees will have to be held weekly or even more frequently, but in many cases where plans have to be made well ahead and production or distribution lines kept working to high capacity, it is better to alter schedules only once a month or even less frequently, to avoid too much disturbance to suppliers, employees, stockists, etc.

In any firm there may be one particular coordination activity which is central to the special policy of the business, involving special customer appeal. For example, design with production, or sales with aftersales service. The chief executive may be the inspiration behind this special customer appeal and he may want to participate continually in it until he is sure that those who carry on in his absence have full rapport with him, that is they see things so much his way that in his absence they make the same decisions as he would have made.

ACTIVITY 6. Make critical decisions on regular operating problems and policies.

(*a*) *Holding company.* If a holding company provides certain com-

(*b*) *Operating company.* At this level the problems will mainly concern

mon services to its subsidiaries or divisions, such as computerized accounting and statistics, or if it lays down certain standard policies, for example on buying, selling, credit or personnel, then these services and policies should be altered only at a comprehensive meeting involving the chief executive of the holding company, his specialist staff and the chief executives of the subsidiaries or divisions.

Such common services and policies should not lightly be changed. Moreover, recommended changes can usually be explored in advance by a subcommittee representing all interested parties, a report from which can be circulated before a decision-making meeting. If possible, the chief executive of a holding company should avoid the time-wasting involved in having a monthly meeting on such matters. A lesser frequency or an *ad hoc* meeting, as needed, is better.

purchasing, pricing and other aspects of competition. The chief executive will include these on the agenda of his regular review meetings already described, if they can wait for a meeting. If he has to act quickly he should bring the matter up at the next regular meeting of all functional heads, to ensure that they fully understand the changes made and their consequences.

ACTIVITY 7. Make critical decisions on non-regular problems and policies.

(*a*) *Holding company.* At this level they are likely to be major financial and legal matters such as a take-over bid made by or to the group, or a large-scale industrial dispute. In a take-over battle, the chief executive will call special top management committee or board meetings as soon as they seem necessary. In an industrial dispute, he will more likely let his specialist staff try to solve the

(*b*) *Operating company.* The problems of pricing, buying and other aspects of competition which arise suddenly will be decided quickly by the chief executive in consultation with his functional heads. He may or may not call an emergency meeting, but he or someone on his behalf will usually have to issue a policy memo. His emergency decisions will not usually be as hurried as they

dispute first, keep himself informed, and let himself become progressively more involved, calling a top management committee meeting or even a board meeting if the dispute becomes really serious.

appear, for he will have thought out in advance the consequences of most of the likely events, and what he should be prepared to do about them.

ACTIVITY 8. Review of financial prospects. (Details of procedure are given in Chapters 14 and 17.)

(*a*) *Holding company.* Because the group's operating budgets and capital expenditure budgets will have been constructed in the light of a cash flow projection made by the company's treasurer (or finance director or accountant), it will not usually be necessary to bring the subsidiary company chief executives in on a monthly financial review of the whole group. But they should receive at least a quarterly confidential summary and they should be informed immediately if the group's finances deteriorate and if this is likely to affect operations.

The group chief executive will usually make a monthly (or in some industries more frequent) financial review with his treasurer and will report on the financial outlook to the board.

(*b*) *Operating company.* It is argued very keenly in Chapters 14 and 17 that every senior executive should know the amount of capital his activities are using, and that a chief executive should be continually aware of the total capital he is already using, also of his likely future needs of capital. From this it is argued that the process of budgeting should be taken logically through to the pro-forma balance sheet.

Hence, it follows that the monthly review of operating results which a chief executive holds with his functional heads should include a financial review. At the bottom of the operating statement, the profit figures should be related to the estimated capital employed to show the estimated return on capital employed, though this will not be the sole criterion for judging results. Forward projections should show the company's financial requirements in the coming months.

ACTIVITY 9. Review of Personnel. (Details of procedure are given in Chapters 13 and 18.)

(*a*) *Holding company.* A major problem for a group headquarters will be to fight against Parkinson's Law and prevent the proliferation of headquarters staff. To this end the group's monthly operating results will need to include a figure showing the cost of group headquarters as a percentage of total revenue. Also a people count, broken down by department, will be made annually as part of the budget process, and monthly or quarterly the actual people position will be compared with budget, any differences being indicated and immediately investigated by the chief executive if not already explained.

The other aspect of personnel requiring review by a holding company is staff development, described in Chapter 13. This will usually involve the chief executive of the holding company plus his personnel vice president or director spending a day or two, once or twice a year, reviewing progress of each of the managers of each subsidiary, in the presence of its chief executive. The group chief will keep so close to his own staff that he has minimum need for formal reviewing of their progress.

(*b*) *Operating company.* The chief executive of an operating company will try to keep so close to all his functional heads and their immediate subordinates that he has minimum need for formal reviewing of their progress. He will be continually watching and judging how they perform, will try to remember their salaries and have a shrewd idea before budget time and before the salary review, how much more, if any, they should receive next year.

13

EXECUTIVE SELECTION AND SUCCESSION

Most chief executives will readily admit to having made some serious mistakes in appointing staff to key executive positions. Possibly a rare exception is MR. BELLAMY, who asserts: 'I am extremely fortunate in picking people. I just happen to have this. And I say to my staff, I don't care what you do, so long as you get it right. Use any kind of test available on the market, take any kind of training, you must get this right.'

Alas, easier said than done. Selecting people from outside the organization is usually more difficult than selecting them from within. But either way, there are pitfalls. Members of the survey were asked what steps they took and what factors were important in bringing up their 'batting average' of successful appointments over failures. The following is their evidence.

What do they do to try and improve the score on external appointments?

MR. ASCOT is a very large and successful employer:

The people chosen must be intelligent, able to grasp things quickly, and have the same thoroughness in probing a problem that we can expect from all our staff. We get a detailed reference from the previous employer, but we also have a battery of tests which we give to every applicant. It shows various aptitudes, preferences, skills and levels of interest. Educational background is also important, and finally one must learn how to evaluate people at interview. But one can still make mistakes.

MR. EXTRAMAN: It does an organization a lot of good to have outside experience brought in. Some of our former graduate trainees have come back after 10 years and they are far better men than if they had stayed with us. They have had a lot of experience, as well as development of their personality. Those who stay with us tend to be protected. We need people to come in from outside to bring ideas as well as experience.

MR. ARMSTRONG: In appointing key people, you must never hurry. At times I have had to look for as long as two years to find the right man. You must keep to your objectives and standards, rather than place a time limit on yourself. It is not always possible to have genuine references on people. One relies very heavily on personal interviews, and I get colleagues to see potential appointees. I like to see them several times, and I use industrial psychologists. They sometimes see something flagrant that I might miss. We also use an executive search firm. We make a world-wide search. I don't care where he comes from.

MR. DILLMANN: I judge people for promotion by their personal attitude, their knowledge and how they fulfil their tasks. They must be capable of learning, of promoting new things and taking interest in other than their special field.

MR. BEATTY: Very often I seek someone whom I have worked with before, for example when I recently wanted relief from the day-to-day activities in order to spend more time on forward thinking, I appointed as managing director someone I had known in my previous job.

MR. AYLWARD: I select my key men by buying their businesses. My one criterion for buying a business is: 'I want that guy.' My chief finance officer has 101 other reasons, and they must all be right. The figures must add up before I sign the deal, but it is the chap I want. I have done a dozen acquisitions in the last three years and have made no mistakes yet. I did 18 in the previous six years and there was only one exception in that lot; he wanted to go and run a different type of business. How do I know the man is right? Age is not a factor for me, unless he is near retiring. But I can tell. I make it my business to. I play golf with the guy, drink with him, get my people at him and sit back and watch. We have got here the darndest array of ethnic groups in the world. But I don't have an anti-Jew Gentile or an anti-Gentile Jew. I don't want a bad one in here who has got any prejudice against any race. You quickly see what the guy is like if you sit him down with your mixed bag of people and watch how he performs.

How does a chief executive get to know and be able to judge the people two or more steps down the ladder, with whom he is not in direct regular contact?

The difficulty of judging people two or more steps down is put succinctly by MR. CLEMENTS:

Naturally we try to judge by previous results, but the real problem is that we sometimes attribute success wrongly. A man is in fact able to disguise his results because he is, for example, in charge of a department and one does not know whether he produced the results or whether he has a very able subordinate for whom he is taking the credit.

The same problem is put in personality terms by MR. ASPINALL:

In selecting people one must be aware of the fact than an extrovert type frequently attracts attention beyond his true ability. We must watch out and not be taken in by the wonderful great guy who is really quite shallow, and not overlook the introvert who is really quite capable but doesn't grab you by the arm and tell you about it.

A similar view comes from MR. DEGENHARDT:

You have to look closely that you don't get a salesman who merely sells himself. He must have a clear, analytical mind, and be able to manage people. He must be frank with people. If he is not, they won't be frank with him.

It is not, of course, the type of personality which one needs to be wary of, but what it may hide—as explained by MR. ACLAND:

One must have a fairly good reading on the emotional reach of a man. His intelligence is obvious but this emotional reach is more difficult.

Special projects involving work in committee by people of different levels provide one opportunity to get to know the people further down. But there can be plenty of other opportunities.

'Last night I had ten of our up and coming executives to

dinner,' said MR. BOWLES. And he added—as already reported in chapter 8: 'I don't believe in a hierarchial system of seeing only the person immediately below. You can see the people further down provided you never give them an order or instruction or put them in the position of being disloyal to their immediate boss.'

MR. ATWELL: I don't skip over, I go through channels. When I want to find out about somebody, I get the top man to bring him to talk about something. Sometimes the one who talks the least has most behind what he says. He doesn't have to be a good salesman to let you know he is a good operator. I learn more by listening than talking. The super-salesman is sometimes whistling in the dark to keep up his spirits. It's not difficult to see whether a person is ambitious or whether he has reached the end of the line or is only interested in one thing, whether he knows what the firm is doing, whether he knows how to handle his own people, whether he realizes the effects of what he is doing on company policy, whether he is oriented towards the company.

MR. AUBREY: I get to know the people two and three steps down through these means. In addition to our monthly review, we have a more detailed quarterly review where the marketing and sales management come in and make their forecast presentations. They have a precise format for the numbers they must present but they also must tell us about their objectives, their market share and their plans for marketing and expansion. This goes on for two to three hours. Also there are product meetings and I like to know when they are on so that I can come in on the summary or show up for lunch.

Also we have an annual management conference which lasts about two days; the people below my operations management committee and one step below that all come.

Also as a company every two years we do a manpower review where the personnel manager and the division manager in my presence go over every manager or potential manager in his unit—his position today, his potential, at what stage he is ready for another job, should it be in a different area or the same area?

Also there are social occasions when I get to know people. All these together—you just work at it.

What can a new chief executive who comes in from outside do to get to know quickly his new staff, including those further down?

MR. BOOTH had his own solution to this one as already reported in Chapter 7:

I spent a lot of time initially, a bit in each department, doing a consulting job. I even set up the objectives for the department and formed the budget. This whole process took me nine months but it gave me a fairly clear picture both of the problems and of the people. It meant that I worked a 15-hour day.

MR. ATTFIELD: I have made 27 changes since I came here. I had to fill three or four positions from outside but I filled the rest from inside, and I was greatly helped in choosing people by the Management by Objectives programme which I ran, using an outside consultant. This programme consisted of a two day seminar followed some time later by a three day workshop. I had to put 116 people through them both. This was the best way for me to get to know my own staff. In the seminar they were taught the system and then in the workshop they actually prepared their list of objectives and their budgets, and learnt to use the system.

However well you judge a man in his present job, how can you avoid the Peter Principle, and not promote him beyond his level of competence?

There appears to be no real answer to this except to be tough when you find out:

MR. CLEMENTS: We sometimes promote a man who was doing well into a higher position that he does badly. This way we lose a good sub-ordinate and gain a bad boss. The whole organization suffers. But when we find out we just have to tell the man. It is no disgrace not to be able to do everything, and if a man rises above his level of capability he has got to be told; he has got to reconcile himself to the facts.

MR. CLIFFORD: The real skill isn't so much in knowing the people to select but knowing the people to fire. As much money is lost through failing to fire the wrong man as in failing to select the right man.

MR. CHISHOLM: We have made many boobs in appointing people. Now, whenever we realize we have made a mistake, we change immediately. We have had to face the fact that we are running a meritocracy. Every time we have tried to keep someone and we have said it will get better, it never does.

In the larger groups, however, there may be good reasons for proceeding more slowly—as MR. BISSETT explains:

If you suspect you have made a mistake, it is usually about two years before you can do anything about it. You have to give the man a chance. You have to say to yourself, maybe I haven't given him the right opportunities. And in any case, you have to avoid your firm getting the reputation for quick hire and fire. Once you got that kind of reputation, people wouldn't come to you.

MR. BERESFORD's group is world-wide; he knows the difficulty of uncovering trouble at the other end of the earth:

In one case where something was going wrong in a subsidiary abroad, I said to three of my colleagues, let all four of us go separately out there and have a look round. Then when we have all come back and compared notes, we might have enough information to make a decision.

From all three countries in the survey comes similar evidence of the type of man-to-man (or man-to-woman) frankness which is needed to cope with a job situation which is not working out, or which may not:

MR. DOBLER: I have had a woman in charge of the overseas patent department for 12 years. Now that I want to drop my overall responsibility for this work, I want to promote her. I have challenged her that she must tell me honestly if she can handle the job. Equally, if she cannot handle it, she must be brave enough to come forward and accept an outsider as her superior. She has agreed to take the job on these terms.

MR. CHRISTIE: You've got to keep promoting people until you find they can't go any higher, and then drop them back if they are not succeeding. I come round to the same side of the desk and talk to the man very frankly: 'Look here, you can leave in a huff or you can drop back in salary and start over again with us. You can do one or the other but we must be honest with each other—this is terribly important.' And I usually find he wants to stay.

MR. ARNOLD: People change, but there is a halo effect which carries on. A man can have a very good reputation for past performance and then his health declines and he becomes 30 per cent effective because he is no longer motivated. At this stage he should be prepared to get out into another position either within the firm or outside it. We know from sport and sporting heroes that the public doesn't expect you to be top all along, they just expect you to be a good dog. When you see someone failing the important thing is to get together with him frankly and arrive at a joint conclusion on the facts. Then you must examine your organization to see if it is possible for him to be adequately fitted into another position. If it isn't, you've got to arrange for a separation.

MR. AVERY, however, believes that there are ways of avoiding many of the heartbreaks of failure:

The only way to be really certain about appointments is to do the same thing with people as with products and put them to tests. For example, if the treasurer is to be made chief financial officer, before you have to make that decision you give him certain decisions and responsibilities that would belong to the role of chief financial officer, and watch how he reacts. If he cannot handle them, you know where you are.

MR. CLARK has even tested outsiders:

If the post is very important I try to get the man to work on a trial basis, so that we can have a look at each other. Two or three weeks' exposure is usually enough. During this time there must develop a mutual respect for each other's management skill and commercial sense. It is possible for a man to have his trial period during his holidays from his present post.

How important are formal systems of reporting on and rating managers, in assessing them for promotion?

Less than a third of members of the survey mentioned using such systems, but amongst those who do use them are some very firm supporters of their value:

MR. DENYER: We are in the motivation and service business. When we take on new staff our problem is to educate them along these lines, so we have a system by which they work right through the firm and we receive detailed reports on them. This is my chief guide to selecting them for future promotion. It is in this type of business, where the disciplines have to be so precise, that a system of reporting is particularly valuable.

MR. ALEXANDER: We now use highly trained appraisers. This began when we made our big merger. I realized that we had a wonderful opportunity to cast off the dead wood and choose the best staff. We knew our own staff well, but not the others. I engaged some very well-known consultant appraisers from Chicago, but to test them out I first got them to test the people we knew very well. We were astonished to find that after four hours of testing on our own people, they were able to report in very great detail things that we had taken years to discover.

MR. ARCHER: Three of our group vice-presidents retire in two years' time. We have been indulging in long-range planning to be ready to take care of this situation. There are ten to twelve promising young men who know these vacancies are coming up. This creates a very dynamic situation. They are working their tails off. We are looking for people who are aggressive, result-minded, have initiative, are reliable, are ingenious, and are able to make a plan and achieve it. We have a system of appraisal forms, and for the first time we have made a manpower inventory. We are concerned to find out firstly what is their potential, what kind of job could they do, when they will be ready to do it and what additional training they need.

Our Management Performance Appraisal and Plan of Objectives is a document which is concerned with setting down firstly the responsibilities of the person being appraised, secondly the results achieved by him in the past year, thirdly his performance rating as to whether he is outstanding, above average, average, below average or unacceptable, and fourthly the specific objectives he is required to achieve in the coming year.

Our Management Inventory is a triplicate set of documents, the top copy of which is held by the personnel department, the second by the immediate head of the person being recorded, and the third by his superior, the division head. The first part of the inventory gives the name and background education and employment history with the company, and previous employment history. The second part records the performance of the individual in the current year, in the last year and two years ago. The third part is a potentiality forecast, indicating whether the person could go two levels higher, one level higher, or not advance, and whether he is ready now or will be ready in two years or four. It is concerned with the actual steps of advancement that are possible and the reasons why.

MR. ANTHONY: For 20 years we have had career descriptions of our people and appraisals and an executive development programme, but we felt it wasn't enough to help us select the right people. So we developed a management man-power planning programme. The end point of this is a number of meetings each year, one for each company in the group and one for the corporation as a whole. At these meetings the audience consists of the president, that is myself, the group vice-president who is relevant and the personnel vice-president, and the chairman of our management development committee who is on the board and is also head of a management training organization.

At one of these meetings the head of a particular company will come into the conference room and on the wall he has got the organization structure of his company. There is a plaque for each person and on it is his age and years of experience and his photo. On the table in front of us is a book of appraisals of the people in this company by each man's superior and that man's superior and by the personnel man, and also by his functional counterpart at head office. There is also his performance record.

The head of the company goes through every person on his wall chart and discusses him, and also discusses who could take over his role in an emergency, who is ready to move into the job if it were available now and who would be ready in four years' time. We write down follow-up minutes of the meeting, concerning what promotions, development courses, etc. need to be taken.

We find that putting the situation up on the wall and going through it properly every year and talking about it means that we actually take action instead of merely putting off a lot of the personnel steps that are so easily postponed until it is too late.

The appraisal form on each person includes five inches of space describing the results of his performance in the last year, $2\frac{1}{2}$ inches on his methods of getting results, $1\frac{1}{2}$ inches on his personal qualifications, also comments on his greatest strengths, his greatest weaknesses, his potential, and plans for his improvement.

The survey also revealed cases where formal appraisal and rating systems do not fit easily into the circumstances.

MR. DAMM: This firm is very traditional, being 180 years old. We do not have any special tests for selecting people for promotion, nor do we have any personnel planning, for development of the executive team. It is no good hoarding a reserve of good people. If a man is really good and you have no position for him, he will leave. If he remains with you, waiting, when you haven't a position for him, then he is not very good.

MR. BRADLEY: We watch for the case where a branch manager says So-and-so is a good type, I will bring him on, train him up for promotion. This is the way the branch manager himself gets promotion.

But it's a hit-and-miss affair because there may be a good man under someone who is not fit for promotion. It is difficult to see the good subordinate under the mediocre manager. We have a staff development manager who is supposed to try and spot these good people. When he came to us, he wrote job descriptions for all our staff. He is a very capable graduate of a famous university but unfortunately when I asked him whether he would do a period as a branch manager, he shied away from it. He said he was a professional. This was a great mistake. He has learnt his profession but not his trade. He could have been of much greater value to us if he knew what it was like to run a branch. If I took on a man like that again I would make it a condition of his appointment that he must be prepared to spend a period running a shop.

MR. DODEN: When selecting people for appointment, I watch them very closely over a longish period. Integrity comes before everything else. Also I am concerned whether they can really become interested in the job. Not long ago I had to pick someone to take charge of my administrative services company, which was getting in a bit of a mess, due to the opening of my new warehouse and dispatch centre that is computerized and highly mechanized. The people in charge of the various functions there just didn't seem to be able to cope. It took me a long time to realize that the man to put in charge of it was my production director. Not an obvious choice, because he was not running a big production plant as he might have in another industry, he was mainly ordering production from outside firms. But it came to me that the way he handled people and the tidy administration he ran, showed that he could do the job. My staff were very critical of this appointment, but having made my decision I would not listen to any further argument. Within weeks, everybody was congratulatory about it, saying that he was a natural choice.

How common is it for a firm to select in advance the successor to the chief executive, to take over in the event of his untimely death?

Almost two out of three of the chief executives asked this question said that their successor had already been chosen. Here are some typical comments:

MR. ASKEW: We have a recorded planned succession in case of need. It would be like opening a will if I were hit by a truck.

MR. BOND: The succession here is all arranged. All the board members know who will succeed me.

MR. DACKWEILER: The man in the next room is my provisional successor, because my son is only 22. My sister and I have laid it down that it will be a responsibility of the supervisory board of directors and workers to decide when and whether my son can take over.

Some chief executives are planning to phase themselves out:

MR. DOBLER: I have provided for my succession when I leave the firm in five years' time. The commercial director will take over, and I am preparing a new organization structure to meet this situation.

MR. BOSWORTH: I am leaving at 60. For the succession I am training up a young cousin, aged 24. He is a born business man. He smells when things are wrong and doesn't wait for the computer to tell him. He is also very shrewd about people. But he hasn't yet got the integrity that is essential for a good business philosophy—for developing a good company image. I mean it like this. If Rolls-Royce produced a Mini, it would be a disaster. Nobody expects them to produce a Mini. My young cousin could no doubt bash around and make a lot of money quickly if he was in charge, but he would spoil the company's image. He will have to learn.

14

THE MEASUREMENT OF OPERATING PERFORMANCE

Surely management accounting contains codes of practice which determine how a company's operating performance is reported to the chief executive and how it is compared with budgeted performance, past performance, etc?

By contrast with the widely accepted conventions and practices of historic accounting, there is a bewildering array of styles of reporting in management accounting. This is clear from having discussed the reports they receive with 103 chief executives, and having seen examples of the documents in 71 cases (care being taken, by showing me out of date copies, and by other means, not to reveal any company confidential information).

Is it possible to develop a logic to the conventions of management accounting—a logic as precise as that of historic accounting?

A definite conclusion of this survey is that such a logic can be developed. And this chapter will be devoted largely to developing a logic out of the variety of methods used. Case examples will be quoted when they illustrate points in the logic.

Is it realistic to separate management accounting from historic accounting?

Decreasingly so. One of the problems of recent decades has been this separation. But the more one looks at the management accounts presented to those chief executives who appear to have the best reporting systems, the more they look like conventional historic accounts done very quickly and up to date, and compared with budgeted and past performance.

In other words, it has become clear from this study that the logic of management accounting must be the same basic logic as that of historic accounting. There should not be two types of accounting, only one. Within it, however, there needs to be a distinction between a budgeted income statement or profit and loss account and an actual income statement or profit and loss account, likewise a distinction between a budgeted or pro-forma balance sheet and an actual balance sheet.

If we look at the control of a business in this light, we can even hope some day to get rid of that modern misnomer, the cash flow projection. For this is designed to show how much cash a firm will have, or will need, at certain moments of time in the future, yet one of the great conventions of historic accounting is never to confuse a flow with a moment of time.

The income statement or profit and loss account shows the flow of revenue and expenditure in and out of the business during a specific period, such as a year. Anyone who wants to see what it would be like to run his business on a cash accounting basis can do a cash profit and loss account, showing the flow of cash in and out. This would be a true cash flow statement. But it would not tell him how much cash there was in the business at a particular moment of time. The balance sheet tells him the assets, including cash, and the liabilities of the business at a particular moment of time. Anyone who wants to look forward and estimate how much cash the firm will have or will need at some future moment of time should really try to construct a budget balance sheet for that date. If he finds the figures will not balance, then provided everything else is accounted for, the difference is probably the missing cash—the extra amount of cash he will need to find in order to run the business in the future.

Projecting forward the balance sheet is only one step on from a practice being used by an increasing number of firms, of having a monthly balance sheet for each 'profit centre' unit of the enterprise. In the survey, for example, MR. DODEN and MR. DENYER reported this practice from Germany, MR. BLISS from Britain and MR. ARCHER from America. In fact the phrase 'balance sheet' was actually used. But in many other cases on both sides of the Atlantic, regardless of the words used, the same basic system was being practised, because each company or unit in the group was being charged interest on the capital it employed. This could not be done without assessing the amount of capital, hence constructing at least an approximate balance sheet for the unit.

Why is the practice of having monthly balance sheets confined to profit centres?

A true profit centre can be any section of a business which could by itself make a viable business, selling to outside customers at real prices and being charged real prices for any raw materials, equipment or services used. A profit centre can be very small, for example each specialized monthly magazine in a house publishing dozens of monthly magazines. By contrast, MR. ALEXANDER points out that in his oil company he 'cannot push de-centralized profit responsibility further down than the main divisions'. In the United States he does not have to integrate oil production with refining, for profit centre purposes. The price of crude oil to the refinery is not an arbitrary internal price, it 'is fixed (by an outside authority) in relation to the conservation of fuel. Hence there is no problem in regard to transfer prices from an oil producing division to a refinery.' But each producing division and each refinery with its market must be regarded as a profit centre, however large these units may be.

Only where prices and costs relate to the market place, so that profits can be measured realistically, is it possible to estimate true earnings on capital employed, and hence to charge a rate of interest on the capital employed in order to see whether or not there are any net earnings left over after all costs have been met.

Why is it necessary to estimate true earnings on capital employed? Why should the return on capital

employed be such an important measure of the worthwhileness of any particular business activity? The answer to this is central to understanding the logic of a management control system. Although this answer is generally known to most experienced businessmen, it is worth restating here in a particular way in order to lead into a logical basis for analysing business activity and deciding just what figures, how often, and with what comparisons, should be presented to the chief executive in order to give him the best information possible for planning and controlling his business.

The reason why the return on capital employed is so important, is simply that a businessman almost invariably has to spend money before he receives money from his customers. In other words, he has to have capital, and he risks losing this if the customers do not buy as much as he expected.

If we look back through history to the Merchant Adventurers of the Middle Ages, we see merchants spending money on sending ships abroad, loaded with local products for sale, with the object of bringing back goods purchased at the other end of the journey. Obviously nobody would take the risk of doing this unless he hoped to get back more money when the ship returned and its cargo was sold, than he spent on the venture.

The same is true today of businessmen spending money on factories, shops, new products and so forth. But if you are continuously spending on these things, you cannot judge your success by looking at each separate item, particularly as some products go on selling for years, in contrast to the single-voyage ventures of the Middle Ages. Therefore the measure of modern success is not how much surplus you have made on the money spent on a particular voyage, but how much surplus you made in a particular period, usually a year, on the capital at risk during that period.

Hence we get the conventional income statement or profit and loss account, showing the revenue received from sales during the period, less the expenses incurred, and finally the profit or loss made, and closely allied to this is the conventional balance sheet, showing the value of fixed assets employed such as buildings and equipment, plus the current assets such as cash, stocks, work in progress, and the value of bills owed by customers, less the current liabilities such as bills owed to suppliers. The net total of assets must exactly balance the value belonging to those who provided the capital, for this is what ownership involves. These assets may of course have grown or shrunk in value since they were provided, just as the value of the cargo of a returning merchant adventurer's ship may be different from the one he sent out, but it is still exactly equal to his ownership of it. Hence the two sides of the balance sheet remain in balance.

Incidentally, the trading activities of the Merchant Adventurers are still part of our everyday language, for people still say: 'I will do such and such when my ship comes in.' We live and work and hope that it will be laden with a rich cargo.

What is the relevance of the merchant adventurers and of historic accounting conventions to the logic of a management control system?

They are seen to be entirely relevant if we look back again at the activities of a typical merchant adventurer. Before his ship was fitted out and loaded, ready for sailing, he could strike a balance sheet setting out all his assets and liabilities and showing his net total of assets—which as we have seen was exactly balanced by what his business owed to him personally. He could also make out a pro-forma profit and loss account, showing his budgeted expenditure on the venture and his forecast revenue from sales when the ship returned, and hence the profit he expected to make. Adding this profit to his present level of assets he could make a pro-forma balance sheet for the end of the journey, and on the assumption that the journey had been successful, this pro-forma balance sheet could contain a lot more cash. However, some of the traders who bought from him might not pay immediately, and indeed some of the goods might not be sold quickly, so the pro-forma balance sheet could contain a substantial amount of accounts receivable, and a lot of stocks, or inventory. There might even be some costs of the journey not yet paid, so in the liabilities section of the balance sheet there could well be some accounts payable.

Hence it was possible for the Merchant Adventurer to budget realistically ahead for both the profit and loss account and the balance sheet, taking any date that seemed relevant either during or after the expected completion date of the voyage. He would know from experience that events would never turn out exactly as budgeted, but in this respect he would be in a similar position to the modern businessman, who can also budget forward and make pro-forma income statements and balance sheets.

Though it is not yet a common practice for businessmen to do this in such a logical and complete form, some of the most astute self-made businessmen, untrained in accounting practice, have come close to it as an instinctive business practice. Here is the experience of MR. CLIFFORD who built up a multi-million pound business from scratch, and has already been quoted in Chapter 5: 'In the early stages of building my business, every Saturday night I did my own balance sheet. I added up the value of all I possessed, subtracted what I owed. What was left was the value of net assets to start the next week with.'

And here is the experience of MR. DODEN, another self-made business success: 'I do the balance sheet myself, month by month. I keep it in a drawer. I plot on a chart the total balance figure and the relation between the different parts, to see where the money is coming from as the firm grows—how am I financing it? By doing this myself it hits me harder, it is more effective.'

But surely, when there are so many able and well-qualified accountants in the business world, it is not necessary for chief executives to do their own week-end sums and keep private little charts in their desks?

Certainly not. But it is a useful guide if we turn to the instinctive habits of very successful businessmen, original capitalists, to find the right logic for a management control system. And it is argued here that the most useful logic, indeed the only complete logic lies in the traditional income statement or profit and loss account and the traditional balance sheet. Only by taking into consideration every item of these two documents can a complete system of budgeting and control be established. Here in brief are the steps of the logic.

1. Examine each item of the income statement or profit and loss account, and each item of the balance sheet. Decide how frequently each one changes and how significant it is to the business, hence how often and in what form you want to see it.
2. Ask yourself also what lies behind it (e.g. personnel figures lie behind wage and salary costs), and hence how often you want to see these.
3. Then insist on seeing frequent and regular, usually monthly income statements and balance sheets.
4. When budgeting forwarding to a particular date, do so on the basis of trying to construct every item in the profit and loss account and the balance sheet for that date.
5. In most cases, start from the expected level of revenue, then estimate all the costs of obtaining it, and so build up the budgeted income statement. Then use the accounting profession's experience—and your own—of business ratios to build the various items in the budgeted balance sheet (e.g. if you know your expected ratio of stocks to sales, stock requirements can be calculated for the expected sales revenue). When you have constructed every item and found how much the present level of your finance throws the balance sheet off balance, you know the amount of extra finance to budget for, in order to meet your future cash and other needs.
6. Make regular, usually monthly comparisons between the budgeted items in the profit and loss account and the balance sheet, and the actual results realized for those items, also comparing, where relevant, the profit and loss results with those of a past period such as a year ago, and the balance sheet figures with those for a past moment of time such as the end of the last financial year, or in some cases, a year ago.
7. Carry forward and compare the cumulative, that is the year-to-date totals of items in the income statement or profit and loss account, as well as comparing the monthly figures.

Business ratios were developed by financial analysts, for analysing the published accounts of companies. But they can be equally well used in reverse for constructing a budget or pro-forma balance sheet for some future date of a business. They are in fact used by accountants and treasurers in constructing cash flow statements. But I recommend, as a result of this survey, that the best way for the chief executive of a business to look at his future financial requirements is to look at a series of forecast or pro-forma balance sheets. If he does this, he is always looking at the same layout, a complete layout of all the relevant items—fixed assets, stocks, work in progress, accounts receivable, cash, the lot. Moreover, when comparing budget with actual, he is not only judging the performance of the business against plan, he is judging the accuracy of the forecasts of various items, and so improving his own skill in handling the balance sheet. This is crucial, for in the words of MR. DODEN, already quoted in Chapter 5, 'to run a business successfully you must be in balance, that is you must have this feeling about a balance sheet, that if you deduct something here it will show up there. One must have this simple understanding of double entry.'

This logical system of analysing your requirements of a control system has been presented in brief, as a guide to where we are going, but we will now build up various items one at a time and relate them to the findings of the survey concerning the frequency, importance, reliability, etc. of various items.

But first, a question. Does the use in a management control system of the conventions of historic accounting mean that we should revise the view expressed in Chapter 5 that a chief executive needs to know only the principles of accounting and the layout of the income statement or profit and loss account, and the balance sheet?

Not at all. The professional practice of accounting contains an enormous amount of detail, some of it specific and some of it requiring business judgement, which does not have to be known by a chief executive or by most of his colleagues in senior management. It is almost enough that they understand the principles of double entry and the layout of the two main documents. But there is one thing more. As MR. CASEY pointed out in the survey, 'the chief executive must be involved in basic coding. He must say that he wants certain things analysed, but leave the actual coding system to the accountants. To be fair to them, however, he must keep them well in the picture on new products and new activities which might require a change in the coding system.'

It quickly becomes obvious to every experienced businessman that the revenue and expenses, assets and liabilities presented to him in the accounts can only be entered under their respective headings if the bills and payments, etc., passing through the accounts department are coded up in sufficient detail, accurately and easily so that the necessary analyses can be made. Somebody's salary, for example, might be part of an overhead item in the profit and loss account, part of work in progress in the balance sheet. A printing bill might be part of the budgeted cost of the publicity department, but also part of the cost of launching Brand X.

Failure of a chief executive to have a sympathetic understanding of coding problems can lead to endless frustration through not getting the right information at the right time, or through paying too much for it. It is no exaggeration to say that many of the troubles of the last decade in installing computers could have been avoided if top management had paid less attention to the computer itself and more attention to the types of analyses they needed and the coding requirements for putting the necessary information into the computer, prior to analysis. No computer can ever print out, for example, an analysis of sales of cashmere sweaters by size and colour, if size and colour have not been coded into the sales accounts. But would the cost of such coding be worthwhile, could it be done on a pre-punched sales tab, or would a periodic sample analysis of sales be adequate for the particular business? These are the sort of questions which no chief executive can avoid if he is to understand the problems of his accounting and control staffs, though he will want to avoid unnecessary interference with their work.

How does the systematic analysis of a company's management control requirements actually proceed? Firstly, the income statement or profit and loss account and the balance sheet, set out in the greatest possible detail, should be studied item by item. We give below, in Figures 14.1 and 14.2 typical lists of the main items in these accounts, so that we can go through them one at a time and draw attention to points made in the survey. These are symbolic financial statements purely to pinpoint the main items being discussed. They are not meant to be typical of any particular type of business or representative of all business. Moreover, my endeavours to cope with transatlantic differences in terminology mean that they will appear as unsatisfactory hybrids to everybody. Nevertheless, they must serve as a check-list for the items being discussed one at a time.

Figure 14.1

TYPICAL ITEMS IN AN INCOME STATEMENT OR PROFIT AND LOSS ACCOUNT

(as known internally to the management though not usually published in this detail)

Sales revenue		000
Less		
Production costs (where relevant, or alternatively costs of merchandise)		
Raw materials	00	
Components bought in	00	
Labour		
Direct	00	
Indirect	00	
Power, light, heat and other services	00	
Depreciation and interest on plant and equipment and on working capital	00	
Plant repairs and maintenance	00	
Factory overheads	00	
	000	

Transport and distribution costs		
Supplies	00	
Warehouse costs	00	
Labour	00	
Depreciation and interest on vehicles, working capital, etc.	00	
Overheads	00	
	000	
Selling costs		
Printing	00	
Advertising	00	
Salaries and staff expenses	00	
Rent, rates and service costs of premises	00	
Depreciation and interest on capital used	00	
Sales overheads	00	
	000	
General overheads		
Rent, rates, insurance, light and heat, cleaning and other services	00	
Staff salaries and expenses	00	
Professional charges, directors' fees and expenses	00	
Depreciation and interest on capital used	00	
Pension fund	00	
	000	
Total cost of sales		000
Net profit or loss after meeting all costs		00
Total capital employed in these operations		000
Net return on capital employed, after interest deductions		00%
Net profit or loss plus interest on capital used, and deducted above		00
Gross return, including interest, on capital employed		00%

NOTE: In this income statement or profit and loss account every sector of expenditure has been charged interest and where relevant depreciation on the capital it employs. This means arriving at the bottom at a net profit or loss after all costs. It also makes possible the estimation of net return on capital employed, and after adding back the interest charges, gross return on capital employed.

Figure 14.2

TYPICAL ITEMS IN A BALANCE SHEET

Assets Employed			
Fixed assets			
Land and buildings		00	
Plant and equipment		00	
		—	000
Current assets			
Stocks or inventories		00	
Work in progress		00	
Accounts receivable (debtors)		00	
Cash		00	
		—	
		000	
Less current liabilities			
Accounts payable (creditors)		00	
Taxation		00	
		—	
		00	
Net current assets			000
			—
Total assets			000*
Financed by			
Common stock or ordinary share capital		00	
Reserves			
Capital surplus	00		
Retained earnings	00		
	—	00	
Loans		00	
		—	
Total finance (equal to total assets)			000*

NOTES:

1. The above balance sheet has been set out in vertical, or mid-Atlantic style, beginning with the assets and ending at the bottom with how they have been financed. This avoids misunderstanding as to which side is debit and which side credit. The majority of balance sheets do now in fact appear in vertical form.
2. If the balance sheet is that of a profit centre which is not a company, the financial section of the sheet will not contain any share capital, it may consist entirely of a loan from the company. Even

in the case of a profit centre which is a subsidiary company, the share capital may be small and the main item in the financial section may be a loan from the parent company.

3. There will be an additional item, additional finance required (or surplus finance not required) in a budget or pro-forma balance sheet, to reconcile the current actual finance with the requirements at some future date, and so make the two starred items of Figure 14.2 actually balance.

Sales revenue

In the survey, 50 per cent of the chief executives saw sales figures monthly, 35 per cent saw them weekly and 15 per cent saw them daily. Those who saw them monthly did so in the course of seeing a monthly profit statement. Those who saw them weekly or daily did so mainly for reasons of working discipline.

As MR. BLOOMFIELD reports: 'For some firms, sales are important, for some costs and for some stocks. In our case it is sales. We have a daily sales total and analysis by representative, by territory and by outlet. The daily figure is accumulated over the month and compared with the budget and with last year. If the variation from budget is more than x per cent, somebody gets on to the problem straight away.'

MR. DAUTZENBERG reports: 'I see daily orders of the salesmen, these figures being only 24 hours late (from the computer), and so I know the shipments a few days in advance. We have no stock problems so I know that what is ordered will be shipped. The day's figures are shown cumulative for the month, also exports are shown cumulative and the preceding month is cumulative up to the same day. These figures are analysed by product. They give the short term trends.'

MR. ASCOT has a special disciplinary procedure: 'We do a mid-month revision of each store's plan so that the store manager can take such steps as are necessary to keep his profits up to budget.'

This situation is not unique to retailers. MR. ASHBOURNE is an engineering manufacturer, and this is how he handles the same problem: 'We have weekly reports on orders and shipments. We up-date our orders every month at the half-way level and show what has got to be achieved in the remainder of the month to hit the target. Then at the end of the month we immediately revise the figure for the next month'.

MR. ARGENT reports: 'I receive a daily sheet showing the orders, the shipments and the backlog, and the total to date for the month of orders and shipments'.

MR. ATTWATER sees daily figures on production in actual units, not value. The figures show both the daily production and the week to date, also the 13-week period to date and the year to date.

To some companies, daily figures would be meaningless. For example, MR. BOYD is in a branch of retailing where sales fluctuate widely according to the day of the week. So he receives weekly sales figures.

In general, the reporting of sales more often than monthly is done for one of two reasons—(*a*) to pursue those who are lagging behind budget and see what can be done to bring them up before the end of the month; or (*b*) to co-ordinate production and sales and see that an excessive backlog of orders does not build up. Frequent sales reporting can stimulate and aid production departments in keeping up with orders. In these cases we must distinguish carefully between sales orders received, and invoiced sales representing the goods which have been despatched.

When sales figures are used as a discipline, it is at least as important for the chief executive to be known to see them, as for him actually to see them. As MR. ABBOTT points out: 'The system becomes self-policing when a manager sees his own figures and there is the threat of the sack if he does not perform.'

Sales analyses

Even when sales totals are reported daily or weekly, a sales analysis by product line is not in most industries made more frequently than once a month, sometimes once a quarter. MR. DAMM produces branded consumer goods. Monthly he sees a complete sales analysis by product, showing both number of items and value, and also discount. This appears only three to five days after the end of the month, it is done on a computer and is very up to date. Such an analysis is a first essential to effective market research, and hence to a comprehensive policy for keeping in close touch with customers' needs.

Sales contracts

For medium-sized contracts, monthly reporting is usual. MR. CLARK arranges it this way: 'Each area head has to report the gains of contracts and their value, also the loss of contracts. He has to list separately all large contracts under negotiation and all new developments of significance on old contracts. But we count as our sales only signed contracts, not the ones people think they are going to get.'

MR. DANNEWALD is in insurance: 'Monthly I get figures showing new policies written. For new business there is a production plan covering the current year, and the actual figures are compared with plan every month, also with the plan to date. They are analysed into different types of insurance, and by area.'

Where major contracts are obtained involving perhaps years of work, usually in engineering, and valued at millions of pounds or dollars, different arrangements must apply. MR. BLUNDELL reports: 'We have a form called "Advice of New Contract" and these forms are circulated whenever there is news of new contracts signed.'

MR. ARGENT: 'I receive a report of large pending orders and this is carried forward from one month to the next so that one can see what has happened to orders that were pending.'

Sales forecasts

The budgeting process involves sales forecasting, as will be discussed in Chapter 17. But a budget can go wrong soon after the start of a year. Should it be changed or not? Some members of the survey have quarterly reviews of budgets, some have them half-way through the year. Some have a rolling system of forecasts that runs alongside the original budget. Here is MR. DAUTZENBERG's method: 'I have monthly sales forecasts for three months ahead. That is, at the end of November there will be a sales forecast for December, January and February, at the end of

December there will be a sales forecast for January, February and March. The production figures are based on this for three months forward.

'We make revisions to our yearly budget whenever they are necessary. This is done only after thorough discussion and it is not done very frequently. Nevertheless, we have to recognize the effects of changes in the law and of Government or other activities which we cannot forecast. So we cannot hold the same budget against somebody whose conditions of working have changed.'

MR. ALLEN has a similar system with slightly different emphasis on the degree of accuracy: 'We budget annually and we revise our forecasts every month, forecasting three months ahead. For example on September 1, we have a final forecast for September and a second estimate for October and a first forecast for November. However, we still keep the original year's forecasts in the monthly layout of comparative figures, so that each set of figures as it accumulates is being compared with the original estimate.'

Market research

Budgeting and striving to achieve targets can never be self-contained, as Mr. Clements was quick to make clear: 'Performance comparison against targets is important, but the processes of analysis and comparison against competitors are also equally important.'

Some of the continuing and essential work of market research will be done by the permanent staff of the business, but some by its nature may have to be commissioned from an independent professional firm.

When is a sale actually effected?

Bedevilling some sales statistics is the question of when a sale has actually been effected. Some firms, like MR. COLE's, both hire and sell the same equipment. This complicates his financial picture: 'The figures every four weeks show turnover, both hire and sales, and an analysis of where it comes from, what depots and what products.'

And there are others who never know when a sale will become a bad debt. MR. ATKINSON has a chain of watch and jewellery shops and he has all the problems of credit selling in his trade: 'We have to look at orders, shipments, purchases, collections and receivables. Orders are divided into those received, those approved and those held, as some orders have to be approved for credit. We do an ageing report on accounts receivable, looking closely at those which are well overdue.'

Costs of production, distribution, selling, etc.

The detailed monthly profit and loss account circulated to members of the management of each profit centre of an efficient business, usually shows a break-down of the costs that go into achieving sales.

Sometimes each item of cost is shown as a percentage of sales revenue, the idea being that a manager in charge of one particular function, such as advertising, can be reprimanded if his costs rise as a percentage of sales. His colleagues can join in censuring him because he is seen to take a higher, and hence presumably an unfair share of the total revenue for running his department.

MR. BOOTH's firm is typical, in that he sees sales figures weekly but also has 'a four-weekly analysis of performance, breaking down all costs and giving them as a percentage of sales as well as giving the absolute figures.'

The trouble with this system is pointed out by MR. BERESFORD: 'You can budget a lot of costs, including performance in your factory, but if your sales are down, bang go your percentages.'

Anyone with experience of watching the effect of a drop in sales, will know that some costs, the variable costs, shrink more or less in proportion, while others, the fixed costs, remain virtually static and hence they rise alarmingly as a percentage of sales revenue.

There is another disadvantage, although a less weighty one, in showing costs as a percentage of sales revenue. As MR. BENHAM points out: 'It is of more concern in measuring expenses, to compare actual against budget, both monthly and cumulative, and to show the percentage variance. Our computer stars a variance of more than a certain percentage so that we notice it more readily.'

If percentage variance from budget is to be shown, and if the percentage that each cost bears to sales revenue is also to be shown, there can be a confusion between two sets of percentages unless they are shown on separate sheets.

When budgets are first made up, there is a case for expressing each budgeted cost as a percentage of target revenue, so that each contributory to the operation knows his share of the expenses. But on balance it seems unwise to repeat this list of percentages in future monthly comparison tables. There is yet a further factor, which is best explained by MR. ASKEW: 'We adjust budgeted costs for the level of sales achieved. If this is not done, one is comparing actual expenditure against a budget expenditure which is not real in relation to the sales achieved.'

MR. ASKEW's point deserves more attention than it usually receives. If a sales target is not achieved and the company is for this very reason wanting to keep costs as low as possible, it is ridiculous for some department to be applauded for their good performance in keeping costs below the original budget, when their level of costs should have been much lower still, to be in keeping with the level of sales.

Costs should, wherever possible, be reduced in absolute amount if sales fall, and they should not be allowed to rise proportionately if sales increase. They should in this case fall when expressed in terms of unit output. This latter point is made by MR. ATWELL: 'Because of the dramatic effect on costs through a change in output, in our type of mass production where fixed costs are high, our budgeting is adjusted according to the actual output, so that people cannot spend money they are not entitled to when output goes up.'

All budgeting is weak if those participating in it do not have an understanding of how costs vary with sales, and hence with output or level of capacity used. MR. BERESFORD considers that:

'Enormous damage is done by failure to understand fully what costing is, and by the too great readiness of people to accept the costs put before them. They should insist that all the assumptions relating to cost are set out. So many decisions are wrong because there is a faulty profit calculation due to faulty costing. The proper preparation of cost figures and the proper reporting against them is vital. This is what we should be teaching our young men. The distribution of overheads is a particularly difficult matter.'

This subject is of special interest to MR. DACKWEILER, who is a part-time professor of business administration as well as chief executive of a family business: 'I was one of the first in Germany to look closely at the cost of operating time and to have a cost per hour for operating each department so that with this being recalculated monthly, we could apply the correct level of overheads.' MR. DACKWEILER has done important work—one might say pioneering work—in how to make staff cost-conscious: 'All our figures come straight off the computer and are bound up into convenient-sized booklets. The computer does all the headings and lines on the tables, at the same time as it prints the figures. All these layouts for our tables are stored in the memory of the computer. And we don't use abbreviations. Headings are spelt out so that everyone can understand the figures.'

MR. DACKWEILER's type of relatively small, high-precision products, manufactured in large numbers, lend themselves to a smooth flow of costs, and hence to monthly accounting. By contrast MR. ANDERSON is in chemicals where there are very high research and development costs and special promotion costs. His monthly accounts are therefore more difficult to interpret: 'Every month there are a significant number of non-recurring expenses and next month a different set. The only certainty about non-recurring expenses is that they will recur.'

Wherever work is a long time in progress before completion, there is an accounting problem in making sure that the costs shown on an income statement relate to the items actually sold and shown in the sales revenue. Equally, from a production point of view, there is a problem of relating time schedules to costs. It is easy to spend two-thirds of the money without having completed two-thirds of the work.

MR. BLYTH is in heavy engineering, and he points up the paradox: 'Standard costing is needed to show the level of work in progress, on the assumption that the costing has been standard. But it is also needed to show the variation from standard costs when the operation is complete.'

Here are six examples from the survey of widely different efforts to keep a check on production progress.

MR. ARCHER has a machinery manufacturing business, parts of it more sophisticated than others: 'In the computerized companies, every morning each foreman receives a report on the previous day's production and on the amount of scrap. In the non-computerized companies he receives this weekly, at the beginning of the week relating to the previous week.'

MR. DOBLER has a building equipment manufacturing business. He considers that in this industry, watching the percentage utilization of capacity is most important: 'This is almost never below 98 per cent, though in a recession it went down to 75 per cent. It is usually high because even though we are in a Catholic area and are not supposed to work at week-ends, we enjoy good relations with the Church. The manufacturing is continuous process and several hours of work are lost in setting up again if we stop the machines, so we are able to work through at least two week-ends a month. But measurement of utilisation of capacity depends on not allowing production people to have more than one month's production in stock, otherwise the figures are meaningless. Provided this is watched, measurement of utilisation of capacity is most important, as this is where you make the profit.'

MR. BACON makes consumer durable goods. He has a daily report of output from the works, scheduled and actual, showing up any arrears and the reasons why.

MR. DEMMLER makes consumer supplies. He and his colleagues see a daily output figure for the previous day. When the directors enter the office at 7.30 in the morning, they come in via the Sales Department and see not only the previous day's output but also a forecast of invoiced sales for the current day, based on the previous day's orders and on the weather forecast. The next day, the forecast for the previous day is compared with the actual, as a check on the accuracy of the forecasts.

MR. ASHFIELD has an aerospace manufacturing business. In the works they have computer readers into which a workman puts the job card and the details of the job he is working on, also his own card identifying himself. He clocks up the time, so that automatically the computer is able to provide statistics relating to production time, transit time from one job to another, queuing time when there are items waiting their turn, individual productivity, unit cost and man-hours spent on particular jobs.

MR. ARROWSMITH has an aerospace manufacturing business: 'Weekly I receive status reports from each location, and these draw my attention to anything unusual. Basically these cover what has happened on a programme, the man hours expended, the standard hours produced, the flight tests made, and the delivery status.'

General Overheads

The next item on the typical profit and loss account is general overheads. This is the subject of a separate chapter 18 so it will not be dealt with here, except to say it was found in the survey that in business firms not large enough to have computerized clerical procedures general overheads are not usually assessed and re-allocated more often than once a quarter. In between times, the same figures are used for profit calculations.

Net Profit

Nearly all the firms in the survey produce monthly income statements or profit and loss accounts. The reason for this periodicity is put neatly by MR. DILLMANN: 'We have monthly accounts. If you have them in any shorter period they make you nervous. Also if you get people reporting too frequently they spend so much time making reports instead of doing business. On the other hand, if you have a longer term than one month, it takes you too far away from the things that happened for you to be able to do anything in time.'

The typical profit and loss account shown in Figure 14.1 has the depreciation and interest on capital employed taken off each functional activity, so that after all costs of sales have been incurred, there remains only a net profit or loss. By contrast, in published accounts, depreciation on all relevant assets will more likely be deducted from a gross trading profit; also any real loan interest but no imputed interest will be deducted to produce a net profit from which any dividends will be paid, leaving hopefully a balance available for reserve.

It was noticeable in the survey that the chief executives with the greatest understanding of the cost of capital were using the former method in their internal accounts. Witness these examples:

MR. BELLAMY: We charge everybody for their working capital and for their expansion capital. They have to earn at the going rate.

MR. AYLWARD: We have monthly cash control. Our executives are judged as much for money use as for operating performance. Each is charged for the money used. We look particularly at sales, profit and return on investment for each of the profit centres.

MR. BIGGS: Looking at the use of money is just as important as looking at sales progress. If debtors go out by two weeks, that's a lot of money gone in interest payments which it would take a massive sales drive to make up.

MR. DENYER: We have a monthly profit and loss account and a monthly balance sheet, so it is easy to see when we should stop something which is not bringing in an economic response.

It is far from easy to re-organize the administration of a business so that the chief executive receives profit figures quickly enough to be useful in decision-making. Here is the story of MR. BOLTON's struggle and triumph against the bureaucracy of a big business:

When I became chief executive I asked the divisional heads to provide me, on the last day of the month, with an estimate of the profit for the month and of the profit for the year—extending forward to the end of the current year. I also asked them for an estimate of the capital employed world-wide on the last day of the month, this figure to be supplied within three days of the end of the month. The chief accountant of the group told me that these tasks were impossible, so I fired him. I was then in a unique position to recruit a new chief accountant who was specifically required to provide what I wanted, and the criterion for choosing him was whether he was actually able to do this—not just whether he promised to do it but whether he could, by what he showed me, demonstrate that he was actually able and willing to do it. I wanted not only the profit for each major activity but also the variance for the month compared with the previous month and with budget. I also wanted an estimate of the tax bill and bank interest, U.K. and overseas, the group return on capital employed and the earnings per share. In addition I wanted the sales related to the average working capital.

Ways were in fact found for getting all these estimated figures. Subsequently the accurate accounting figures came, and we were able to compare the estimates made three days after the end of the month with the actuals. On our graphs we used dots for the estimates and a continuous line for the actuals, so that one could see, spread around the continuous line of the accurate figures, the estimates and how wide of the mark they were. We found that on the whole they were pretty good.

This system of comparing estimates with historical records has sharpened the divisional heads' appreciation of what are the true variables that they must watch and try to control.

The typical items in a balance sheet include the following:

Fixed Assets

There is no major problem bringing these into a monthly balance sheet, since new additions are known, and rates of depreciation on existing assets are known. In an inflationary period there is, of course, a longer-term problem of reconciling depreciated values with market values. Financial advice will have to be taken, but we will ignore this problem here. A whole book would need to be written on it.

Current Assets

Estimates of stocks or inventories are not usually a problem even when it is impossible to do a proper stock-take. MR. DODEN'S method is typical: 'I have a monthly balance sheet, showing my liquidity and stocks. These stock figures are estimated on the basis of x per cent of sales value being stock value.' MR. DODEN is a manufacturer. It is the same for retailing and wholesaling, and on the other side of the Atlantic—as witness MR. AYLWARD: 'Every unit in the enterprise produces a monthly profit and loss account giving sales, all expenses including wages and profits pre-tax, and comparing them all against budget. These are estimated profit and loss accounts without waiting for actual stock-takes. They are based on the previous average gross profit, using this on the sales figures to estimate stocks. But each quarter the figures are worked out completely and I have to make my report to the public and to the security analysts.'

In some types of business, the difficulty of estimating the value of *work in progress* handicaps the completion of monthly accounts, both profit and loss accounts and balance sheets. MR. BLUNDELL makes heavy industrial plant, and he explains: 'On big contracts, the vital thing is the work in progress. We are continuously doing a paper check on stock and work in progress but we do a physical check annually. Payments to us are related to work done. We count a sale as being achieved when we have either a signed contract or a letter of intent. Once we have this we get on with all the preliminary engineering work and this enables us to recover overheads. We also have short-term contracts and work on the replacement of components, etc. These jobs give early results. But at any one time we are likely to have many millions of pounds-worth of stock and work in progress. Therefore figures for these items are crucial to our accounts. Fifty per cent of our turnover is subcontracted and so our company results are very much influenced by the subcontractors' performance.'

To the layman the problems of MR. BLUNDELL and MR. COOPER would appear to be similar. They are both engaged in heavy industry. But whereas MR. BLUNDELL produces engineering capital goods, with consequent nightmare accounting problems, by contrast MR. COOPER produces building supplies on a continuous process basis. His accounting problems are much simpler: 'We have by 10.30 in the morning a report each day on the previous day's deliveries. On Saturday of each week we have the week's figures for production, deliveries, transport and engineering. We have a full balance sheet and profit and loss account by the 16th of the month up to the end of the previous month, all double entry and ready to be audited, with all cost breakdowns. We show the figures cumulatively as well as for the month, and compared with last year.'

But surely critical path analysis has overtaken this problem of knowing the status of work in progress and its value to date?

Such is not the experience of MR. ASHFIELD's firm, a notable contributor to the spacc programme:

PERT is particularly useful for beginning a project, for planning it. One must make out a network, and this is a check that you have included everything, and included each item in its logical order. PERT is an aid to the definition of tasks. But after that there is not much in it. Up to 200 events can be done better by hand calculation, so it is only the more complex networks that are better done by computer. Moreover, other forms of cost control that you have to carry out, under your contract, are at least as good as PERTCOST, and one does not want both.

One reason why PERT is of limited value to the company is because there is so much engineering work when we start a new project, and PERT is really hardware oriented, that is it is easier for keeping track of particular hardware jobs that have a starting point, but with engineering the work is not like this. If you have a certain stage of design work to do, the important thing is to identify in one plant or another the engineering design team which could most suitably do the job.

The system the company works to for Government contracts is called Cost Schedule Control System. For this and for each of the complex modern systems, it is important that the same people commit themselves to both the time schedule and the resources, and hence the budget.

Accounts receivable are a problem for some firms to fit into monthly accounting, as witness the experience of MR. DECKER, whose firm makes a wide range of industrial and domestic products: 'Our major problem with budgeting is that some customers concentrate towards the end of the year. For example, the railways won't accept an invoice until the end of the year. Also some big firms want all the invoices in quickly in order to reduce their profits before the end of the tax year. Again, decorative laminate is sold to the furniture industry, which has seasons. It is only saleable really during the building season. All budgets have to be adapted for the seasonal cycle that hits them.'

Not only the budgeted profit and loss accounts but also the budgeted balance sheets have to be adapted. Goods which have to be produced out of season but not yet sold, show up as a rise in finished inventories.

Accounts payable can create similar problems, as we saw in the experience of MR. BLUNDELL, whose sub-contractors were slow in sending in their invoices.

Although in both cases the accounting profession has procedures for accruing revenue and costs respectively, in proportion to the amount of work done, this puts a strain on the estimating skill of non-accounting staff who have to advise their accountant colleagues as to what has actually been achieved.

Cash is not a major problem for monthly accounting, except for the matter of cheques drawn but not yet paid through the bank, money in transit and money held in different currencies.

Forward estimating of cash requirements to the end of the current financial year and broadly for three to five years ahead, was naturally found to be common in the survey. But the logical system of management control developed in this chapter suggests that special emphasis should not be put only on future *cash* requirements, but on constructing future pro-forma balance sheets as a whole, so that cash, inventories, work in progress and all the other items can be seen in their proper relationship and in the same format as they will appear in the actual accounts. Any additional finance required will be clearly indicated under this heading in the financial section of a budget or pro-forma balance sheet.

How often does the chief executive of a business really need to know his cash, inventories and other balance sheet items?

The answer can only be 'as often as possible provided the figures are meaningful and help to build up a pattern of relationships in the chief executive's mind'.

We have already seen that the value of work in progress is difficult to estimate in some firms even once a month, but MR. ARROWSMITH, an aerospace manufacturer, sees weekly status reports on it. Other items in the balance sheet are usually not so difficult, and the frequency of their reporting depends very much on the degree of computerization which it has been possible to achieve.

MR. ASCOT is president of a large retail chain, and such is his company's degree of computerization that he can say: 'We have a daily cash statement, so that we know how much money is in the till for running the business. The treasurer moves the funds around from one bank to another as required. We also know daily the inventories, the accounts receivable and the accounts payable.'

However, only 29 per cent of the chief executives in the survey see a daily cash statement, another 12 per cent see a weekly cash statement and the remaining 59 per cent see it monthly. Only 6 per cent of those in the survey see inventory figures weekly or more frequently. Another 85 per cent see them monthly and the remaining 9 per cent less frequently.

Is a month the right interval for budget figures and performance comparison?

Those who agree with the general idea of monthly accounting do not all use the calendar month, with its varying number of working days. Some use 13 lunar months of four weeks each in a year. Some use periods of 5:4:4 weeks, making up a 13-week quarter. Some use decades, taking three decades into the month.

The vast majority, however, use calendar months and do not worry too much about the variations because they are judging cumulative figures, that is the year to date, as well as the current month. Also it is quite common to have quarterly reviews which are much more thorough than the monthly presentation of figures.

MR. ANTHONY has his group's budgets broken down into quarters before they are further divided into months. This helps to make due allowance for seasonal effects: 'They (the subsidiary heads) are entitled to divide the year's plan up into quarters in any way they think appropriate to local conditions. This means they are living very much in the present. Of course the person who lives so much in the present that he ignores what he is expected to do in the whole year is going to end up in a mess. But equally we think that it is important that a person shouldn't just work for an annual plan, he should be very realistic about the current quarter.'

What are the advantages in having a standard type of format for monthly performance comparison?

MR. ANSELL gives one: 'All our monthly figures and reports are in the same format, even the charts, so that they can all be interpreted equally well, and for that matter filled in by people in any division or company.'

MR. CLIFFORD gives another: 'I don't leave it to the managing director of a subsidiary to send me the figures that he thinks I should have.'

Nevertheless, some adaptation is needed from one company to another, according to the type of business, and where this is needed in MR. CLIFFORD's group, he designs the form himself.

Is there a one best format for performance comparison, revealed by the survey?

The best, in the opinion of the author, after seeing 71 formats in America, Britain and Germany, is that of MR. DEDERICHS's company. Its layout is given symbolically in Figure 14.3. There is a full profit and loss account for each activity in the group. For each line of the account there are three columns, showing the budget figure, the actual, and the difference for the month, then alongside in a separate table the cumulative figures. On a following page are graphs (illustrated in Figure 14.4) showing again the monthly figures month by month for the year to date and the cumulative figures on another set of graphs alongside. The company uses blue for last year, green for the budget and red for the actual figure of the current year. They are planning to draw these graphs on a computer, the figures being already produced by computer. At present the graphs have to be updated by hand each month. The same graphs that are in the chief executive's folder are also on the wall of the Board Room, behind a lockable iron screen. MR. DEDERICHS says: 'I seldom go through the figures because I know them from the budgeting period. Hence I am usually only looking at the graphs and if there is an odd one I look at the figures relating to it.'

The use of colour on graphs by MR. DEDERICHS has meant hand colouring of copies until the advent of colour photocopiers.

Figure 14.3

SYMBOLIC REPRESENTATION OF MR. DEDERICHS'S FORMAT FOR PERFORMANCE COMPARISON

(Name of business activity)

	Month of April			Cumulative Jan. to April		
	1970	1971	Diff. +or−	1970	1971	Diff. +or−
Sales revenue ...	0000	0000	+000	00000	00000	+0000
Cost of...........	000	000	—00	0000	0000	+000
Cost of...........	000	000	—00	0000	0000	—000
Cost of...........	000	000	+00	0000	0000	+000
Cost of...........	00	00	—0	000	000	—00
Cost of...........	000	000	+00	0000	0000	+000
Cost of...........	00	00	+0	000	000	—00
Profit	000	000	+00	0000	0000	+000
Cap. empl	00000	00000	+0000	00000	00000	+0000
Return on cap...	00%	00%	+0%	00%	00%	+0%

Figure 14.4

SYMBOLIC REPRESENTATION OF MR. DEDERICHS'S CHART SYSTEM FOR PERFORMANCE COMPARISON

(A few key items from the previous page are illustrated)

(Colour distinguishes this year's actual from budget and from last year's actual)

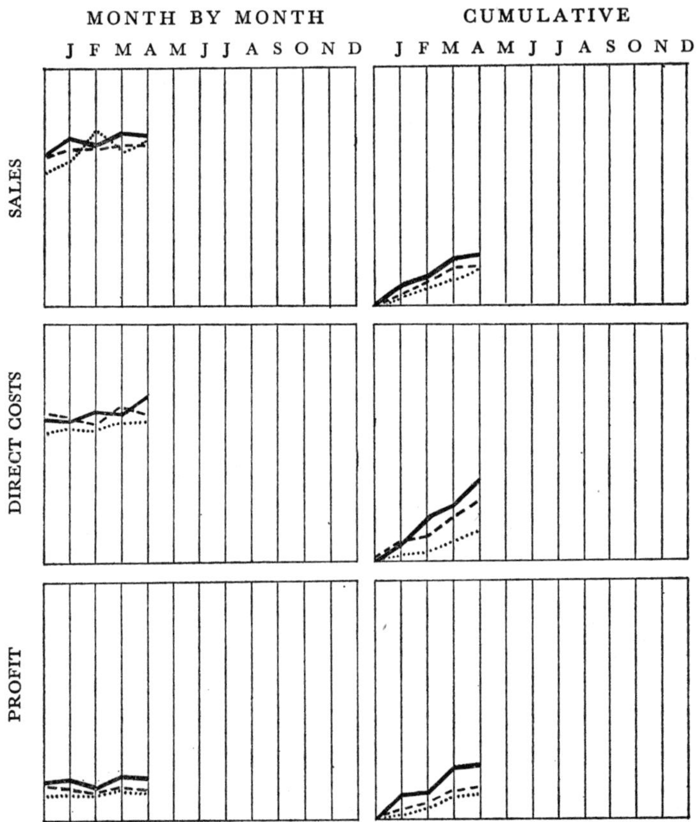

It was noticeable that Mr. Dederichs shows last year on graph only and does not show the actual figures in a table. He concentrates figure attention on budget and actual. Could not last year be ignored altogether in monthly performance comparison, since it was

presumably taken into account when preparing the budget, and it is now history?

Not in the experience of MR. ADAMS, who is a retailer: 'It is last year which gives you a trend. Retailing cannot be done on a basis of budgeting only. One must always look back when making forward decisions.'

MR. ARTHUR runs an oil company, but he supports the same view: 'On the retail side we look more at last year. The closer you are to the market the less you are able to plan accurately. We have awful economic wars. Four men on four corners of a street can precipitate a price war and the company is forced in to prevent its dealers from going bankrupt. There is a fool born every minute.'

The other important reason for not ignoring last year applies particularly to the company with quoted, or listed shares. Says MR. BOND: 'The reason why we compare with last year is because of the City [of London]. The financial world cannot know our budget figures, they can only compare our present performance with the past. This is how they judge our share values. Whatever budgets we may have set, it is important that our figures should compare well with the past. If they do not, and our share price goes down, it costs me a lot more to buy another company on a share exchange basis.'

Should monthly performance comparison tables, when circulated, be accompanied by written reports explaining them?

This depends on where they come from and the meeting system that follows them up (already discussed in Chapter 12). MR. ACLAND controls a diverse group of widely scattered companies, each with its own chief executive and accounting staff. He says: 'I have a weekly summary of sales and orders and a monthly more detailed breakdown of revenue and expenditure, with comments attached on why activities are not on target, if they are not.'

In this type of case, a subsidiary chief can add comments immediately he receives his figures from his own accounting staff, and before sending them to head office.

If written reports are not to delay the accounts, they need to be very brief. MR. BOWLES receives both figures and comments: 'The written report with each set of accounts is never more than a page, on average, although it may be a bit longer if the situation is bad and shorter if they are doing well.'

However, a written report is not a good place to break bad news. Explains MR. ANTHONY: 'I have an organization that is supposed to tell me these things. They should tell me before the figures arrive. If I don't know in advance what is going on, I raise hell.'

In contrast to the written report is the verbal presentation. MR. ARROWSMITH's company uses this method of explaining the figures: 'Monthly I see complete accounts. They are presented by one of our financial men on the multigraph and discussed in detail. This presentation is before the whole presidential staff. We have the sales by product line and by operating division, the profits by division and the expenses by division, also research and development expenditure, the cost position on each project, fixed assets authorized and spent, personnel totals divided into indirect and production, receivables, inventory and a cash projection, also sometimes labour rates. All are compared with the past and with plan. In addition status reports are done in four parts—technical, scheduling, financial and sales. We have status reports on any designated programmes, that is any projects which are specially important or are behind.'

How is it possible for the man at the top of a big and diversified group to see the detailed picture of each unit under his control?

MR. BELLAMY is in charge of a big group, and this is how he sees the position: 'Every unit manager gets on the 12th working day of the month the results in full for the previous month, and the same table of figures is received by local management and by the top. It's an amassing job at the top. I receive about 200 of these unit management reports. Each group of reports for each sector of the business has a collating sheet on top of it, summarizing the results of the group. Then at the next level there is a collating sheet for the bigger units within the next group level, and so on right to the top.'

What about looking at longer-term trends?

MR. ASHFIELD has a chart room in which all the firm's activities are shown plotted over the past 10 years (where relevant) as a background to the monthly short-term figures.

For the less sophisticated situation, a common arrangement found in the survey is for the chief executive to have different coloured bound files ready to hand, say a black file for the current figures, a brown file for future budgets and forecasts, and a red file for the past 10-year trend.

What about progress on capital expenditure—an activity which does not fit into the format of an operating report?

MR. BEST had the clearest format for this in the survey: 'The table is set out so that we see the total budget of capital expenditure, the approvals outstanding, approvals agreed to date, payments to date against approvals, the balance of approvals not yet paid, the balance of approvals not committed, and the individual project budgets for the current year. This system enables me to stop off expenditure and to know how much I can stop off, at any moment if there is a cash crisis.'

Are monthly operating reports ever used to compare sections of a business and stimulate competition between units?

Not to a great extent, since most businesses consist of departments performing different functions and working together to achieve common aims. But there are exceptions, particularly unit stores in a retail group. MR. DEGENHARDT has such a group: 'All the top 220 managers get the semi-net profit and a running list showing which stores are doing best. The running list is in terms of semi-net profit per square metre of selling space, which is a rough measure of return on investment.'

What other reports are needed monthly to control a business, in addition to the operating reports?

They are as varied as the types of activity. Here are two very different examples. MR. ARCHER has a manufacturing business: 'Every month we have a report on research and development, broken down by project, showing the amount of money spent so far and the total estimated to complete the project. Every month we have a capital expenditure report showing the amount spent and the amount committed, compared with budget. Whenever a new plant is built we have every month a progress report showing its progress against plan, both in money terms and in terms of completion.'

MR. ASCOT has a large retail business: 'There are monthly reports on customer service, manufacturers' warranties, new installations, credit sales and collections, defaults and delinquencies, shipping centre development, profit-sharing, the pension plan, the sample sales of the bigger stores, and there is a weekly report on women's fashions. Also there is a monthly comparison of our stores against other stores, and there are reports on old merchandise, the catalogue operation, an out of stock report, customer complaints, insurance, and acceptance credits. In essence, each major function or activity has to make a monthly report. The style of report is laid down as a firm discipline so that one report can be compared with another and results can be followed up. It is laid down by discussion with the audit department, the format then being approved by top management.'

Lastly, MR. CLEMENTS has a research-based engineering firm: 'We have a very tight system of financial control and a parallel system of technical monitoring of performance. This is particularly important with research and development, where one cannot tell from an ordinary budgeting process how effective the expenditure is. One needs a system of technical monitoring by experts in the particular branch of activity.'

Are there any general conclusions from this survey of chief executives, as to what knowledge they need of

accounting and what knowledge others need who are in line management positions leading towards the top of a business?

It is easiest to state what they don't need—a detailed knowledge of accountancy practice. This comes out in Chapters 5 and 6 as well as in 14.

One of the attributes of a successful person is that he recognizes useless knowledge—from his point of view—and sticks to learning what is essential to his task. What the chief executive and the would-be chief executive should concentrate on is:

1. An understanding of the basic principles of double entry (but not of the detailed professional practice).
2. An understanding of the income statement or profit and loss account, and of the balance sheet.
3. A detailed knowledge of—
   (*a*) how each item in these accounts reacts in practice on the others,
   (*b*) their relative sizes,
   (*c*) their constituents.
4. How each may be compiled realistically for budgeting ahead.
5. How the progress or change of each may be compared regularly, budget against actual, and in some cases against last year.

We will look in detail, in Chapter 17, at capital expenditure budgeting. Suffice it to say that an item missing from the conventional balance sheet is forward commitments of capital expenditure—money which may not have been actually spent but is so tied up with completed sections of a project that it is very likely to be spent unless there is a major economic downturn. One of the advantages of a cash flow statement is to bring together every source of revenue or cause of spending and show the effect of them all on the cash position at various forward moments of time. This is essential information for the chief executive, but I believe it would be better to put it in a series of forecast or budgeted or pro-forma balance sheets, showing a comprehensive breakdown of assets and liabilities at each chosen forward moment of time.

It seemed clear from the survey that relatively few firms yet do this. Actually only five revealed to me that they do it,* but I was only asking specifically for information on it during the last 25 interviews when I realized how important yet how rare it was. So my guess is that the real percentage of firms producing pro-forma balance sheets is probably around 10 per cent and unlikely to be higher than 20 per cent. Here are the five examples. They are all American, two of them internationally famous groups and the other three subsidiaries of international companies:

MR. ARROWSMITH: Some companies follow two different tracks, a budget system which is kept separate from historic accounting. But to us the budget has always been a complete balance sheet and profit and loss statement for the future, for each period ahead.

MR. ATTFIELD: We have to do our forecasts like a balance sheet because we have seasonal sales. Also some of our food products require different periods of ageing to be different qualities. So we have a problem of working out what inventories we can finance.

MR. ATWELL: We do a complete monthly projected balance sheet, month by month for the first year ahead and then quarterly for five years ahead.

MR. ARTHUR: When we add a new project on to a division we do a pro-forma or imaginary financial statement, including this new project, to see the effects on the total.

Finally, MR. AUBREY's case example is given in some detail because his set of operating reports is so well thought out both for control of the business and for its educational effect on staff:

We have a daily sales flash, by product group. Invoiced sales figures are compared daily and cumulatively for the month and for the year to date, against forecast and against the previous year.

We may make some internal revisions to our forecasts if for example there is a new product introduced, but we try not to change our overall forecast reported to Head Office. One product may come

* I must make it absolutely clear that we are discussing internal information, for the chief executive and his colleagues, not published information.

forward and another one back. If you don't hit the target, you don't move the target but you sharpen up your sights.

We have monthly operating statements both by company and by product, a monthly balance sheet and a breakdown of inventories by major categories. The monthly operating statements are compared with budget and last year, and they are also cumulative. The monthly balance sheet is compared with the previous month and with the last year's end.

For cash, we have a new forecast every quarter for the next 12 months, and then more broadly for each of the next four years. We do a pro-forma balance sheet for the end of the year, but for the quarters we do a cash flow statement which shows all the major changes in the balance sheet, all the expenditure for capital items, all the changes in inventories, receivables, etc. They are listed in the same order as in a balance sheet.

The treasurer does a quarterly presentation, and this is an educational process for the staff, but we have also had a university business game, and some of my management committee felt that by working with the numbers, they got to understand these things better.

In conclusion, the case for the pro-forma balance sheet is summed up in these words of MR. BOLTON, who as we saw went to so much trouble to produce up to date estimates of capital employed, but like most members of the survey, had possibly not heard of the pro-forma balance sheet: 'Utilization of cash is one of the most difficult things to get over. It is essential to identify the total capital employed on a product.'

15

SELECTION OF KEY CONTROL FIGURES

Is it true that each industry has its own particular key control figures which provide the chief executive with a quick guide to how his firm is doing?
This is only partly true, and then only over the short term. For example, it used to be said that as furniture uses a lot of space to display properly, a quick guide to the profitability of a furniture retailer's shop was sales per unit area. However, the growth in sales of packaged furniture has certainly knocked the universality of this key ratio.

For reasons already discussed in Chapter 14, the only ultimate business test of the success of a venture must be the profit made on the capital employed. Almost all businesses need capital to start up, and even in those cases where capital is not needed, if a business firm wants to rise above its competitors and establish a more permanent and unique relationship with its customers, it inevitably has to invest capital. Hence the return on this capital becomes a universal yardstick of whether the business has been able to return to its founders more (or less) than they put into it.

Nevertheless, there is something in the idea that a particular industry can have a quick way of watching its own progress in between the dates when the profit figures are due. So a question was asked about this in the survey. Participants were initially asked which are the key indicators that in their industry tell them most, at a glance, about the way things are going.

Surprisingly, this question was not easily grasped and required quite a lot of explanation, so half-way through the survey it was re-worded in the following fashion: 'Suppose you went on holiday to the South of France/Bahamas, and you phoned the office, which are the key indicators, and so forth, that you would ask about?'

This revision of the question brought some interesting information about chief-executives' holiday habits and attitudes, which is given at the end of this chapter.

What was discovered in the survey about the frequency of use of various key indicators?

Nothing shone out as the dominant indicator. Sales or order figures were mentioned in 55 per cent of cases, and profit figures in 42 per cent of cases (these percentages being completely unchanged by the alteration of wording of the question half-way through). No other indicator came anywhere near these figures. The cash position was mentioned in only 10 per cent of cases and stocks in only 4 per cent.

Since the two most obvious business indicators scored only 55 per cent and 42 per cent respectively in the survey, did the participants have a lot of special indicators of their own, peculiar to their industries or even to their firms?

They revealed surprisingly few, and the interviewees gave no cause to believe that they would be against revealing information of this kind. In fact the nature of their answers supports the view that watching the progress of a business involves watching so many variable and interacting factors that there cannot in most cases be any overriding key indicators.

As already mentioned in Chapter 14, one family of indicators, known as business ratios, are useful in constructing pro-forma balance sheets, once the planned levels of spending and the forecast levels of sales are known. They were originally designed to be useful to the financial community outside the business firm who, looking at the published financial statements, have the task of seeking out any signs of impending trouble. But a chief executive is the receiving point for many types of internal information and therefore he is less likely to need indicators of this kind. Moreover, the widespread use of modern budgeting techniques reduces the likelihood of also needing special indicators. Though a knowledge of key ratios may be used in constructing the budgets, once they have been built there will be a tendency to rely mainly on comparing actual results with the budget.

Nevertheless, a few special indicators had been constructed by participants in the survey and they are presented here along with other typical comments on key indicators:

MR. BOSWORTH: The key things we have to watch (in our furniture business) are sales input or orders, sales output or invoices, and the delivery periods relating to them. If we have an input of 100 and an output of 75 and delivery is 8 weeks, which is what we are scheduled for, I am very concerned about what has gone wrong in the works. But I am hopping mad if the delivery period is 12 weeks.

MR. AUSTIN. The thing I want to know immediately, every day for the previous day, is what is the relief factor. We make our trailers available on a per diem plan, under which the railroad only pays for the days that they are actually using a trailer and if they know they are not going to be using it they can file a form with our local depot which puts the trailer on relief and then when they want to use it again they file a second form. The ramp inspector on our behalf has to countersign the form after he has been to the ramp to make sure that the trailer is there, and not in use. Then he contacts another railroad and sees if they want it. This plan has been a very important factor in building our business, because it appeals to the railroad, but of course the percentage of relief in the use of our trailers is very important as to whether our business is profitable or not.

MR. CHISHOLM: Everything here is done on the basis of exception reporting. I particularly watch for lost sales, by item, due to stocks not being available. The computer reports these branch by branch. But it also projects forward and reports where sales are going to be lost next week, so that we can do something about it and move stocks in. This system is based on last year's pattern of sales. We stock for four weeks in advance. We use a system of exponential smoothing. Suppose the average sale from last year has been 1·4 of an item in a particular week, the stock is 6, the sale in the latest week is actually 2. We add on to the 1·4, 2/5ths of the difference between 2 and 1·4. This gives 1·64. We multiply by 4 because we stock for 4 weeks ahead, this gives 6·56 and we round it up to 7, the nearest number above. As the current stock after selling the two items in the latest week is 4, we send 3 more garments, in order to bring the total up to 7. This way we are always stocking ahead for 4 weeks on the basis of expected sales.

MR. DOBLER: I used to receive daily figures of cash, incoming orders, shipments, and royalties. This is the way I built the business. The figures came daily and were accumulated monthly. But now I feel that daily figures are a waste of time and I am concentrating on monthly figures.

MR. CLARK: We have an important key indicator, which is assessed daily. We need to bear in mind that our disposal centres are moving further and further away from where we can collect the waste products. So we need some way of looking at the capital costs per vehicle and the mileage done, and assessing the profit margin above the expenses of running. Our indicator is best described as returns per mile, or more accurately, per wheel, because the indicator takes into account the type of vehicle. By means of this indicator we can see immediately whether a branch is working on a profitable basis or not, and if not, make immediate investigations.

MR. BOND: The key figures for us are the cost of production per barrel in each brewery and the margin that each marketing company is effecting on their sales. If the sales slip, the overheads stay much the same, so the margin slips. In this business we have to be very cost conscious and very profit conscious.

MR. ACLAND: The type of key figure one looks at depends on the nature of the division and on the situation there. In the area of our special chemical division in Southern California, for example, there is currently a lot of unemployment and it so happens that we need a lot of commission salesmen. We have just interviewed 1,000 and taken on 40. I have looked closely at this situation. By contrast in another division which is highly seasonal, I am always making seasonal comparisons. By contrast again, in recent months I am always looking at collections and receivables because money has been so dear. Again, by the nature of our investments, I am always looking at the progress of capital expenditure—how the spending is going and the percentage of completions.

MR. ATTWATER: Our production efficiency percentage (in this

overseas subsidiary) is reported daily and is based on United States standards of what they would produce per day.

MR. BOOTH: We have weekly sales totals for each store and the ratio of staff costs to sales. Lunchtime on Monday for the preceding week we have the figures, and they are compared with the previous week and the same period of the previous year. Of course these figures eliminate new stores which are just getting under way.

The management accounts are set up around people, both horizontally as well as vertically. For example, though the managing directors have the responsibility for maintenance in their own companies, the maintenance chief has his budget right across all companies, for all maintenance.

MR. BEST: If I know, and I do know every week, the production figures of all our 30 plants around the world, and the net sales to third parties, I know whether I am operating at a profit or not. But also a statement of cash in and out is most vital, to know whether we are alright financially. And lastly, I must have cost information on critical products, those that are near the margin.

MR. CAIRNS: In my business the cost per square foot of material produced has been related to machine capacity so that we can see quickly whether we are working at a worthwhile capacity. Unfulfilled orders are another key.

MR. CHILDS: We use a computer bureau and have the week's figures out by Wednesday of the following week. The key indicators for us are the immediate orders, the forward order position, the stock position and the cash position. Our orders are broken down into retail, mail order and export. All actual figures are shown against forecast. We also watch closely the despatches and promises for despatches, to insure that the scheduled dates are met.

MR. BAXTER: I not only watch all the figures closely myself, but I expect my key people to watch. If someone walks in here with a problem, my first question to him is: 'Do you know what the present situation is?' And when he has answered that and shown me that he does understand the overall situation of the company, in figures, I say: 'Now let's get your problem into group perspective.' The key items here are stocks, credit, cash, discount. Also I watch rebates from manufacturers as a measure of buying power. I have computerized these. A quarter of our profits (as wholesalers) is rebate.

MR. CLEMENTS: In analysing a business I look for anything I can find, but I have several specific indices:

Rate of return on capital employed.

Sales turnover on capital employed.
Sales turnover to stocks.
Average number of months of debtors.
Sales per head.
Output per £ of fixed assets.
Rate of profit on turnover, gross and net.

Another significant index is average number of days of credit outstanding. The profit and stocks of a business, as calculated at any time, are synthetic. The most significant thing is, where is the cash? The quickest clue to what has happened to a business is the cash. Is it in capital assets or not? And if in assets, how much would they be worth, if they had to be sold? A daily cash watch is most important.

What do the people on holiday telephone the office about?

Here are the answers given:

MR. ASHBOURNE: If I was away I would ask how are the orders, and I wouldn't have to ask about profits, because they would be cabled to me in code.

MR. DODEN: We are running so much on schedule that if I was away and phoned the office I would only ask for sales figures.

MR. ALLEN: If I were in the Bahamas and phoned up, I would want to know the weekly billings, and at the right time of the month I would want the financial figures, particularly the earnings per share. I would also ask about any major labour problems.

MR. DOEBEL: I phone daily when I am abroad. I would be particularly concerned with whether a special client had accepted the concept of (an advertising) proposal put to them, because on this could hang 10 million marks. I would also ask, at the right time of the month, how profits were going.

MR. BOYD: If I were away and phoned up I would want to know last week's sales. We have them roughly by Monday but more accurately by Wednesday.

MR. ATWICK: If I telephoned up from the Bahamas I would immediately ask if there had been any surprises this month, any strong variances from budget. I would also ask about incoming orders and the backlog, and inventories and receivables.

MR. DERKUM: I always phone when on holiday and ask about sales and cost ratios, and the profit and loss statement. I also ask about the monthly balance sheet, particularly the ratio of liabilities to owned capital.

MR. ARGENT: If I phoned from the Bahamas, what I asked about would depend on the problems of the day. I wouldn't leave and go on holiday when there might be a strike, for example. If there was a customer problem, a big customer such as General Motors, I would ask about that. I would leave my telephone number. Sometimes I phone up for no particular reason but just to show them that I am interested.

MR. BOWLES: I phone the office nearly every day when I am abroad. I like to know what's going on. If there was a major problem I'd be asking about it, or if the month's figures were due I'd be asking the finance director about them. The only way to get away from one's responsibilities really is to go on a small boat.

MR. ANDERSON: Whenever I am away for more than a week, I get sent a daily envelope containing any key financial information and changes in trends. I have a very good secretary who knows what I like to look at and what I don't. She is very good at sending me on things of high interest. For example, key court decisions, news on the health of a colleague who has been ill, the newsletter for our industry. This letter will trigger off key questions when I phone up. There will be no routine questions unless a particular issue has been hanging on, for example an acquisition negotiation.

MR. ANSELL: When I am away, the officers of the company send memos on any important problems to my secretary and if I phone up I ask her if there is anything in the reports. If there is, I have the call transferred so that I can talk to the responsible officer. Also we have a world-wide teletype system that I can use just by going into the company's local office. For example I was doing some negotiating in Belgium recently, so I walked across the street into the office and was immediately in touch with head office in the States and was able to get information to carry on the negotiations.

MR. ATKINSON: If I go away the most important thing I want to know is where my management are and their plans for the time when I am gone. I must know a week beforehand, otherwise I do not have a good holiday. Even so I check in every couple of days to ask how sales are going.

What about the attitudes of the chief executives who do not phone the office?

MR. DEGENHARDT: I never phone but I leave my telephone number.

MR. ARMSTRONG: If I were on holiday I wouldn't ring my office. They can get me if there is something vital, but they rarely bother me. I have a home in Florida and I don't have a listed number there. My assistant has the number but nobody else. If I did ring the office, I would ask about a people problem, not a statistical problem.

MR. DECKER: I never phone the office if I am away. They phone me. I am so organized that it is unlikely that any issue will arise on which they can't take decisions. I have a deputy chief executive who is our finance man and very experienced.

MR. AYLWARD: When I am away I never phone the office. Half the time they don't know where I am. I don't go if there is trouble. I have a good wife as regards holidays, if they are on they are on, if they have to be put off that is it.

MR. DANNEWALD: I don't phone the office when I am on holiday, although I am occasionally phoned. But if I did phone I would ask about special problems, not about figures. I normally go away for only three weeks, so the figures can wait.

MR. ARNOLD: Every man in this organization has a back-stop. If he isn't there, his deputy must take the responsibility and make a decision.

MR. ANTHONY: I don't phone the office when I am on holiday. If they call me, it had better be something darned earth-shattering.

MR. ATWELL: What's a holiday? I don't take them. If I am away from the office I receive a basket of mail every day.

MR. DITTMER: I don't telephone when I am on holiday. One must have a chance to get away so that when you come back you find that someone else is running the business better than it ran when you were there.

Author's Note: MR. DITTMER gets the 'prize' for being the most amusing of the 103 chief executives interviewed. He had me in fits of laughter a number of times.

16

USE AND NON-USE OF CHARTS

Is the use of charts widespread at the chief executive level?

Members of the survey were asked whether they used charts to help in the understanding of figures, and 27 per cent said they did not, whilst 73 per cent said they did.

Some very precise and apparently well-thought-out reasons were given for not using charts, and these are given here, before presenting an analysis of the advantages and specific uses of charts.

REASONS FOR NOT USING CHARTS

MR. CAMERON: I have no charts. I prefer to remember everything in its proper relationship.

MR. CHILDS: If I had to have charts on the wall I would feel that I had failed. I have more products and prototypes in my office than anything else.

MR. BLUNDELL: I can picture figures in chart form. To people who appreciate figures, charts are hardly necessary. You just need to remember the past figures, to give you a trend.

MR. ATWELL: I just like to watch the figures, but I'm a figure man. If I have a visitor who happens to be a chart man, I give him charts.

MR. ATTWOOD: I can see trends without having to have them visualized for me.

MR. BOND: I like the feel of the money that I get from the figures.

MR. DANNEWALD: Figures give me all the proportions and trends that I want.

MR. CHISHOLM: We do not use charts. The computer is programmed to print out moving averages, which of course give us the trend.

MR. BATCHELOR: There is no need for charts if one is numerically skilled. Charts really don't work because you have to get down to the figures in the end. They delay getting down. A chart doesn't give the amount, in cash terms. It can be misleading. I can recall a case where people should have been arguing about the chart that didn't look very serious. It's the total cash that matters.

The sharp angle on one particular chart doesn't matter if that operation isn't contributing much, whereas the more gentle angle on another chart may matter a lot if a lot of money is involved.

MR. CLEMENTS: It is a fallacy to say a chart enables you to 'see at a glance'. There are not many easy ways of doing things. The trouble in this country is that we so often find out after things have gone wrong. We don't care enough before. We should check, check, check. This is the secret of success. We should worry in advance, not after. The managing director of an operating business ought to know what's happening long before he gets any charts. It is very seducing, this sort of thing. In any case, the presentation of the information is not the critical thing in the management process. Critical analysis of the market, etc. is.

The sloping of a curve and the spacing of the units make a hell of a difference to the impression got from a chart. There is a limit to what you can get from either figures or charts. It is important to send in a checking-up team once you feel things are going wrong.

Finally, a line on a chart does not give you scope for accumulation of data on the background. It is like television for culture. It is too easy.

Well, there you are. If you still have the courage, after that blast, to say you like charts and to admit that you don't remember all the figures in their right relationships, read on.

What do the others say about the advantages and specific uses of charts?

THE SPOTTING OF TRENDS

MR. CASEY: The ability to spot a trend is the most important skill in a manager.

MR. CAIRNS: Only a graph can show the real change.

MR. BERESFORD: On charts you see the trend quickly, but you can't in figures. Also you have got to compare with the economic climate. This is what our economists do for us.

MR. BOOTH: I believe in the importance of trends. For example, are we selling more fruit and vegetables? I have just taken on a business graduate to set up a chart system.

MR. BENHAM: There are quite a few trends in activity that are not obvious from the figures. We plot them on a chart and I can see them in a flash.

MR. ASPINALL: We do charts which not only go back five years but project forward five years. Charts give you a better idea of trend than do a series of figures. They are better at enabling you to see the problems and the opportunities.

MR. ANTHONY: We do a lot of charts but they are mainly concerned with outside trends, for example gross national product, total industrial production, our industry's trend of production, economic trends generally.

TYPICAL EXAMPLES OF THE CHARTING OF OPERATIONS

MR. ATWICK: For every set of figures sent out monthly for each company, the controller also provides a chart. There are eight pictures for each company, showing orders received, shipments, profits, inventories, work in progress, operating costs, overheads and cash. This has the great advantage that if for example the volume of production dips down one particular month, I will have been provided with the break-even curve and the consequences of the dip will bc far more obvious than if I just had the figures. I learnt this charting from Du Pont when we had a plant at Wilmington, and of course I learnt a lot of the other figure work from General Electric, so we had the advantage of these two major companies' experience. The controller does all the charts, up-dating the master charts in each case and making photocopies for each director who receives a set.

MR. DACKWEILER: We have charts showing firstly the turnover of different lines of products, then our analysis of the main items of cost, and then the difference between total costs and total sales, as a two-line chart.

MR. BLYTH: We plot the factory scrap levels and reject levels, also the sales volume of a series of products, to see the trends. All sales statistics are graphed against budget, cumulatively, and also the percentage share of the market is shown.

MR. AUSTIN: We use a lot of charts. We plot the relief rate (see Chapter 15), the income, the expenditure, and separately the maintenance cost. We plot individually by companies within the group, by railroad, by steamship and overall. Why are charts so important to us? Firstly, we need to be able to see quickly whether any slippage is due to an area going up or down, or to a particular customer, or what. Secondly, as regards maintenance, if there is a lot of maintenance we want to know whether it is the doors, or the bottoms, or some other part of the trailers. The charts don't tell us this, of course, but they give us immediate warning better than figures can, that maintenance costs are going up. That causes us to look closely at the back-up figures and investigate what is wrong.

Our charts are done in the departments concerned, for example maintenance charts by the maintenance department. They are then photocopied and the copies circulated to relevant executives.

MR. ANTHONY: We use charts for orders received, orders completed and orders in estimating. We have different lines on the same chart.

MR. CLARK: We have our master schedule of key figures transcribed on to a set of charts which are carefully locked up, but they are updated weekly. My general manager can thus watch the continuing history of each contract and get a pattern, not merely a single figure or succession of figures.

MR. BEATTY: We plot orders, sales invoiced, materials used, labour costs and overhead costs. They are plotted on log paper and compared with the industry as a whole, and we also plot them by type of product. When I was with my last firm, my order intake charts were vital. This was because of the highly cyclical nature of the machine tool industry. There was a 5 to 1 difference between the peaks and troughs of the cycle. I used to be able to predict when the cycle would move up again.

MR. ATKINSON: We chart inventories. We keep a year's movement, and chart by dollars. We show last year's inventory movement and then we overlay the projected movement for this year, and plot the actual. This gives us an indication 30 to 60 days ahead of whether we shall need money, whether we should hold purchase orders or delay shipments. This is quicker than computers. The historical gross profit gives us the inventory accurately enough. Every 10 days when the sales and purchase figures come in we can calculate the inventory close enough within an hour.

MR. DECKER: We use charts as well as figures and words for our five year plan. All the costs are split up in the charts, and the interest on capital used is shown. I keep these in order to see how the thing went, when I get the quarterly reports from the divisions.

MR. BISSETT: Each operating company prepares its main figures in chart form and these are sent up to group finance and distributed to us monthly with the figures.

MR. ATTERBURY: We bar chart each major expansion programme and factory start up.

MR. BURKE: We use charts for works costs.

MR. AYLWARD: I have charts made on anything I want to watch carefully. For example, we recently re-modelled 14 stores. I said to the vice-president in charge, 'I am very interested in the results of this re-modelling.' He provided me weekly with a sales curve, so that I could see the effect.

MR. ADAMS: The treasurer charts the cash flow. And for this he also takes in the situation regarding debt and available funds, so that he is aware, well ahead, of our cash situation. This is seen much better on a chart than in figures, whereas most other activities can be seen satisfactorily by the figures alone.

USE OF CHARTS IN PRESENTATIONS

MR. DAHLMANN: Charts are used for reporting to the supervisory board. You have to be an insider to read figures, charts help the outsider.

MR. ANTHONY: We use charts in presenting our case to the union committee. We compare pay in the machine-tool industry with other industries, the sales of our companies as a percentage of the market, and the area rate of pay compared with the national rate.

MR. DOEBEL: For our clients we plot thc advertising budget and their share of the market.

MR. ALLEN: The corporate planning division does a special quarterly presentation attended by all the presidents of the different companies. Charts are shown on the screen.

MR. DOBLER: If I go to a divisional board meeting or give a paper to the members of my trade association, it is good to show a chart. They are not interested in detailed figures.

MR. BOLTON: I do a monthly report to the board and I compile this by going through the very comprehensive system of charts prepared for me by the central planning organization.

MR. AVERY: We use charts at the end of the year when we do budget presentation to the board. We present the budgets, the cash flow, the capital expenditure summary, all these overall and by company, also a long-range earnings projection for six years ahead. We spend $30,000 per year on visual aids in our budget presentation to the board, then we give each company their charts and they keep them up to date.

MR. DENYER: We use flip charts for presentations. These are kept up to date by the head of administration and long range planning. I do a presentation in July or August on next year to the whole of top management. I start with our sales expectations and work down.

MR. ALEXANDER: Today at our executive committee meeting 100 charts were presented on the screen. These were prepared last night, and they were presented in batches by six different people who were making out a case for a particular decision which had to be made today.

METHODS OF OPERATING A CHART SYSTEM

MR. DEDERICHS (whose figure and chart system was judged the best, in Chapter 14): The charts in my board room and in my own book of figures are produced by the finance department.

MR. ARCHER: My secretary does charts for me and brings them up to date every month.

MR. ANTHONY: We photocopy our charts and pass copies round to all concerned. The rule is that the originator of a chart keeps every version of it. Everybody else keeps the current version until the next one arrives, when he can get rid of the old one.

MR. ARMSTRONG: I have never found black and white charts particularly helpful, but as soon as we have colour photocopying they will be more helpful.

MR. ANSELL: People used to do their own charts their own way, but we soon found it necessary to standardize the method of presenting the same information, so that everybody could understand each other's charts.

MR. CHRISTIE: I insist on one-page reports, and if there is any detail, it must be attached in a schedule. If there is anything complicated, they must try and project it in a chart.

MR. ASHFIELD: In the conference room we have large charts of the current position and the planned future position, on a month by month basis, in locked wall cabinets. These charts are on runners so that they can be displayed one at a time, and also lifted out of the runners for up-dating. At the end of the room we have small translucent charts on permanent display with lights behind them, giving on a year by year basis a ten-year trend.

MR. DEMMLER: As you can see, this office is also the boardroom. This chart cupboard has dividers in it so that the charts can stand upright. There is a display panel on the door. The charts are mounted on board so that each one can be taken out and worked on on a desk, or looked at on the board table, or displayed on the actual door of the open cupboard. When the door is locked, nobody would know our secrets are in there, it's like any other door in the wall panelling.

MR. ARROWSMITH: Charts can be misleading if people don't know the underlying assumptions. To get them on a basis which all can agree, we set up established assumptions about the spreading out of money payments, depreciation, overheads, etc. The financial officer, when giving a status report, will detail his assumptions, and we re-examine the assumptions at least every 60 days in a meeting I hold with the financial people. Sometimes the marketing and technical people have to come into this meeting as well.

MR. ARNOLD: On our charts we plot, for each division, the trend of sales, of profits and of return on investment. In the case of sales and profits, we not only plot the actual against the budget and against last year, but each month the executive in charge of each division has to forecast the month ahead and the month after that. This means he will be continually revising these forecasts, and they may show on the chart a different trend from the originally agreed budget. We want them plotted so that we know how much money we are likely to get in and how much we are likely to need.

MR. DITTMER: I have a wall chart behind me, hidden behind this map of the world, which folds back in two halves to produce chart space. This system is lockable, so that nobody can see the figures without breaking it open.

I also have charts which fit into my planning diary that I carry in my inside coat pocket. These show for each subsidiary the budget turnover, cumulative, and the actual incoming orders and invoiced orders, both cumulative, so that the difference between them at any time is the backlog. They also show the real level of profits last year, the target level for the current year and the real level for the current year, all cumulative. Thus, when I go to visit one of the works, I am quickly up to date on what has been happening and how they are doing compared with budget.

MR. AUBREY: We are great believers in overhead projectors, and use our controller to make his analysis and interpretation of the month's results at our review meeting. The discipline of doing this is important. Each manager has seen his own figures before. Moreover, he has a division controller assigned to him, and as soon as the figures are available he will be sitting with this man analysing them and finding out why they were good or bad. Nevertheless, when the figures come up on the projector at the review meeting, we find there is a kind of group pressure on the management. Nobody likes to see his figures down when the others have good figures.

17

SYSTEMS FOR ANNUAL BUDGETING, LONGER-TERM PLANNING AND CONTROL OF CAPITAL EXPENDITURE

How far ahead is it feasible to budget in the business world where sales and profits are dependent on whether customers decide to buy?

Strictly, only expenses are budgeted, whilst sales revenue is forecast. Nevertheless, the whole process of projecting forward sales and expenses is generally called 'budgeting'.

With few exceptions, the chief executives in the survey budget ahead for at least one year. This is a logical business activity because agreement to budget is a commitment to spend money in anticipation of customer demand, which is precisely what business is about.

As we saw in Chapter 14, capital is the amount of money spent by a business man before he receives adequate sales revenue from customers to meet his expenses. Agreement to an annual budget of operating expenditure is therefore as much a capital commitment as agreement to building a new factory. The operating expenditure will involve tying up working capital and once an annual operating budget has been agreed, it should be possible to estimate how much working capital is likely thereby to be tied up, and hence to project forward a pro-forma balance sheet for the operation concerned.

It is, however, usual in practice to distinguish between annual operating budgets for existing activities and so-called capital expenditure budgets for new or enlarged or modified projects. In some firms the words 'capital expenditure' are unhappily used only for spending on plant and other fixed assets and durable goods such as motor cars which need to be depreciated in the accounts over a period.

At the opposite extreme, however, is the capital expenditure which is called thus because it is spent on a new project, yet the money goes on items which do not necessarily endure. Here are two examples:

MR. DOEBEL: We have a fixed rate of investment in human capital, growing steadily by 20 per cent to 25 per cent per annum. We have to grow because the advertising agency discount of 15 per cent is fixed by law, but costs are steadily increasing. It is human creativity which promotes the agency. We do not spend money on promotion, we just invest in human capital.

MR. BOWLES: The big strategic marketing decisions involve a very big investment. It's called an investment but in fact we blow the money on advertising. It's all gone, we have nothing to show for it if we've made a mistake. Not even a bit of plant we can pat.

There is a case, then, for saying that a tidying up process is needed on forward budgeting, to distinguish between operating expenditure on existing projects, launching expenditure on new projects and fixed capital expenditure which may be spread over many projects and much time, being depreciated over a longer time than its initial construction or installation period.

Most of the chief executives in the survey budget ahead for longer than one year, for at least three reasons:

(*a*) Some items of fixed capital expenditure, such as construction of a new factory, take longer than one year to complete.

(*b*) Some new projects take longer than a year to get under way.

(*c*) Budgeting for just one year is likely to lead to a hodge-podge of decisions. Only by planning further ahead is it possible to develop a consistent set of policies.

The following are examples:

MR. ATTERBURY: Every year we start a new five-year plan. We study closely every facet of the business, set goals, review what we have achieved, and adjust accordingly. What is important is what people have to find out about the business in order to do this, rather than the result, which is immediately out of date. Our plan is only used as a day-to-day tool the first year out. The rest is just a general guide.

MR. BOLTON: We do a ten-year plan, on the basis that I give each division a percentage profit figure I expect, and tell them how much money they can have. There is a detailed budget for the first year, and it is less detailed for the next four years. The second five years are a think-plan which is not quantified. All major capital projects have to be in the first five years' capital budget.

I am hoping eventually to halve our present number of employees by more intense capital investment. But we also have a central register of patents arising from our investment in research and development. This is more important than our actual physical property.

MR. DECKER: In the spring we do the five-year plan and in the autumn we do next year's budget. The five-year plan includes capital expenditure, but it must also be brought into the yearly budget.

MR. BOWLES: We do our capital expenditure budget once a year. We have a very good cash flow. Capital decisions come up to the group board not because of the expense involved, but because of the effect on policy. We must make sure that all policy matters are decided at the top. Here's an example where one can get confused over policy. We bought a wine firm, and then we were offered another one with a bonded warehouse. We found ourselves getting deeper and deeper in wines, without having made a proper decision as to whether that was our business.

MR. ANDERSON: I set the overall corporate goals, and if the total plans don't meet the goals, the staff have to try and get more out of the resources, or get the same out of less resources. They nearly always tend to get the plans front-end loaded, that is most of the expenses at the beginning and the goodies in a later period. If you plot several curves like this, one after the other, the result is no growth.

MR. DOBLER: I have to conform to the budgeting system for the whole group. It is regarded as not good if you are too high above budget, any more than if you are too low. An excessively high level of operations means that the group must find more working capital than they budgeted for.

MR. ANSELL: We have a one-year profit plan and a five-year projection of capital expenditure and financing. We are a new product enterprise, and if a new product is due to enter the market at a certain time and is delayed for six months, this changes the profit plan quite considerably.

MR. ARMSTRONG: Like I.B.M., we are very sophisticated in our planning. You can't change a business much in a year. You can cut expenses, but you can't alter where it is going. Any attempt to work out the implications of changes in the business would take five months to do by clerical methods, and so by the time they were worked out, they would already be out of date. We have computer models, and if a factor in our business changes, for example if the average firm uses our equipment an extra ten times a day, then the computer quickly works out the implications of this for our maintenance services, for our supply of equipment parts, and so forth.

What about the chief executives who do not go in for planning and budgeting?

They are admittedly few in numbers, but they have their special reasons:

MR. AUSTIN: Our fairly heavy cash flow is invested by putting through orders for new containers and trailers. We order them when we see our customers are wanting more, and then the problem is to negotiate lease terms. I do all the calculations myself concerning rates.

MR. COCHRANE: We are not short of capital. We sell our goods very quickly, and capital expenditure control is no problem. We cannot get stores built fast enough because of the difficulty of getting planning permission (building zoning and bye-law clearance).

MR. CLIFFORD: I have never needed to go in for any formal planning. At no time did I plan to open five more shops in the next month. If six came along, I took them. It is more important to have the opportunity to do a thing than to have the reason to do it. Many an opportunity has been lost because people have planned to do a thing and then have gone ahead because they had planned, regardless of changing circumstances.

MR. BLACK: I believe in the maximum amount of flexibility. So many large companies get hide-bound with their budgeting. With an acquisition, there is a right and a wrong moment. We like to take a company when they have just had a bad year.

MR. ARGENT: We haven't yet got long-term planning. In this industry we have problems even doing one year ahead.

What about those who plan ahead but find their plans frustrated by outside restraints?

These examples, it will be noted, are all in Britain—which no doubt helps to explain the remarkable growth record of British industry. MR. COCHRANE's problem in getting planning permission has already been quoted.

MR. BRADLEY: Our capital expenditure is governed by the capacity of the architect's department and of course the taxation problem.

MR. BAXTER: I control capital expenditure by budgeting. Before the beginning of the year, I assess the amount of cash that we are likely to have and we make plans to try and spend it all. But only by forcing ourselves can we spend it, because of planning difficulties. Cash tends to pile up.

MR. BLYTH: If we saw a division doubling its capital expenditure plans for one year, we would strongly doubt their ability to spend the money. There is so much detailed procedure as regards engineering design, estimating, buildings and so forth, that if anybody does get a sudden rise in expenditure approved, we don't in fact find them spending the money.

MR. CHRISTIE: I sign all capital expenditure sanctions over £75. We budget every year for what we want to spend, but we usually spend less than the budget because suppliers let us down.

What are the basic procedures described in the survey for annual budgeting, long-term planning and control of capital expenditure?

MR. DEDERICHS: The yearly budget is done in the finance department. Each division has two staff officers, a planning co-ordinator and a cost and budget controller. There is a permanent planning committee for the whole group and the chairman of it is the planning department head. The members are the planning co-ordinators for each division plus one member of the finance department and one from personnel. This committee delegates detailed work on the annual budget to the finance department member.

The company has a plan of dates for the year which says that at a certain date every department in each division must put its draft budget figures on the table of its planning co-ordinator, and at a certain other date each division must put its combined figures on the planning committee's table. At a certain other date they must go from the committee back to the departments, and then at a certain other date they must go back through the committee finally, and then be put together in the planning department, ready to go to board members for certain meetings of the executive board. We discuss both next year's budget and the five-year plan. Then these must both be put in front of the supervisory board. It is required by law. The supervisory board does not of course refuse to pass the budgets—as a matter of trust. There are fifteen members of whom five are elected by the staff and ten elected by the shareholders.

The divisions in our group are only dealing with costs and prices, they have no accounting capability. All their figures go into the computers at head office. If a division wants to change its budgets to take on more staff, or for any other purpose, the reason must be explained to the group board. Detail below the divisional level can be changed provided the overall figures keep within the divisional budget.

Parallel to these budgets there is an annual personnel plan and also a five-year personnel plan.

MR. BEST: Our financial year ends on February 28. In the late autumn the divisional directors are asked to produce their detailed budgets for next year and these have to be in by Christmas. Then there is a digestive period of 2½ to 3 weeks, when accounting management get through the budgets. In the third week of January, I go through each set of budgets with the divisional managing director. He has a trading budget, a capital expenditure budget and a people budget. When these budgets are approved, the divisions are allowed to go ahead and implement.

Divisional directors then have to up-date their five-year forecast of capital requirements, the first two of these years being in detail. These forecast capital requirements must be with me by May, and I deal with them by mid-May, as soon as the year-end accounts go to the shareholders.

MR. ARTHUR: We don't insist that everything in our budgets is totally worked out in detail. Projects have a natural sequence of information development which causes them to come to a head at a certain time. This cannot be forced. So when the money in the budget comes up for approval in total, that is not the end. When the engineering work is ready, this is authorized, and once the engineering is done, we then have a more precise analysis of the project, of its costs and of its total economics. The responsible executives do presentations to our weekly meetings when their particular projects are ready for approval.

MR. DENYER: Our budgeting system is prepared on the computer, starting with a market report system. All our sales reports are mark sensed, so that they can be fed straight into the computer.

MR. AUBREY: Our fiscal year ends on October 31 and so we attempt to have our initial sales forecasting presented by early August. When we have seen these forecasts and the plans and sales costs of achieving them, we add them up to see if they make a reasonable corporate plan. Then the engineers have to work on the factory costs and the required facilities and supporting services. By the middle of September we have overall forecasts for the next year and for the next five years. Then we work out the inventory levels, etc., and staff groups consider any extra office requirements. In these ways we develop the capital forecast as related to the sales requirements. As there is a 1½ to three year lead time between a spending decision and coming on stream in our field, we must plan for this far ahead.

MR. BRIDGES: In planning a new model vehicle, we work backwards from the planning timetable already used to produce our present models. If, for example, we want to replace an existing model in 1975, then we work back from that date. The head time for getting out a new car is at least three years, and it really pays to work on two models ahead, that is six years ahead. Using critical path analysis, we make out a network and plan the actual programme for completing each stage—assessing the market requirements, making the first design, agreeing the basic dimensions, getting the initial style renderings, costing the project, doing final styling, releasing the model to the design engineers and to the production engineers, and so on. From this programme we know all the dates when the various items have to come up to the product committee for approval.

Every month, in order to see that the scheduling goes right, there is published a programme review which is numbered and runs for seven months either way. These reviews show the actual sales, production and stocks over the last seven months and the expected sales, production and stocks over the next seven months. They enable the programming committee to decide how many cars to make and where. These decisions are then broken down into detail of models, etc. and these decisions are then broken down into further detail of components, etc. by the purchasing and material supply departments.

This is how our type of production determines our form of budgeting. We have of course a supporting monthly financial statement in which our cash requirement is forecast and graphed.

MR. DILLMANN: We have a budgeting system but we are flexible about it. We want the financial plan to fit our project plans, not the other way round.

MR. ATWICK: Each of the 24 plants budgets for one year ahead, including the giving of forecast dates of when they expect the money for capital expenditure. If the total requirement is too great, some items are cut out or the plans are re-phased to spread them over a longer period.

MR. BENHAM: We are bound to get important items that are not in the budget, but then we kick other items out. There are always things in the budget which are not absolutely essential but we hope we will do them. They get kicked out from one year to the next.

MR. ALLEN: For capital expenditure we have three year, two year and one year budgets. I do not pay much attention to the third year in our kind of business. They usually put it in low, and I know it is going to be higher.

MR. DAMM: If we want a new factory, we of course plan in outline for two to three years ahead while the construction is proceeding, but the detailed capital expenditure budgeting is done only a year ahead.

MR. BOOTH: We have categories of advancement and priority, to indicate which new stores are most important to open because of the sites they are on, which ones are so far advanced that we cannot really stop them, and on the other hand which are in such an early stage that they could be postponed.

Our site-finding organization is charged with the specific brief to find certain types of sites. A capital approval form is filled in by the site finding organization when they want to tell us that they have got an option on a site in such a place and that the cost estimates for building a store are such and such, that the likely costs of running it and the likely level of trade are such and such. Also the profitability is projected and the rate of return on capital.

Each case comes up to the director of site operations and if his office approves, it comes up to me. I thus have an opportunity to authorize the production of detailed costings, before the proposal comes up for actual capital expenditure authorization.

There is about a three-year lead time, from when a site is found until a store comes into operation. Once the site-finding organization have had the capital approval form O.K.'d, they seek planning permission, and then the whole matter goes to the regional managing director. He works closely with the development department, which is headed by an architect. When it is ready the project comes up for board approval. Meanwhile it would have been fitted into the capital expenditure budget.

This budget is put up in such a way that there are about six alternative cash requirements, and the main board of the group can choose which one to approve. Depending upon which one is chosen, certain sites will be developed in the coming year and the others will not, according to their priority and level of advancement.

The capital expenditure review every six months shows for each project the cash spent in the year to date, the cash which remains to be spent for the rest of the year, the cash spent prior to the year and also the carry-on obligation for future years if the project is to be completed.

What are the criteria for judging and approving capital expenditure projects?

MR. DEGENHARDT: In planning capital expenditure, we estimate the possible return on our investment. We start with the market research department, estimating the possible sales. We take a minimum and a maximum. We estimate the costs of running the business and the possible profit, and look at our ratio on investment.

MR. ATKINS: Capital expenditure is based on the average annual rate of return. The company has a required minimum figure. If the average annual rate of return is less than 15 per cent there is no chance, if it is 20 per cent there is a really good chance, provided the cash is going to come fairly soon and we have got the cash available.

MR. CLEMENTS: I used to budget capital expenditure on a moving 3-year basis. This is alright so long as the growth is fairly even. But new capital may be required for either expansion or replacement. Depreciation must cover capital expenditure, not the other way round. If you let capital expenditure be limited by depreciation, you are understating the prices of your products. Depreciation that is not replacement is a subsidy in the price. We are working on a new system which will alter the levels of depreciation so that we depreciate at the levels we spend. Operating the business is one thing, calculating the tax contingencies is quite another.

MR. ARTHUR: Some of our projects do not really concern the market very closely, for example technical situation A produces products X, Y and Z, technical situation B replaces the old method of producing X, Y and Z.

Some projects involve going straight from the work of the scientists in the laboratory to a pilot plant producing say two barrels a day, and scaling up to a plant producing 16,000 barrels a day. We have to have evidence from the original scientists, from the pilot plant engineers, from the design staff of the large plant, and also evidence on safety and operability and on pollution. All the relevant people come to our weekly meeting of executive directors to make their presentations and answer questions. There's nothing like being personally involved. The economic staffs who vouch for the economic viability of the project also come. They are each asked to underwrite their proposals.

If we come unstuck, it is likely to be because our price assumptions are wrong, because someone else has been planning the same project.

To what extent is there checking on the progress and the results of a capital expenditure project?

General progress is almost universally watched, but results are sometimes difficult to interpret, and the follow-up is often neglected.

MR. CLARK: I watch capital expenditure by liaising with the finance director. If there is a sudden enormous variation, we send a team of three from the general management services department to investigate. We investigate the man in charge rather than the figures, we just use the figures to highlight the management failure. If there is an anomaly in our budget system, it becomes apparent when we make the investigation.

MR. DILLMANN: Twice a year we look to see how a new project turned out. It is very difficult to separate the project afterwards from its division. After all, we haven't got the original situation any more.

MR. BEST: Capital expenditure projects are subject to internal audit when the project is completed. This is to ensure (*a*) that they are completed to time and (*b*) that they are operated to the designed productivity. We also compare with what happened before, if for example we are replacing an old machine with a new one.

Is it reasonable to centralize all capital spending and allow units of enterprise no discretion of their own?

Small items of expenditure are often allowed up to an agreed figure. In some cases much greater freedom is allowed.

MR. DITTMER: Each section of the business is allowed to spend 80 per cent of its monthly tax allowable depreciation freely. This is at the disposal of their own board. The other 20 per cent is reserved for central planning, so that we can finance new projects or new products.

Control of capital expenditure is also sometimes tied in with operational control, so that a failure on operating results can lead to a restriction of capital availability and vice versa, just as if the subsidiary company were entirely dependent on its own resources.

MR. ATTWATER: A division is allocated capital, after their plans are approved, and if their profits drop off compared with budget, and hence their available working capital decreases, we deduct the drop from the investment capital they can spend. They are thus working truly on their own within the capital provided.

18

CONTROL OF STAFF OVERHEADS

How does a chief executive stop Parkinson's Law from operating in his business? How can he effectively control staff overheads?

Dr. C. Northcote Parkinson's famous leg-pull law states that: 'Work expands in order to fill the time available in which to do it.' Some of his most memorable examples illustrate the problem of empire building at the headquarters of an organization, with the result that the total overheads rise far above the level justifiable by the primary activity of the organization.

A question was asked in the survey on how a chief executive can fight Parkinson's Law and effectively control staff overheads. The replies are classifiable under these headings, with the percentage of replies given against each:

	per cent
It's impossible	11
Through the budgets	17
By head counts	17
By watching profitability, percentages and ratios	15
By the way we are organized	11
By special committee review	9
By staff cuts during recessions	7
By the way we grow	13

The following are selected answers under these various headings:

IT'S IMPOSSIBLE

MR. BRADLEY: Parkinson's Law at head office is a problem; 25 years ago we had six branches and no head office, now we have 15 major branches and a head office costing £150,000 a year.

MR. DAMM: There is no way to overcome Parkinson's Law, except always to think of it and make your decisions based on it. There is an old saying in Germany: 'Never to speak of it but always to think of it.'

MR. CHARLTON: There is a tendency to change a worker for a man with a pencil and think you're advancing.

MR. ALLEN: The line companies stick up their tail. Every month their bonuses are based on their figures. But you can't have the same measures on the staff. They are not a profit centre. It is pretty damned hard to nail this one.

MR. BOYD: Fighting against Parkinson's Law is very difficult. As soon as a man gets a bigger job he wants a bigger desk, an assistant, and so on. We have an expense control department, and a manager must justify anything he wants to this department.

THROUGH THE BUDGETS

MR. ACLAND: There is a personnel budget as part of the financial budget. The divisions have complete control over hourly staff, we only control the salaried staff.

MR. DODEN: Our staff recruitment is very well controlled by our budgeting. They cannot go over the top on expenses.

MR. BAXTER: I check on staff recruitment through the quarterly detailed comparisons against the budget.

BY HEAD COUNT

MR. ARMSTRONG: In addition to budgets, one must also control the number of people, because it is possible to hire more people at the end of a budget year, when there is little effect on the year's figures and yet there is a dramatic effect on next year's figures and the organization loses control of its profitability. I don't believe in having big headquarters. They take too much interest in themselves and battle amongst themselves instead of with the operating units. This last year, because we have had a slight set-back, I have said no additions to staff. None whatever. I have said that I won't listen to any arguments. You will win the arguments. Every case that you bring up will be a good one. But I am not going to let you win because I won't even discuss it.

MR. BEST: The hiring of people is more costly than capital expenditure. That is why we look at it six times a year.

MR. BENHAM: Control of staff recruitment really stems from how good the manager of the department is.

MR. BISSETT: Any appointment on a salary over £4,000 has to come up to me both for approval of the salary and as to what the person is wanted for—that is, the job itself—though I do not necessarily see the man unless he is very senior.

BY WATCHING PROFITS, PERCENTAGES AND RATIOS

MR. BLUNDELL: The real measure is the profitability of the division or company. If it is not making satisfactory profits, overheads are very much in question.

MR. BEATTY: I established ratios between the direct and indirect labour costs, and have given people targets. They are obliged to keep their staff costs to these.

MR. ANTHONY: All our staff figures are on a percentage basis, relating to revenue, and we see immediately if there is any rise. If income dips off, expenses as a percentage rise immediately, and we have to get them down.

MR. DACKWEILER: We have monthly statistics covering the movement and status of employees in each department. The technical staff tend to control the commercial staff and vice versa. We are very open with our information system, and each can see what the other is doing, from the figures that are circulated.

MR. AUBREY: In our system of accounting, most of the charges get back to people who are responsible for products or groups of products and hence have a profit responsibility. Also over the years we have developed a knowledge of the relationship of overhead to turnover. For example, here our general administration costs 3 per cent of turnover. If it went up to 3·6 there would be a lot of questions asked. In the operating departments they have to absorb these costs, and they too would be asking questions. The system is self policing in this respect.

Also we have our targets for sales costs and we compare the figures for Britain, France and Germany, monthly and quarterly. These are similar-sized countries and we ought to be able to see whether we are doing as well or better or worse. The quarterly comparison is sent to all our managers.

BY THE WAY WE ARE ORGANIZED

MR. DILLMANN: We can still control staff costs because we are not too big.

MR. BERESFORD: Each chief executive has an appointed head office director. He must discuss all important matters with him including all key staff employments and salary levels.

MR. AUSTIN: We know from all the paperwork concerning salesmen's calls and ramp inspectors' visits that they are doing their work, and also from our regular visits to depots.

BY SPECIAL COMMITTEE

MR. DAUTZENBERG: We have an O & M team permanently reorganizing the company, sector by sector. They are more likely to cut staff than to increase it.

MR. BOOTH: For staffing above store level we have a manpower audit. This looks at the overall manpower situation, identifies line managers, their responsibilities, functions and salaries, to make sure that the firm is getting good value for money. There are review meetings which go on at each level right to the top.

BY STAFF CUTS DURING AN INDUSTRY RECESSION

MR. ATKINS: In normal times we operate independently, but when the group is tightening up on staff, as at present, they take back control to headquarters in the States.

MR. DITTMER: We have a programme for the whole firm of targets of achievement. One of these concerns reducing staff by 5 per cent at a time. This is our answer to Parkinson's Law.

MR. ARCHER: Until two years ago we had successively better years, but then the machine tool industry began to fold up. A year later our other markets also dropped off, so we have had to trim some fat. I had to issue edicts on both inventory and staffing levels, after I had first asked for cuts and these had not been made. But it must be remembered that my younger staff hadn't been through a recession. Now any addition to staff has to be approved by me, and equally any increase in salary.

MR. ALEXANDER: We cannot do much about Parkinson's Law until we start getting into trouble. If there are good profits, then it is almost impossible to control the build-up of staff, but when the profits turn down, we have to get tough. The industry keeps going through cycles like this.

BY THE WAY WE GROW

MR. DECKER: Output has been doubled in the last five years with almost the same number of people. So far my departments have never been able to get all the people they were allowed to get, because enough people with the right qualifications haven't been available. We have had no problem over Parkinson's Law.

MR. CHRISTIE: Any request for more labour, whether replacement or not, has to come to me personally on a special form. This is how I keep costs falling all the time.

MR. ATTWOOD: Parkinson's Law for us is negative, because we had 16 per cent less people when we were billing 20 per cent more revenue. We continually strive to have fewer, better people, better paid.

19

CONTROL OF PURCHASING

In what circumstances should control of purchasing be highly centralized, and when should it be decentralized?

A question on how purchasing was organized, was included in the survey. Both the question and the answers concentrated heavily on the problem of central buying versus decentralized buying.

Analysis of the replies shows that in 56 per cent of cases, buying was centralized. Within this total, 18 per cent of chief executives handled the buying themselves; in 30 per cent of cases there was a central buying department; in 4 per cent of cases there was a team of buyers specialized on different types of goods; and in another 4 per cent of cases, though some buying was centralized, there were regional buyers for commodities such as steel and cement where distance made the pricing system favourable to local purchases.

Of the remaining 44 per cent of cases, 16 per cent involved decentralized buying but coordination for common purchases, with the nomination of one major buyer to act for all. Another 6 per cent of cases involved branch buying direct from suppliers but on the basis of a bulk discount negotiated by head office. The remaining 22 per cent involved strictly decentralized buying.

Undoubtedly the economies of large-scale buying are a major factor in bringing about the merger of business firms. In the words of MR. BRADLEY: 'As bulk-buyers we can improve profits by 10 per cent in any case when we take over a business, but we don't want to give that away in the price we pay.'

As the cases quoted show, there are three major types of situation for which bulk buying brings economies:

(*a*) Large-scale manufacturers where, even if the plants are dispersed, they use common materials.
(*b*) Large-scale distributors where there are numerous branch outlets selling the same products.
(*c*) Groups of companies which may require different raw materials but which have a common need for transport vehicles, typewriters, etc.

Cases where the chief executive himself becomes involved in the buying usually arise from the fact that skill in buying is crucial to the nature of the market he is in, and indeed it may be fundamental to his product philosophy. This is something he has not yet been able to delegate because it involves the very essence of why his products are different, why they are able to sell better than those of his competitors.

Cases of decentralized buying usually involve companies producing different products in the same group but brought together in a merger, and largely autonomous except for control of overall financial policy. To take away the buying power of these companies would mean to strike at their autonomy and to make them less accountable for their profitability. It is in these cases, however, that there is a tendency for the companies to be brought together in conference, and for the largest buyer of a particular commodity to be nominated as buyer for them all. Achieving this half-way house to centralization may involve an internal political struggle, or shall we say an exercise in firm tact, supported by the logic of economies yet to be realized.

To what extent are the economies of bulk buying due to the guarantee of long production runs for the seller, and to what extent are they due to economies in delivery costs?

This is an endlessly debatable point, and one which needs to be continuously probed by every chief executive, according to the circumstances of the case.

As the evidence presented here shows, in near monopoly cases such as buying from the British Steel Corporation, there is no economy of bulk purchase to be gained from guaranteeing the supplier a large order and hence a long run. But there are discounts for bulk delivery, because of the economies involved. There are some similarities to this situation in the United States where the pricing systems for steel and cement arise from the semi-monopoly of local supply available to each producer who is geographically isolated from other suppliers and who therefore has an advantage in transport costs.

By contrast, wherever goods are truly competitive in one market, bulk purchase results in a true economy of long-run production for the supplier. In many cases the economies of long-run production can best be obtained by vertical integration. To quote again MR. AYLWARD: 'When you have got several dozen stores selling many millions of quarts of milk a week, it is pretty obvious that you ought to buy a dairy.'

What about the case of the overall discount adjusted after the end of the year, according to the value of goods actually bought?

This is a kind of half-way house. It applies where a supplier has a wide range of goods and the customer is uncertain how many of each he will want. It allows freedom to his branches or subsidiaries to do the ordering of exactly what they want, when they want it, but it puts pressure on them wherever possible to order from particular suppliers who give the discount.

These and other cases are quoted in the classified evidence which follows:

THE CHIEF EXECUTIVE HIMSELF DOES THE BUYING—18 PER CENT

MR. DOBLER: I had always thought that the most important parts of the business were sales and production, but others say you make the money in buying. Half my costs are raw materials. So now I look at the big contracts before they are signed, and I use particularly the knowledge I gain from talking to competitors at association meetings—a type of knowledge which my buying staff cannot have. What turned my attention to buying was when Turkish agents came to Germany and negotiated with my suppliers. I watched closely and found that they got up to 27 per cent discount, whereas in the past I had thought my buyers were good to get 5 per cent.

MR. AUSTIN: I do all the purchasing of equipment myself, but not of small supplies.

MR. BLYTH: I keep a close watch on steel purchases myself due to my background. We buy more high carbon steel than any other company and we have to be sure that the price list is carefully worked out, so that we get the right quantity discount, reflecting our big buying. This is a matter of face to face negotiation when they prepare the price list.

MR. CHISHOLM: Major purchasing is done by myself. I choose the items with the help of one woman buyer. Once they have been agreed, and I have done a simple calculation in my head to decide on an initial order, the computer takes over and does all the follow up orders, that is, it uses a system of exponential smoothing to calculate from actual sales and stocks, what the new orders should be.

CENTRAL PURCHASING OF MAJOR ITEMS THROUGH A DEPARTMENT—30 PER CENT

MR. BURKE: We have central purchasing of all supplies except very small items, and we also have central engineering for ordering the equipment for a new works.

MR. ASKEW: We do central purchasing except for certain supplies which are bought locally, for example, pallets and fruit and vegetables.

MR. DAUTZENBERG: We do our purchasing through a department which works on an eighteen months budget because of the need to keep an average eighteen months stocks in order to have the blends of all the crops of tobacco around the world.

MR. DEMMLER: Eighty per cent of supplies are bought through a centralized buying office, including malt and hops and machinery, cars and lorries. But other things like paper and pencils are bought locally.

MR. ALLEN: We have central procurement for most of our supplies. The biggest items are fibre and yarn from the chemical companies, and of course we buy machine parts, dye stuffs, chemicals, etc.

Though the divisions order their supplies through central purchasing, they are in fact controlled by their own level of inventory, which we watch closely. The central procurement is able to bargain big, but it follows each division's schedule for actual deliveries.

MR. DAHLMANN: Our central purchasing department buys for the whole group major common items. Different companies have their own purchasing departments that buy only the things that only they buy, and that only they know how to buy. We keep the purchasing activity as close as possible to the real business.

DECENTRALIZED BUYING BUT CO-ORDINATION FOR COMMON PURCHASES—16 PER CENT

MR. ARMSTRONG: Control of supplies is the responsibility of the divisions, but we have a central procurement staff who set the policy and try to co-ordinate purchases, get better delivery and prices. They may designate one particular division to do the negotiating over a particular product.

MR. CLEMENTS: Our major purchases of supplies are left to the different companies using them. Where one thing is used in common, there is a central control which nominates one buyer for the whole group, but this is the exception. The trouble with centralized buying is that you never know what the actual buying costs, as regards overheads, etc. You cannot allocate your buying costs, either the overheads or the discounts, properly. It is important not to tie up the local man so that he cannot buy and you make him unaccountable. It is safer not to try and save that little bit of money through central buying.

CENTRAL BUYING WITH REGIONAL EXCEPTIONS—4 PER CENT

MR. CONSTABLE: We do central buying except for products which have a regional price variance, usually due to their weight in transport, such as cement or steel. The regional office buys when there is an advantage on price.

USE OF SPECIALIZED CENTRAL BUYERS—4 PER CENT

MR. AYLWARD: We have central buying for the supermarkets and the discount stores. We have five grocery, two drug, four hardware, 16 discount, nine clothing and soft goods buyers at head office.

MR. BOYD: We have 15 buying departments, buying different types of drugs, bottles, photographic equipment, etc. The buyers must justify their buying by the sales.

DECENTRALIZED BUYING WITH CENTRALLY NEGOTIATED DISCOUNTS—6 PER CENT

MR. BRADLEY: 'Each branch has a buyer who buys what the branch can sell, but all the bought accounts are boxed together, and it is on this that the group negotiates its discount. We check on the rate of sale for every unit of stock. Bad stock is the responsibility of the branch manager and the buyer. The trouble is, if they are asked to reduce stocks, they are inclined to reduce stocks of things that sell well rather than reveal and get rid of their dead stock. The commercial management department has to watch the records and chase up dead stock.

MR. BENHAM: Every month a list of suppliers and the value of business done with them is presented to me, showing the actual figures for the month and cumulative for the year. This is done partly to help get the cash flow right, and it is also so that I can ask why so much has been spent with Mr. X or Mr. Y. If anybody is getting a lot of business from us, then we either want a good discount on volume or we want longer credit. We normally get discounts on the volume of business and we get a bill for payment of the discount that has already been deducted if the volume does not reach the stipulated level.

FULLY DECENTRALIZED BUYING, OR ALMOST SO—22 PER CENT

MR. ANTHONY: We have no central purchasing. We don't even have a purchasing man in head office.

MR. BLUNDELL: We do not and cannot have group control of the major purchases of supplies while the subsidiaries work behind different tariff barriers. But we do exchange quite a lot of information. When engineering staff are making estimates they put enquiries through to check on prices of materials and components used.

MR. ARGENT: Our two main companies do their purchasing separately. There are industry controlled prices in the steel industry.

MR. BISSETT: We have a 50 per cent interest with the British Steel Corporation in a special steel company and we get some of our supplies there. But we only aggregate purchases when this makes economic sense. Steel prices are based on quantities and delivery points. So if we put in a bulk order and then wanted our supplies delivered to 50 different companies in various places and at various times, we would not in fact make any savings. The prices charged would have to depend on the deliveries, not on our bulk order.

THE ADMINISTRATION OF BUYING

MR. DEGENHARDT: The stores are never forced to sell any particular merchandise bought by central buyers. The assortment list is given to the department heads in each store and they make their own choice. If anything is left which has been bought and they have not been able to sell, one or two big stores may be asked to take it and mark it down.

We have monthly reports on the left-overs, which are sent to the departmental heads in the stores, who are known as assistant buyers. Twice a year we do a summary list of what is older than X months, X being varied according to the nature of the goods. This list is broken down into buying departments and into stores, so that we can distinguish between genuine buying mistakes and inadequate selling effort.

MR. ASCOT: We do a weekly inventory and we have a season ticket on all merchandise for ageing, so that for example 1.S. means Spring 1971, and when we take our inventory we can see what is old stock. We have a surplus stores system.

MR. ADAMS: Our buyers have budget goals, but we make them as autonomous as can be. The chief control over them is comparison across the group. We have a detailed purchase mark on, or mark up analysis, and a detailed age of inventory analysis. We work on a question basis. Why is somebody else able to do so much better than you?

MR. BEATTY: We watch the percentages of materials to sales and the level of stocks relative to sales, and we chart these.

MR. ATWICK: The budget for purchases for a year ahead is shown in dollars, and the next three months ahead is shown in detail of quantities and types. The controller's office watches actual progress against forecast. Detailed unit figures are compared quarterly, the overall value figures monthly.

MR. COLE: For major purchases of supplies, we keep very close to our suppliers and have every three months a meeting in which we let them know our plans for two years ahead. We might, for example, want to place a large order for diesel engines with one supplier.

MR. DODEN: We obtain very competitive quotations for all our major purchases.

MR. DAMM: We are developing a new planning and control system for the buying department, with automatic buying based on sales forecasts, the production plan, price and discount quotations. It is a mathematical system for optimizing the benefits, to obtain maximum discount for quantity but have the delivery done in stages to prevent over-stocking and yet have adequate stocks. Most of our purchases, such as bottles, are fairly routine. We want them by the hundred thousand or even million. For a small percent of our purchases, day-to-day flexibility will still be needed.

MR. CHRISTIE: The problem of controlling major purchases of supplies is a real pain in the back-side. One thing that helps us is that we pay our bills more promptly than most, so we can beat our suppliers over the head. Also we deal mainly with people who are no more than 50 miles from this works. We are in the heart of England and there are suppliers in all directions. But the biggest problem is to get top buyers who have integrity but are not in an ivory tower. Also they must be versatile, not specialize on one product.

MR. BAYLISS: There is a lot of market research ability about, concerning selling, but there is no equivalent body of buying ability so well developed.

20

USE OF CASH AND SHARE INCENTIVE SCHEMES

How widespread is the use of cash bonus systems for rewarding, in part, the top managements of business firms?

The brief answer is almost universal in Germany, very widespread in the United States, and in a minority of companies in Britain.

In the survey, 45 per cent of the British chief executives asked, said that their companies had cash bonuses, 82 per cent of the Americans said Yes (but 92 per cent of those actually running a company in the United States). All of the Germans said Yes.

How effectively are cash bonuses used?

If effectiveness could be broadly measured by the size of the bonus in relation to basic salary, then the difference would be even more startling. In Germany, bonuses are rarely less than 25 per cent to 50 per cent on top of basic salary, and they ranged in this survey up to five times basic salary. In America bonuses of 20 per cent to 30 per cent of salary are fairly common. Some firms have a ceiling of 50 per cent bonus on top of salary, but a minority have no limit and bonuses can exceed salary, though they are very rarely as high as in Germany. In Britain the majority of companies with cash bonuses for executives in fact hand out 3 per cent to 5 per cent of pay as a Christmas gift, not effectively related to effort or results. Even when a scheme is geared to results, the level of bonus is likely to be in the 12½ per cent to 25 per cent region, rarely higher.

It could, of course, be mere coincidence that, among these three countries, the one which pays the highest bonuses in relation to salary has the best recent history of economic growth, and the one which pays the lowest bonuses has the worst recent history of economic growth.

How widespread is the use of share incentive schemes, including stock options and restricted stock?

Here the differences are again remarkable. Every American chief executive in the survey who was in charge of a company in the United States had a stock option or other share incentive scheme. By contrast only one of the 16 German chief executives had such a scheme, and his company has American affiliations. In Britain 35 per cent of the chief executives asked had recently installed incentive share schemes in their companies, and from the author's personal knowledge of the rate at which these schemes have been increasing, by the time these words are published the percentage may well be nearing the half-way mark. These schemes have not yet, however, been installed long enough to have any measurable effect on British economic growth.

Why should there be such differences in systems of top executive reward in the three countries?

It seems to be partly a matter of the tax system, partly a matter of general political climate.

In the United States, with its long tradition of capital gains taxation, the stock option rose to be an almost universal method of adding to the rewards of senior business executives. But the current less favourable tax treatment of options, their limitation to five years, and parallel with this the steady reduction of the maximum earned income tax rate to 50 per cent may well alter this position. There is an increasing interest in Phantom Stock schemes by which executives receive dividends on a notional amount of stock accredited to them, which does not actually exist. They do not own it, they just receive the dividends on it, as if it did exist.

By contrast in Germany, where there is no capital gains tax on the small shareholder, but there has been a major rebuilding of the national economy, attention has been concentrated on paying immediate bonuses for immediate efforts and results. The bonuses have climbed very high, but rising tax rates have begun to make them less attractive.

One type of bonus system for quoted or listed companies which is fairly widespread and seems effective in Germany, provides a cash payment which is related to the individual's salary and to the dividend paid to shareholders. This scheme comes very close to being an American-type Phantom Stock scheme. However, Share Incentive Schemes may well grow in importance in Germany as the next generation of senior executives becomes disenchanted with their net take-home pay after tax, and look round for some other reward.

One of the most interesting paradoxes between Germany and Britain is the difference in effect of pension schemes on bonus and salary levels. The German position is put well by MR. DANNEWALD: 'The supervisory boards of companies in Germany are always wanting fixed salaries to be lower than the bonuses because the fixed salaries are the basis for pensions. By paying more in bonus and less in salary, they keep down the pension bill.'

In Britain, fixed salaries are also generally the basis for calculating pensions, but due partly to the high rates of income tax and surtax which existed for so long, there had grown up a lack of interest in bonuses. Fixed salaries suffered equally from high tax rates, but at least they were eligible for pension, part of which could be taken in a tax-free lump sum. The fixed salaries paid to the heads of large companies in Britain, though not high in relation to the total earnings of equivalent German executives, were nevertheless high in relation to the amount of net income left after paying income tax and surtax. But all of this salary qualified for pension and brought the prospect of retirement with both a pension and a considerable tax-free lump sum.

The tax system before the 1971 Budget in effect turned British senior executives into bureaucrats who could not expect to have wealth during their working lives however hard or effectively they worked, but who could expect to retire on a moderate amount of wealth that was largely unrelated to the prosperity of the companies they controlled. It would have been difficult to devise a more cunning method of ensuring that British economic performance was inferior to that of other, comparable nations. But all this has been changed.

What are the sorts of rationalizations offered by British chief executives to explain the poor bonus situation in their companies?

Here are some comments:

MR. BAYLISS: It is difficult to compare one executive with another because of their entirely different functions.

MR. BEATTY: We have no cash bonuses for management level. I attach more importance to getting the right people and stimulating them into becoming dedicated to the business rather than to the money they receive from it. Unless a scheme is well-designed, it can become more of a disincentive. For example, a scheme based on return on capital employed can encourage a manager to restrict growth in order not to risk achieving a high return on capital.

MR. BERESFORD: The different divisions have different levels of profitability and if you ask a man to go to a job where the task is harder and progress is likely to be slower, you have a real problem if there is a bonus. We used to have a bonus but it degenerated into being automatic. In any case there is not much hope for a good system while taxation is so high. Also 60 per cent of our business is U.K. and 40 per cent is overseas, and this makes the problem very difficult. And where do you draw the line, what about the other people not in the scheme who are equally good?

MR. BLACK: We used to have a proper system of bonuses. But when you are mainly engaged in an industry where the results are so appalling, and the worse the results, the harder everybody has to work, the only thing really is to have personally-assessed bonuses. I do the assessment.

MR. BLOOMFIELD: I abandoned my bonus scheme. It came to be regarded as a right. It wasn't geared directly to results.

MR. BLUNDELL: We used to have a bonus system but it was amalgamated with salary. It was extremely hard to determine a bonus that had any relation to the true part people played in achieving the profits. We find it more important to provide for pensions adequately rather than bonus income. Our industry is rather complicated. By contrast, on the Continent the salaries are substantially augmented by bonuses related to profitability. Perhaps after all it is the high tax rates which have kept us off bonuses here.

MR. BISSETT: It is difficult to have cash bonus systems in an integrated company serving an integrated market. You could share out part of the profits, but you are not really motivating the man. You get better motivation by dealing with his salary.

One division, the engineering division, does have a system of cash bonus payments. But this division consists of a lot of small companies, each with its own market. The head of this division sets profit figures arbitrarily as targets for the heads of these small companies. If a man exceeds his budgeted target by x per cent he receives a bonus of y per cent on his salary. It is a simple system and effective for this type of division.

Recently we have introduced a share incentive scheme for 45 senior executives. The company lends money to them to buy shares and they have to keep them for ten years or up till when they leave. The money is lent interest free. I insisted on a 1 per cent payment as a stop loss provision. When an offer is made, it is only open for 48 hours, and becomes invalid if the market moves 10 per cent either way from the price of the offer.

Why should MR. BISSETT break off his discussion of cash bonuses and their inadequacy for motivation in major sections of his group, in order to talk of a share incentive scheme for which the same arguments about an integrated company would appear to apply?

The answer would appear to lie in the period of high personal taxation through which Britain has passed, and the history of the Inland Revenue's fight against stock options—firstly in the Courts, and having lost there, through Section 25 of the Finance Act 1966 which made stock option gains chargeable to income tax and surtax.

The subsequent winning over of the Treasury and the Inland Revenue to acceptance of new types of share incentive schemes, has opened up new prospects for rewarding senior executives in step with rising prosperity of the company they control—and subject only to a maximum capital gains tax rate of 30 per cent.

But we need to cross to America to hear MR. ARTHUR state the true justification for stock options and share incentive schemes:

> The purpose of stock options in large corporations is to balance the options that a man gives himself—up to 100 per cent options—when he goes into business on his own. Options provide a quid pro quo for the executives of large public corporations. They put them in a better position later in life. The corporation needs good men, as much as the small business. Options put the entrepreneurial spirit into a large corporation. They are also an indication of a successful job done, and they provide a success feeling parallel to that of the entrepreneur who went his own way and was successful.

What MR. ARTHUR says about large public corporations, one of which he controls, is equally applicable to non-owning executives in small corporations. Their needs too can be met now that there are schemes available which either avoid or overcome, as appropriate, the problem of valuing shares that have no public market.

The speed with which, in both Britain and America, new types of Share Incentive Scheme have developed in recent years to meet new situations, so that there are now no less than five types* available to meet specific company needs, is a tribute to the determination of chief executives to provide their key staff with 'the owner's eye'.

It was a former president of Du Pont, Mr. Crawford E. Greenewalt, who first developed a corporate understanding of 'the owner's eye.' His observations had led him to conclude that what made an executive look upon the company with the same care as an owner, was not whether he owned a large percentage of the stock, but whether the shareholding he was building up was likely to be significant in relation to his retirement income.

Looking ahead, if the company was successful, would he be

* A follow-up and related book on 'Share Incentive Schemes' by the same author classifies and analyses the main types of American and British schemes, with examples.

rather well-off in relation to what he would have been if he had had only a pension? This is the crucial question. There is a world of difference in outlook between the person who understands how wealth is created by winning more customers at satisfactory margins and who plays a positive role in achieving this, and on the other hand the person who feels that so long as he jogs along for the rest of his time and does a satisfactory job, he will retire on a pension.

The Greenewalt concept is best illustrated with figures. Supposing a scheme aims to provide a key business executive, by the time he retires, with a portfolio of company stock built up progressively over the years and worth say five times final salary, which we will call X,000 in any currency the reader cares to imagine. The aim of the scheme, then, is to provide a capital sum before retirement of 5X,000. But we know that, due to the risks of business, an executive is most unlikely ever to achieve the figure of 5X,000. If the company does well, his stock is likely to be worth at least 10X,000, and if it does badly, his stock is likely to be worth only 2X,000 or even less.

Anyone projecting forward to his expectations of final salary and multiplying this figure by 10, has a vision of a capital sum which is likely to be very substantial in relation to his other assets. This is something well worth striving for, well worth devoting that extra attention to the job, master-minding every aspect of it and developing and maintaining close rapport with colleagues. It is this prospect of comparative wealth, if the firm succeeds, or on the other hand relatively little if it does not, which makes an executive see the business with the owner's eye.

From the Greenewalt concept came two important further developments. Firstly, the understanding that to the executive above a certain level of responsibility and income, a stock investment plan of some sort and the prospect of capital gains are essential parts of his total remuneration package. Whilst take-home pay will be of primary interest to meet his personal and family needs, it is capital gains prospects which align his interests with the prosperity of the company.

The wheel has turned full circle. When company law first

developed, it was usual to require directors to be shareholders. Today so many of the key men are not directors, and moreover, a minimum stock requirement would appear to debar the impecunious man of talents. But the ingenious devising of so many types of share incentive scheme has made it possible to bring the key man of talents into stock ownership regardless of his personal asset situation and regardless of the type of company he works for.

The second development from Greenewalt was a realization of the importance of gradualism in a share incentive scheme. A company could quickly denude itself of its best executives if they could make sudden major capital gains and then retire early. Methods have therefore been developed for the successive allocation or issue of shares, or the successive vesting of rights in shares, so that from the participating executive's point of view, there is always something in the pipeline. There is always something worth waiting and working for, even whilst he is receiving benefits along the way.

Such, then, briefly is the recent history of the developing philosophy of share incentive schemes, and of the efforts on both sides of the Atlantic to harness executive talent towards the optimum promotion of corporate growth.

At this point, however, we may well repeat MR. BERESFORD's question, quoted earlier: 'Where do you draw the line?' What about the others employed by the company who are not in the scheme? Mr. Louis Kelso, a San Francisco attorney, has developed a comprehensive theory of universal capitalism. He points out that if capitalism provides a good economic system, of almost universal application to the problems of supplying and distributing goods and services, then clearly the system should be applied almost universally. That is, as many people as possible should contribute both labour and capital, and positive steps should be taken to see that as many people as possible own shares. He further points out that the modern corporation is the ideal vehicle for promoting universal capitalism. Its ownership is almost infinitely divisible into shares which are easily transferable. It is the ideal vehicle for moving towards a two-income society in which capital and labour work truly in harmony because as many people as possible have two incomes, one from work and one from ownership.

But how, it may be asked, can a share scheme for senior executives be extended downwards to people whose incomes are lower and therefore whose greatest need is for immediate cash salary or wage—who cannot afford to have any significant proportion of their income or their savings at risk of fluctuation in value, and who should not carry major risks for the additional reason that they do not carry the major responsibilities for the success of the enterprise?

A notable German contribution towards answering this question may be seen in the ratio system used by MR. DAHLMANN's corporation and others in the survey, for distributing bonuses that are related to the dividend level. The ratio system moves from 5:1 at the top levels to 1:10 at the bottom levels, that is at the top the bonus income can be as much as five times fixed salary level, so that five sixths of the top man's income is at risk. By contrast, at the bottom pay level in the firm, bonus income is no more than 10 per cent of salary, so that only one part in 11 of an income at this level is at risk. Nevertheless all are in the scheme: 'The higher the responsibility, the more your income should depend on bonus', says MR. DAHLMANN, 'but people are basically the same at all levels, so they should all participate.'

The principles of this ratio system can be used for progressively extending share schemes downwards so that all can participate, all can feel a collective attitude of identification with the corporation, but at the higher levels where decisions are made and results are more directly influenced, there is the greater incentive effect, the greater commitment and risk.

Though MR. DAHLMANN lives on one side of the North Sea and MR. COOPER on the other, and being in different industries they have possibly never met, yet it is interesting to note that MR. COOPER runs a share incentive scheme which employs a similar scale of risk/responsibility to that which MR. DAHLMANN uses for cash bonuses,

MR. COOPER's industry is capital intense, and he encourages

all employees with a certain minimum period of service to buy shares. But these are highly geared shares so that what a participant pays is small in relation to what he expects to gain if the company is successful. At the bottom level of employment the total permitted purchase of shares is worth £10, at the top it is £500. Between these figures is a ratio of 1:50, which is the same as between MR. DAHLMANN's 1:10 at the bottom and 5:1 at the top. Any such scales of risk/responsibility must be arbitrary. It is, however, significant that they are in use for both cash bonus and share incentive schemes. Broadly, cash bonus schemes seem suitable for extension right down a company which is skilled labour intense, like MR. DAHLMANN's, and share incentive schemes seem suitable for extension right down a company which is capital intense, like MR. COOPER's. Both are in my experience appropriate at the top level of all firms. How far down they should go and what scales should be used, will vary greatly with the nature of the business.

PART III

PERSONAL WORK METHODS

21

EFFECTIVE USE OF TIME

How does a chief executive keep himself free enough from meetings in order to be able to get on with his own work?

He usually doesn't, during office hours. According to the survey, the average proportion of his office hours spent meeting with and directly contacting others is 74 per cent. This proportion varies, however, enormously from man to man. Table 25.1 gives the distribution of percentage of time spent in contact with others, in contrast to working alone (or with secretary).

Table 25.1

DISTRIBUTION OF PERCENTAGE OF TIME SPENT AT WORK IN CONTACT WITH OTHERS

	Under 50% of time	50–59% of time	60–69% of time	70–79% of time	80–89% of time	90–99% of time
% of sample	5	18	22	22	24	9

Surprisingly, this percentage does not appear to vary in direct relationship to the outwardness of personality claimed by the chief executive. On the contrary, the claimed extroverts have a 71 per cent average time spent in contacts and the introverts have a 76 per cent average. Whether this means that self-styled introverts think they spend more time with others, or try harder to do so, it is impossible to say. The only thing that seems clear is that the bulk of a chief executive's work during office hours has to be done in contact with other people, listening to them, persuading them, reconciling them, making decisions with them.

How, then, does the paper work get done?

By regular overtime of a few hours a day. The effect is to alter the balance between contact work and quiet paper work. MR. BARRATT claims that he spends only 30 per cent normal office hours doing paperwork, but when the overtime is added in, the proportion is around 50 per cent.

Some people arrive early, some work late, while some do both. MR. BELLAMY does both. This enables him to spend virtually the whole of normal office hours talking to people.

MR. BEST arrives early and does the mail first, because he likes personally to see any complaints from customers and shareholders. He does not start seeing people until 10.30 a.m.

By contrast, MR. CHRISTIE spends the whole day motivating customers or staff, so that he starts his paperwork about 5 or 6 p.m. and goes on to 9 p.m.

If you write to a chief executive and do not receive a reply for a couple of weeks, it may be that he is the type who lets his correspondence mature. MR. BAKER does this, but once a fortnight he has a blitz on paperwork, stays very late and clears it all up.

MR. ANSELL has a weekly blitz: 'I like to work on Saturday and I try to encourage people not to come and see me on Saturday so that I can clear up my desk ready for next week. But I don't read operations reports during the week-end. I try to keep a free week-day in my diary occasionally to catch up on my report reading. When I am going through the figures if there is something I don't understand I phone through straight away. Mostly they can answer it immediately. There may be a rise in costs or a fall in revenue or profit and I want to know why. All the people who report to me are on this inter-office phone, and I just press the button. I am not likely to phone anyone else in the firm, unless it is to commend them on something I have heard they have done rather well, just as a morale booster.'

How far can paperwork be avoided?

One task in particular, the analysis of operating performance reports, is impossible to delegate.

MR. CAIRNS does this mainly in the car while being driven by his chauffeur. On the other hand some figure-men do not need quite so much time for this task. They do it during meetings. MR. BAXTER says: 'I don't spend a lot of time absorbing the figures quietly, I absorb them by talking to people about them.'

Aeroplane journeys can be good for getting the reading done. American chief executives have the most experience of this. MR. ARMSTRONG's case is typical: 'I read a lot on planes, I have to travel so much. I spend 95 per cent of my office time talking and listening. Listening is far more important. I remember a famous industrialist saying once that he never learned a darn thing when he was talking.'

Another case is MR. ATWICK who lives in the south-west of the United States because he likes the desert climate. He has offices in New York and San Francisco, with two dozen manufacturing plants scattered about the North American Continent and overseas. He flies into New York on a Monday, then on Tuesday he goes out to the West Coast, or to visit plants, then at the end of the week he usually flies back home. He carries two large brief cases with him on all flights, and gets through a lot of reading, including the journals important to his science-based industry.

MR. ATWICK does about 30 telephone calls a day to various plants and offices. He has a time-zone chart which enables him to tell at any moment which places are in working hours. He does not write letters, for he says that 'if you take up your time dictating letters you don't have time to collect information'. His secretary is very good at doling out letters that come into his office, but she keeps a photocopy with on it an indication of whom it has gone to. MR. ATWICK can glance through these photocopies and if he wants to add a comment, he does. Then the photocopy goes on to the relevant executive.

Apart from wasting time, writing letters and memos has

another disadvantage. As MR. BANFIELD explains, 'Most subjects I deal with require a dialogue, not a monologue.'

In some types of business, however, a lot of paperwork is essential, confirming arrangements with important customers, with branch offices or with licencees. MR. DERKUM has a discipline for ensuring that it gets done: 'I have forbidden the staff to have any meeting before 10 o'clock. They start work at 8. Hence everybody gets two hours to do their correspondence and to keep their secretaries busy for the day.'

Also there are some businesses where a lot of background reading is essential, and it is not necessarily science-based, as in the case of MR. ATWICK. By contrast, MR. DAMM produces consumer goods and he says: 'There is a lot of reading to be done of consumer women's magazines and daily and trade press and also new books on business management and the state of the economy and law, bearing in mind that business must defend itself against hostile political influences.'

Is it really necessary for chief executives to spend very long hours day after day on the job?

For most of them, yes. And on top of the business hours may be outside activities connected with trade or professional associations or charitable causes.

MR. ANTHONY's case is typical: 'I work here from 8 a.m. to 6.40 p.m. About 80 per cent of my time is spent talking to people and 20 per cent working quietly. I am a trustee of a Musical Arts Society and I have a 7.30 in the morning meeting tomorrow. I also have a meeting this evening of a Housing Community Association. It is a three-man committee of myself and two coloured people.'

Long hours are particularly important when a business is newly established. As already reported, MR. CAIRNS admits to doing 16 to 18 hours a day during the first year of his business. But significantly, at least eight of these, for four crucial months, were spent doing his own systems analysis, so that he had well-designed order forms and other documentation, catering specifically for the needs of his business. This painstaking work at the beginning meant that he could relax more when the business began to grow and his systems moved smoothly into top gear.

For the really organized person who can design the flow of information towards him so that the key facts for his type of business are carefully summarized and highlighted, vast periods of overtime do not seem to be essential. MR. CALDER is in this category. He arrives at his office at 10 a.m. and leaves at 6.15 p.m. He comes to town four days a week, spends Friday at home. He does not work in the evenings, he takes eight weeks holiday a year. His financial empire has grown 88-fold in profitability in five years. He can perhaps be excused a touch of frank immodesty when he says: 'It is quality, not quantity, which counts.'

How do you go about improving the quality?

The secret lies largely in improving the flow of information towards you, using of course some of the methods described in earlier chapters. A first step, however, may be to analyse how you spend your time now.

MR. CLARK employs a consultant to do a periodic assessment of the way he spends his working day, and reckons to have saved a day a week by this method.

What you do after the analysis has been made, will depend partly on where your main skills lie, where you can make the greatest contribution. For example, MR. BAINBRIDGE spends about a day a week 'collecting information without meetings—working on figures, reading papers, looking at what is on the market, talking to other operators (in his line of business)'. By contrast, MR. CHILDS spends such time as he has on his own working on his product range, where his real creativity lies.

But surely the nature of some business makes it difficult for the chief executive to control his own expenditure of time?

To some extent this is true. MR. BEST tries to visit all his factories throughout the world, and his major sales offices, at least once every two years. As he says, 'One of the prime functions of a chief executive is to be seen, to talk with the charge hands, the foremen and junior, middle and senior management. Also you must know what you are talking about so you have got to be briefed. Most employees are proud of being able to say that the chairman stopped and talked to me for ten minutes. He was interested in how we were doing such and such and he knew all the facts, by God!'

This sort of 'essential' programme would seem to be enough to try the strongest hearts. It appears essential because, in the words of MR. CHAPMAN, 'the branches tend to feel very isolated, but they feel better if the chief executive comes and listens.'

However, a big group must be divided up in such a way that there are local chief executives who are important in the eyes of their own staff. The need for this is put forcibly by MR. BAYLISS: 'It is not right in a complex multiple business for the chap at the top to try to be *the* personality all over the place. This only succeeds in diminishing the managers that the employees see.'

Some visiting, however, is essential for keeping in touch and collecting first-hand information. As MR. AVERY explains, 'if you sit at your desk for too long your glasses fog up'. He arranges a system of annual visits to plants in the period immediately before the company's annual meeting of shareholders. He makes these visits his fact-finding tour, so that he is fully informed for the meeting.

MR. ACKLAND has a smaller, though still substantial group. He visits his plants quarterly, and holds the budget review meetings at each plant, taking his headquarters staff with him. This way they kill three birds with the one stone. They are seen, they learn, and they decide.

In a more compact organization, such as that of MR. BERESFORD, it is possible for the chief executive to have a weekly schedule, beginning and ending at head office, and taking in visits to operating units mid-week.

Does not a programme of visiting, to collect information and to be seen, involve a chief executive in being button-holed to make *ad hoc* decisions as he goes along?

Not in the experience of MR. BISSETT, who spends a day a week visiting factories and also sees a lot of people in his office 'so that they can tell me what they are doing'. He says: 'I am better informed than anyone else in the group, as a result. Moreover, I get an opportunity to judge the kind of people we employ.' But he is not buttonholed for immediate decisions because: 'I have always made it clear that I don't make decisions. They can get decisions quite quickly through the proper channels. The local companies and divisions take their decisions up to authorized levels. Also our central executive committee meets twice a week, one of these meetings being to consider new projects.'

Surely it cannot be true that some chief executives don't make decisions?

MR. BISSETT means only that he makes them with his colleagues in the right place at the right time. Between meetings he is collecting information, which is the real key to effective use of his time. Then he lets his mind work on the facts. But collecting facts involves talking to a lot of people, as well as reading reports and watching operating results.

Is there a danger of doing so much talking and reading that the mind has little chance to do creative work on the collected information?

There are some people, like MR. BATCHELOR, who says he does 'more thinking with people than by myself'. Creative work largely 'comes from contacts'.

Other chief executives, like MR. CAVELL and MR. BAILEY, wake early in the morning and ideas come to them. But for MR. CALDER they are likely to come when he is on one of his long holidays.

When the ideas come, writing them down frees the mind so that it can get on with the next sequence of thoughts. It also helps to make the ideas indelible.

Good commercial, technical and managerial ideas come at all times if an efficient system of information collection has been devised, and provided that some time of relaxation has been left for the mind to work on the facts.

Is not this emphasis on fact-collecting slanted too much towards the need for good long-term decisions? Is it not neglecting the need for a chief executive to be responsive to the immediate situation around him?
On the contrary, a man is all the better able to make quick decisions, all the more responsive to the immediate situation, if he is continually collecting and mentally sifting information. A lot of the decisions which a chief executive appears to make quickly are already more than half thought through. He has pondered on what he would do in a certain eventuality, and when it arrives he acts promptly.

22

STYLE OF OFFICE LAYOUT

Is the modern chief executive conventional or unconventional in his style of office layout?
The survey shows some 52 per cent to be conventional, 35 per cent to be unconventional, and another 13 per cent to be verging that way.

What do we mean by 'conventional'?
It starts with the traditional desk. Most executive desks are expensive versions of clerks' desks. They are therefore quite irrelevant to the role of a chief executive.

Why is a conventional desk irrelevant at the chief executive level?
A chief executive spends a lot of his time talking. In fact, as we saw in the last chapter, on average he spends three-quarters of his time talking. It would take a real idiot to design a conventional desk as an effective piece of furniture for talking.

In fact it was never so designed. It was meant for clerks. Historically a clerk has been someone who performed a semi-independent administrative function, completing perhaps one section in a chain of paperwork. His desk was everything to him because he probably shared a room with others. He needed drawers in his desk to keep his personal chattels, his pencils, his pending papers and reference documents. He did not usually receive people, unless they came to him in a pliant role, to have their documentation completed.

When clerks were replaced by machines, and the number of managers grew, these managers had slightly superior clerical desks. And so on, right up to the chief executive, who had a very grand, chief clerk's desk. By comparison, it cost a lot of money, but it was still a chief clerk's desk.

What has caused so many managers now to break away from convention?

There have been many studies in the last 10 years of how the Executive Spends His Time.* They have thrown light on the relatively little amount of an executive's time that is spent doing paperwork of a kind which needed a clerical-type desk. They have, moreover, shown that for most of the work done by executives, and particularly for the work of a chief executive, a conventional desk has positive disadvantages.

What are the disadvantages of a clerical desk, for executive work?

Firstly, it is a class barrier, an unnecessary authority symbol, a positive handicap to the flow of verbal information. It puts the man who is behind the desk in a superior position to his visitors, possibly inhibiting their frankness of conversation. Says MR. BAKER, chief executive of a major international group employing young managers of many races and nationalities: 'I often sit on the sofa with my visitor for discussions. You have to eliminate people's fears. I'm not at all age-conscious, but they may be. Once people lose their fears, they talk freely.'

The second disadvantage of a clerical desk is that it handicaps the conducting of paperwork, if more than one person is involved—as is so often the case. Only the top man himself is comfortable. Very often the others present cannot even get their knees under the edge of his desk in order to sit up to it. Even if the desk is modern and has an all-round overlap for visitors and secretaries, these people are still second-class citizens when it comes to doing paperwork comfortably.

* See for example a book of this same title by G. Copeman, H. Luijk and F. de P. Hanika, Business Publications Ltd., London, 1963.

If the disadvantages of traditional desks are so great, why do a majority of chief executives still have them? This is the sort of change which people keep postponing, because it isn't urgent on any particular day. Cost is an important factor. Says MR. BANFIELD: 'If I had a new desk, others would want one too.'

So the compromise solution in many cases is to move to the boardroom for every meeting of three or more people, or to have the board table in the chief executive's room—which denies its use to others—or to have a low coffee table and set of chairs in one corner of the room. But however tastefully a coffee table arrangement is laid out, it is second-best for serious discussion, involving paperwork. Only a very athletic person can hope to enjoy leaning forward from a low, easy chair to correct a document on a low coffee table. MR. BOLTON is a big man and he will have none of this. He has a round table in his office for small meetings, but it is of conventional height, so that people can sit up comfortably and work on figures.

The other important reason why so many chief executives retain their traditional desks is because they do not use them very much. Says MR. ACLAND: 'I visit my staff quite a lot because it is easier to get out of other people's offices than to get them out of your own.'

The great travellers do not need a desk. MR. ATWICK spends so much time visiting plants, that he is mostly in the offices of a local subsidiary head. And after his discussions, when he wants to contact his other plants, all he needs is a room with a phone.

Then there are the go-getters who have an age problem.

MR. CHILDS has used his tremendous marketing flair to build up a business very rapidly from almost nothing. He says: 'I very rarely sit behind a desk, we sit round a table or I sit in someone else's office in front of their desk. Being young, I find it difficult to get people to work under me. They have to work with me. I tend to avoid too many reminders that I am the boss. My office is more a sort of general recreation area. There are more models of new products in it than anything else.'

What are the unconventional chief executives doing to break away from the traditional clerical-desk-made-bigger?

They are breaking away in a number of directions. First, there are those who have realized that they are running a whole business, not just one clerical function, so they do not need the clerk's conventional drawers.

Says MR. CAMERON, who sits at a table-like desk without any drawers: 'I like to have out on top the things I'm working on. When I'm not working on a subject, my secretary can take it away.'

Then there are those who have already realized that they spend most of their time talking, holding a continuous series of mini-meetings. A few of these have added a table to the other side of their conventional desks, to make a T-shaped design. Though this is a fairly good working arrangement, it must be provisional. Nobody today would deliberately design a chief executive's desk shaped to symbolize his superiority and rub home the fact that his visitors are 'below the salt'.

During the survey a number of interesting desk shapes were seen where a designer had tried to break away from the conventional desk and make some provision for meetings, but had not really understood the problems. MR. DILLMANN sits at an L-shaped desk, MR. ASPINALL sits on the inner side of a gracefully curved desk.

A happier and simpler arrangement is that of MR. BEATTY, who still has a traditional desk but it is placed in one corner of the boardroom, where it has become a mere receptacle for pens and other personal effects.

He says: 'I prefer to sit at the side of the board table, so that I can spread my things around better and receive people better.' The advantage of sitting in the middle of one side is also well understood and explained by MR. BLYTH: 'I often need to talk with three or four people at a time. They come alongside to look at things, so that we can look at them together.'

MR. DECKER also sits at a table, so that people can sit round it with him, for a meeting. All his colleagues also have tables.

What, then, is the logical design shape for a table-type desk, best suited to the needs of the chief executive? In my opinion, this can be seen in the office of MR. BEST, who has a table-desk which is shaped like a flat octagon, with slight curves to improve its appearance. Its general shape is illustrated in Figure 22.1. MR. BEST sits at one of the long sides and so has plenty of room for working, but the arrangement is also very good for meetings: 'I can have two or three people in around the table and they can not only talk but also look at figures. There is nobody sticking out at the end.'

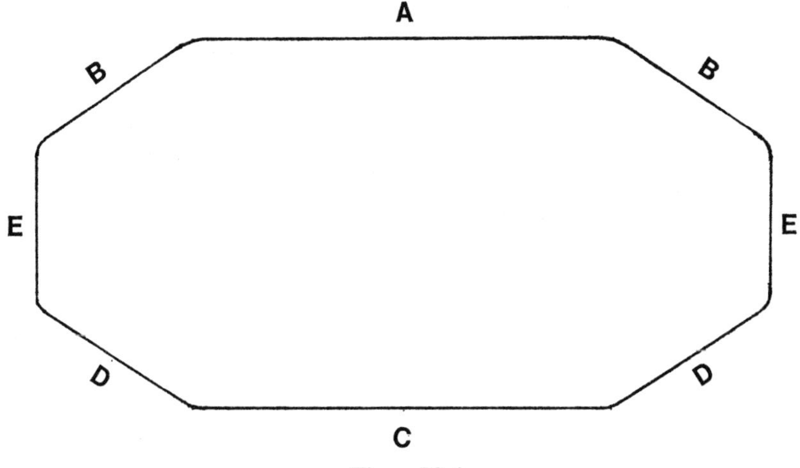

Figure 22.1

In an emergency he could accommodate eight people, with one at either end, but most meetings of a chief executive with his immediate colleagues or with outside visitors or with a special project committee do not exceed six. In the words of MR. DEGENHARDT, 'meetings with more than five people are a waste of time.'

What are the conventions for efficient use of a flat-octagonal desk? These can be seen by referring to Figure 22.1. The chief executive sits at A. If one or two colleagues join him to plan or review something in detail and look at the same charts or drawings, the two positions B can be used. If they join him to hold an interview, the interviewee can sit at position C. If a colleague drops in on the chief executive for an informal talk, he is more likely to sit at one of the positions D rather than C. If there is a meeting of up to six people, the positions A, B, C and D are used. Only if the meeting is enlarged to seven or eight, will the end positions E be used.

While maintaining the principle of the flat octagon, it is possible to design a slightly more tapering and extremely elegant shape. In perspective, which is the way a desk is usually seen by a visitor, a flat octagon can make a most attractive desk, as is clear from Figure 22.2.

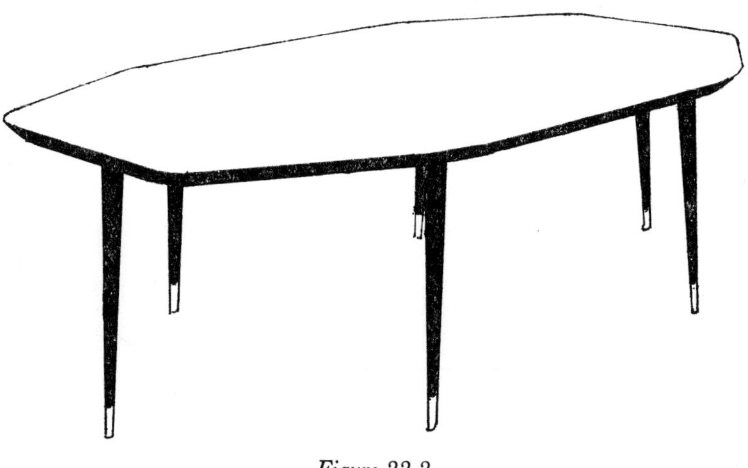

Figure 22.2

23

ACCESS TO CONTROL DATA

If a chief executive sits at a flat-octagon table, not a traditional clerical desk, where can he keep his control reports, other papers and personal belongings?
He will usually have storage units within reach behind him, or elsewhere in the room. One advantage of having a specially designed cabinet behind him is that his phones can sit on it and also IN and OUT trays, so that his table-top desk is uncluttered for holding meetings, spreading out and discussing plans and budgets, etc.

Before looking at the special storage problems of chief executives, it is pertinent to ask: do they need to have storage space, other than for a few pens, paper tissues and personal items? Why cannot the rest be passed out to a secretary to file? Do chief executives in fact keep much paperwork, and in particular, do they keep back copies of control reports in their offices?
The survey shows that 62 per cent keep very little in their offices, and in particular no back copies of control reports. The other 38 per cent keep much more.

How is it that some people are able to keep very little?
The answer does not lie solely in having a good secretary. She keeps very little too. The main answer lies in the way control figures and reports are prepared so that they are fully self-contained, with all relevant comparisons made, so that the chief

executive finds no need to keep past copies to refer back. He can literally throw away each regular report when the next one arrives.

There are some types of business where, if the chief executive kept past copies, he would quickly have to move out of his office and turn it into a paper store. MR. CAVELL runs a construction company which was small when he took over, but now has 1000 contracts current at any one time. Clearly he could not keep much detail on these, so he does not keep any.

Another non-keeper is MR. CHAMBERS, whose work is related to the construction industry, and therefore reported to him project by project. Past figures, particularly last year's are of no interest to him. He is only concerned with how each project is going against the budget. Like MR. BEST, a manufacturer in the fast-moving electronic field, he takes last year into account when making up this year's budgets, but afterwards ignores it as no longer relevant.

A non-keeper who does not even have a procedures manual in his office is MR. BLYTH, whose business is world-wide and so he does a lot of travelling: 'I would not look up a procedures manual if something went wrong. I would call for somebody. It might be the company secretary, or whoever was relevant. I would expect him to have a copy and I would discuss the matter with him rather than look it up. It's a question of size of operation and also the fact that I am out of the country so much. I cannot keep manuals and other routine stuff, I have to rely on other people.'

MR. ATWICK is the biggest traveller in the survey. He keeps nothing. But his schedule is carefully arranged so that control reports reach him by air, on time. His inventories and receivables for the month are due on the 10th of the following month, his earnings figures are due on the 14th. Wherever he is in America, they arrive on time, though there is a little delay if he is abroad. A thick file of control figures and a thick file of charts each month—he takes them everywhere by air with him in his bag until the next lot arrive. Then he destroys them.

MR. BOLTON is a non-keeper, but he has a personal assistant

who spends much of the time bringing up to date his figures and charts, replacing old pages with new in his loose-leaf binders and putting in slips of paper to draw the new pages to his attention.

Most chief executives, however, manage without a personal assistant. They have very good secretaries. MR. BAILEY is not untypical in having had the same secretary for 18 years. She knows the business and knows everything he is likely to want, so that from his point of view, it doesn't matter whether a report has been thrown out or just put in the OUT tray. She can always find a copy.

MR. ANTHONY has a well-organized routine. New figures arrive in a computer print-out sheaf. He goes through them and then puts them in his out-tray. The next morning he finds that his secretary has taken the binder out of the appropriate drawer in his back cabinet, taken out the old sheets of figures and destroyed them, and replaced them with the new lot.

MR. ATKINS likes to be able to refer back, if need be: 'I keep one set of figures, my secretary keeps the previous one and then the third one back is destroyed.'

MR. DITTMER does not need to keep back files: 'I have my little charts in my coat pocket, so if I visit anyone or they come to see me I can look up the back trend before we meet.'

If so many chief executives are in a position to throw away old reports, why is it that some insist on keeping them?

One reason is that anyone running a group headquarters with a small staff is inclined to keep everything because he cannot quickly refer to divisional records. As MR. ATKINSON explains: 'Each new set of figures is fully comparable when looked at on its own, but it does not actually give last month's or the previous month's figures. It only gives the current month and the cumulative totals. So if you happen to want last month's, you've got to keep it.'

MR. DOBLER keeps back copies of control figures in a big cabinet in his office, for reference. If for example he is going to a trade association meeting and he wants to have a chart prepared in order to put across a point, he must have easy access to each past month's figures.

Then there is the problem of checking on accuracy. Explains MR. CLEMENTS: 'I only compare with previous figures if I suspect that the bloke is not telling the truth. If I remember that a previous figure was different, I get out the previous set to compare.'

The words as well as the figures may need checking. Says MR. ACLAND: 'I am always interested in what the commentary was. When discussing a problem with someone I can say, "but you said so and so last year". This helps to make people more realistic in their comments.' Another reason why he keeps the back monthly reports is 'because of the seasonality of some of our products. I like to look at the trends.'

Manufacturing is not the only area where there are advocates of looking at trends. MR. ADAMS is head of a large department store group, and he says: 'Retailing is this year compared with last year, hindsight looking back. We sometimes go back four or five years. We keep our figures.'

There is, however, a limit to what one can learn from trends, when it comes to looking at individual product figures: In the words of MR. BAXTER: 'Why compare this year's sales of white shirts with last year's? After all, they are dearer, they are made of different material, and fashions in shirts change.'

Is there no compromise between keeping masses of figures and keeping none? For example, is it not possible to keep just a summary of key figures?

MR. BATCHELOR keeps only one piece of paper, the monthly summary, and he also has a file on the annual budget, so he can make overall comparisons at any time.

MR. BAMBER is relatively new to the top management of a retail group. Though he had worked in it before, he did not then have close knowledge of all operational figures. To help him get accustomed to the scale of different parts of the business, he has a practice which could well be imitated by other new chief executives. Every month the key operating figures of each store are copied into a specially designed pocket book, and while being driven around in his car, he spends time familiarizing himself with them.

MR. BAINBRIDGE does a similar job for himself, condensing key figures into special binders that are always with him.

MR. BLOOMFIELD also works on the key figures month by month, except that they are set out across a wide sheet so that he can watch the trend of monthly movements. His secretary sometimes inserts the figures, but he likes to do it himself: 'I can then remember the figures better and I take more note of them.'

MR. DODEN keeps his business figures close to him: 'They are entered up by my secretary and I carry the sheets around with me everywhere. If you ring me up in the night, I can reach out from my bed and read out figures to you. I used to have them in a pocket book, but they are too elaborate now.'

MR. ARMSTRONG keeps a condensed version of group figures: 'I get piecemeal reports coming at me all the time on different divisions and I look at them and put them in the out basket. But I also have a group data book. My assistant keeps it up to date, and it is kept on my desk so that I can refer to the figures on any activity at any time. I don't look very often because I remember most of the figures that come to me on the piece-meal reports.'

MR. DECKER can throw away the special reports that keep coming to him, because 'the statistics department send me regular summaries of all the key figures, including the number of people employed as well as the profits, the sales revenue and so on. My secretary inserts these in a special file which sits on my desk for handy reference.'

Is it not really a waste of time for a chief executive to do the kind of detailed work on figures and files that some participants claim to do?

That depends on how many hours he is prepared to spend on the job. MR. CHRISTIE is one of the most successful men in the survey. He has built up a large manufacturing business from nothing in 15 years. But he does all his own filing and keeps his own figures. What is more, he keeps them for 10 years back. He works long hours and personally pursues every detail of the business. He employs no secretary. 'If I want to write a letter,' he says, 'which is rarely, I dictate it to any girl who happens to be around.' He has a very effective management style because everybody reacts attentively to his quietly confident voice, whether on the phone or in person. And filing is not beneath him, for he recognizes that every time he looks at a piece of paper and puts it in a physical file, he is in fact also storing its contents in his mental file.

Are there some types of chief executive who, by the nature of their business, really need to do quite a lot of their own filing?

In most businesses there is a need for the chief executive to keep close to him the personnel records of his key people. As MR. BASSETT explains: 'If someone wants to discuss his salary, I want it close to hand.'

Also there are some cases where a firm has a limited number of key clients or customers. MR. AUSTIN hires out expensive and highly specialized equipment to a relatively few customers, each of whom is very valuable to him. He therefore has a range of lockable cupboards behind him, some of them containing suspension files. He keeps in there highly confidential notes on meetings held with important customers, 'because I do not want these seen by filing clerks or mis-filed and unavailable when I want them. I cannot stand mis-filing. If a customer phones up I have got to be able to open a drawer and reach for a document immediately while he is still talking on the telephone.'

The habit of keeping his own files is not confined to any one type of personality among chief executives. It might be thought that the introverts would be inclined to hoard and mull over their own paperwork. But the extrovert who has thoroughly delegated the detail of his business is inclined to regard the policy-forming paperwork that does come his way as too vital to be out of reach. MR. AYLWARD is one of the most obviously extrovert personalities in the survey, and this is his description of the contents of the cabinet behind his desk: 'Everything I have got is here. I don't keep anything outside. Contracts, corporate meetings, acquisitions, mid-year meetings, projections, the training of black people, operating results, public relations, real estate, speeches, it is all here. I don't need to prepare a speech when I am talking about the company for God's sake, but I do on other subjects.'

MR. ATWELL is another believer in doing his own filing: 'I file all the daily and weekly and monthly reports myself, back several copies, so that I can refer to them quickly. I always want available enough information to keep my people honest when they come in here. If somebody tells me something, I jot it down and it should be consistent with what they say next time. If they don't know, they should say they don't know and not make up a story.

'I also have things filed forward for reference back. For example, you say that the draft manuscript will be ready in April. I have just marked your correspondence April 15 in big letters, and put it in the out tray. My secretary will bring it to my attention again on April 15, and if the draft hasn't arrived, then I will either check with you or have it filed forward a little longer and brought back to me, when I can check again.'

Why do chief executives with special filing problems usually have to have a special range of cabinets built for them?

Because their need for special storage facilities has not been logically thought through by the office furniture industry, any more than has the need to get them away from clerical-type desks.

However, MR. BENHAM has thought through these problems and he has within easy reach of his table-type desk a specially built cabinet which could possibly suit the needs of a wide range of chief executives. This type of cabinet is illustrated in Figure 23.1.

It not only copes with his need for drawers, for telephone stand space, for key reference book shelves, for IN and OUT trays and PENDING trays, it also copes with his special filing needs.

The normal filing cabinets with suspension files, designed to store letters, are not really suitable to the needs of most chief executives. Those who do need them can in any case have a suspension filing cabinet elsewhere in the room. But MR. BENHAM has recognized that the main filing need of a chief executive lies in having quick access to key operating figures and to standard reference material such as organization and procedures manuals. These items, whether typed or handwritten or computer-printed, are usually kept in a loose-leaf binder with a semi-stiff cover. They do not fit well into a filing cabinet and they do not stand up well on a shelf. They need to be held vertically by special dividers, as shown in Figure 23.1.

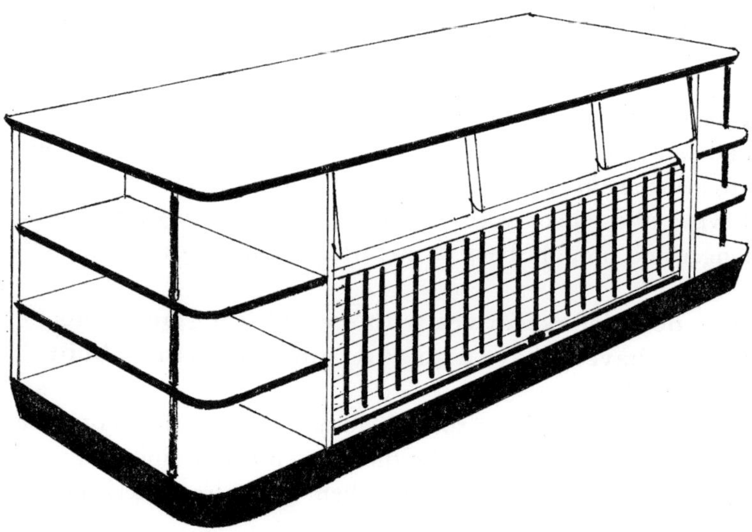

Figure 23.1

Says MR. BENHAM: 'I wanted this special filing unit because I like to be able to put my hands on the board minutes, the accounts, production figures, the order intake, and so on, whenever I want them.'

The sort of unit which MR. BENHAM has designed would also meet the needs of MR. DOBLER, who keeps on a bench behind him a classified and indexed file for pending items to discuss with key staff. The classification system includes special current projects as well as the names of heads of main functions of his business who come to regular meetings with him.

MR. ASKEW also has a filing system for distinguishing carefully between regular operating reports and special project reports on matters that are not yet in top gear.

It will be noted that the cabinet shown in Figure 23.1 includes plenty of pending tray space at each end. Thus it is possible to devise a unit which meets the needs of MR. BENHAM, MR. DOBLER and MR. ASKEW. A chief executive's cabinet can be designed which keeps all his essential files and reference data close to hand, yet clear of his work-table, which will be used on average three-quarters of the time for meetings.

PART IV

CHIEF EXECUTIVE ATTITUDES AND CHARACTERISTICS

24

PERSONAL MOTIVATION

What causes a chief executive to be more highly motivated than most people? Or is it even true that he is?

The survey included a late question on motivation, deliberately kcpt well away from the early question on what business is for. Significantly, the answers to these two questions seem to overlap only in the case of self-made business owners—the original capitalists.

The question on motivation was put in such a way as to assume that a successful chief executive is more highly motivated than most people, and to seek his explanation of his own high level of motivation. There was only a one per cent denial of high motivation, the credit for success in this case being put squarely on luck—which was also mentioned as one of the contributory factors in a few other cases.

There was relatively little reference in the replies to innate drive and ambition, or even hard work. And only three per cent of those in the survey were able to tell a 'rags to riches' story, crediting their motivation to a tough start in life.

In fact, as the following analysis shows, the greatest number of replies fall under the heading 'Work is Fun', with 15 per cent. Next comes the competitive instinct, with 10 per cent, and the desire to prove oneself, also with 10 per cent.

After this comes the desire to create or accomplish something of special significance, with 8 per cent, and next but closely allied to it is the striving for perfection, with 6 per cent.

Together, so far, these answers make up 49 per cent of the total, and only after this comes the expressed desire for more money, with 5 per cent. The rest of the answers all score below 5 per cent.

Altogether the answers have been classified under eight headings plus a miscellaneous category, and they are given here under subject headings, in descending numerical order. Near-duplicate replies have been eliminated.

WORK IS FUN—15 PER CENT

MR. BERESFORD: I was fairly aimless at University, and then when I started at this firm the work seemed to be drudgery, until I realized that you've got to enjoy it by doing it as well as you can. So I went on doing that.

MR. EXTRAMAN: Motivation changes once a man has got financial security. I'm motivated now because I have got a place to go. My old lady doesn't want me at home. I like it here, and anyway I can go out and do a deal.

MR. BELLAMY: Work is the fun of life. I was in the army during the war for seven years altogether, and I thought at the time what a soul-destroying job this is, unless one becomes deeply interested in it. I finished up as a staff colonel. I never went home on leave for three years, the work was so fascinating. If I were a wealthy man I'd pay to do this job, I find it so interesting.

MR. ANSELL: It is more fun to be successful than otherwise. Some people aren't prepared to pay the price. You have got to work and enjoy your work.

Author's Note: When I was being driven back to my hotel in Mr. Ansell's Cadillac, his chauffeur mentioned that Mr. Ansell hadn't taken a vacation for 16 years. 'And,' said the chauffeur, 'when I said to him once: "When are you going to take your vacation?" he replied, "I am on vacation. I enjoy what I am doing here."'

MR. DANNEWALD: To be effective your work must have an emotional connection with what you want done in life. Insurance interests me very much. I am concerned about the responsibility of the insurance industry in the total economy. Insurance firms are big capital-holding companies, and 40 per cent of the German capital market comes from the insurance industry. It gives me satisfaction that my industry can help in influencing our lives and diversifying our democratic system, making it a pluralist society.

MR. ALEXANDER (a former business school professor): I always thought that teaching business subjects was a poor substitute for the action—for the market place. I find the market place a great deal more fun, even when you don't win. The final appraisal is whether your organization will accept an idea, which is not just a theory, and whether it proves profitable or not.

MR. CAVELL: I could retire, but what would I do? I enjoy this. There is tremendous satisfaction in having started humbly and proved myself as good as the other chap. But there is always someone higher, and while one is successful one wants to go on.

MR. AVERY: Some people belong to the 'thank God it's Friday club'. I belong to the 'thank God it's Monday club'. This place gives me the feeling that I am building something of lasting value. We all wonder what the hell we are in this world for.

MR. CHESHIRE: I get a lot of pleasure out of building something and making it go.

I AM COMPETITIVE—10 PER CENT

MR. ANTHONY: I would like to think that my motivation is based on the highest motives—utilizing one's abilities in the service of mankind. But I have been told by others that I am the most competitive person they have ever met. However, I get no feeling out of beating people.

MR. CASEY: To me, the excitement of business is so much greater than was the excitement of science. I have an intense desire to prove that my theses are right by getting customers to buy the products. I suppose I have a kind of paranoia, a desire not to be beaten, not to be second.

MR. DACKWEILER: My motivation is the sporting one—to be better than my competitors.

MR. CAIRNS: I have been excited by competition right from schooldays.

MR. CLARK: I am naturally competitive because I feel inadequate, and inadequate people feel they have got to go and prove themselves.

MR. ASCOT: In any opportunity of work that is offered I like to evaluate myself with others. But to make a good job, one must have the ability to seek advice, follow it and take it. In this complex world no one man is all-knowing.

MR. CHATFIELD: I get satisfaction in achievement, in beating the next man. When you see it in the figures, you've got something to work to.

I WANTED TO PROVE MYSELF—10 PER CENT

MR. ASHBOURNE: I wanted to prove I had the ability to run the business. People always doubt it when you are the son of the boss. You never get any credit for anything you do.

MR. BOWLES: I was an unsuccessful schoolboy. I was unpopular, not very good at games, certainly not very clever. Since then I just go on proving to myself that I am different from that.

MR. DAUTZENBERG: I had a personal goal of achieving something outstanding. I felt that with my qualities I should.

MR. ANDERSON: I have always been extremely competitive with my father, both in the company and outside. For example, I am an avid golfer, solely because he was good at it and he used to relish beating me. As he got older, of course, I could beat him even though I wasn't an outstanding golfer myself.

MR. BAXTER: I have a desire to be seen to be successful. Not necessarily have my name in print, but people who know that I am doing this job should know that I am successful at it.

MR. BOND: The important thing in motivation is acceptance amongst one's colleagues. They like a leader. You can't be a leader unless you are a pretty positive character.

I LIKE TO BE CREATIVE AND ACHIEVE SOMETHING—8 PER CENT

MR. DAHLMANN: Schumpeter defined motivation as an instinct to create something. It is not a question of intelligence.

MR. ASPINALL: The truly motivated people are those who get a zest out of accomplishment. Doing something worthwhile and helping the progress of the world. Personal satisfaction out of making a contribution to the health and welfare of mankind. It is only rather shallow people who are motivated by power and a desire to get their name in the paper.

MR. ARROWSMITH: Motivation comes from the satisfaction you get out of making a sale, seeing how the performance of the product compares with what you sold, building for less than you thought, seeing your employees develop and progress, not having your stockholders too unhappy. Pride of accomplishment, and doing for your family as well as you can.

MR. BAKER: I feel the importance of taking part in the development of this planet. We try to get under the skins of the local people in every country where we operate and make them feel we have a tremendous interest in their success.

I STRIVE FOR PERFECTION—6 PER CENT

MR. ARMSTRONG: My father and Henry Borden influenced me greatly. I always wanted very badly to do the best I could in any field. In my experience the thing that limits people is their emotions. One must be able to take a beating from day to day without blowing up.

MR. CLIFFORD: I went into the forces in 1923 and couldn't get out, of course, because of the war until 1946, so I couldn't start my own business before that. But basically I had always felt that I had a competency that wanted putting to the test. When stationed abroad in the 1930s it was important to learn to swim. I discovered then how, by learning to swim properly, a small chap like me could easily beat someone who had been a natural swimmer all his life and was much bigger and stronger, but had never taken the trouble to learn properly.

MR. CHARLTON: We like to be the cheapest with the best product. When you want to grow a business, you are on a treadmill, and you can't stop. Your shareholders are your bosses.

MR. CLEMENTS: I am motivated by the system because whatever has to be done, has to be done as well as possible—better products at lower cost to satisfy consumer demand. That's how the system works.

I WANTED MORE MONEY—5 PER CENT

MR. DODEN: A business which can't make money is not worth having. I want a lot of money. Personally I am restless. I want to be in a position to move around and to do it in style.

MR. AUSTIN: I was always after my boss's job. He was always making more money than I was. I didn't want authority for the sake of it, I wanted the money.

MR. CALDER: Ambition is a moving thing. I remember how I wanted my first £10,000, then my first million, and after that I was in the money game, which fascinated me.

MR. AYLWARD: My original ambition was to increase my salary to $25,000. When I reached that, I wanted to be a millionaire. Now that I have independent financial security, I want to run the company independently and to build it to a billion dollar company. I don't know after that what my next ambition will be, but I'll have one.

MR. DAMM: I went into business rather than the Civil Service because in business your potential pays off. You get a real reward. But in the Civil Service, whether you are good or bad, you get the pay scale.

I WANTED IT BIGGER AND BETTER—4 PER CENT

MR. DENYER: After becoming plant manager, I began to see what I was going for, and my motivation increased.

MR. BEATTY: I always wanted to be in a position where 'the buck stops here'. I became chairman of a private company and then wanted to become chairman of a public company too, which I now am.

MR. DITTMER: I came from a subsidiary with 1,000 employees to run the group with 20,000, because I wanted the challenge of working with a bigger staff, bigger responsibility and new concepts.

I HAVE A RESTLESS DISSATISFACTION—3 PER CENT

MR. ARCHER: Very few times in my career have I been able to sit back and say I have done everything perfectly.

MR. BLUNDELL: I would have been bored very quickly by routine work and no responsibility, no challenge.

I HAD A TOUGH START—3 PER CENT

MR. ATWICK: My motivation possibly comes from the fact that I was raised in a very backward community on the south side of my home town, which was looked down on. It was a tough life during the depression, and I worked to get out of it.

MR. BAILEY: I had a high regard for my father, who was a very able engineer. He went blind and had to resign. It was terrible to observe him so completely frustrated. The family were hard up and I realized at 16 that I would have to make it for myself. I achieved scholarships. Then the war gave me my chance. At the age of 22 I was in charge of 300 engineers on the Normandy beaches.

I HAD A MISCELLANY OF REASONS—36 PER CENT

MR. DEDERICHS: I always tried to understand what my boss did and learnt from him.

MR. BRADLEY: I am motivated by an interest in development, growing instead of standing still. It was J. S. Mill who said: 'I can perceive a situation in which your capital and income remain stationary but you are still developing in the art of living.'

MR. BAINBRIDGE: If I have an idea, I like to follow it through, not have it called in question.

MR. BEST: When I joined the company I said to myself, one of these days I'll be the head of it.

MR. CHAPMAN: The dribble effect of success, success, success. One must have early success to keep steaming. I have met a lot of better engineers or characters who chose the wrong thing or the right thing at the wrong time. They have been buffeted by fate, have ended up good employees, not employers. So one cannot be arrogant about it.

MR. BENHAM: Sheer, blind luck. I have never had the ambition to be the managing director of any company. I was sick and tired of the frustration of trying to accomplish something in my last firm, and I was invited to start an electronics company. I set down a plan and accomplished it. I was invited then to run the whole group, and they worked on me for three or four days until they persuaded me to take it. One's success is a combination of good fortune in being in the right place at the right time, modest ability and a high level of integrity.

MR. BRIDGES: To get to the top of a big organization you have got to have a lot of luck, for example you have got to have the right age relationship. If I had been five years older or ten years younger I could never have got this job. But at the same time you've got to have been seen performing.

MR. DOBLER: I could have left this firm when I sold it to the big group. Profit is an incentive, but consciousness of being responsible for people who have believed in you and trusted in you, is even greater.

MR. ABBOTT: We've got a lot of debt in the company and I'm working for the banks.

MR. DEGENHARDT: All my family were professional, but I like to get things done through other people—to convince my colleagues.

MR. BOLTON: The British are extremely inventive but bad at exploiting the products of their own inventiveness. I am determined to demonstrate that in the case of my company anyway, they are not that bad.

MR. DERKUM: I get great satisfaction out of the fact that the company is placing confidence in me and I don't like to disappoint my company.

MR. BLISS: I won a scholarship to Cambridge where I got a first-class degree. When I joined the company I could see that I had come into an old-fashioned business at a very difficult time and that I had to work very hard to hold on to my job.

MR. ATTWOOD: There are two kinds of reward, physical and psychic, and the psychic rewards become increasingly important as you assume greater responsibility. Accomplishment, power, social acceptance, these are the major motivations. The lowliest employee gets some minimum psychic satisfaction when he is told he has done a good job.

MR. ACLAND: My motivation now comes from motivating other people. In some ways it is a messianic role. If I left here I would go into teaching.

MR. BIGGS: The motivation system involves enthusiasm and forward thinking. It is self generating. Some day I may wind down, but then I am bringing on other people behind me. They don't have to be all one pattern to be successful. If anyone moulds himself on me and he isn't a me, he'll fall flat on his backside.

MR. COCHRANE: When you get to a certain stage the job becomes part of you. Money is no longer an object. You can't even keep it. You want to do better for the world, leave something behind so that they know you've been here.

25

REQUIRED QUALITIES

What do chief executives consider, from their own experience, to be the qualities most needed in their job? This open-ended question was asked near the beginning of each interview in the survey, in order that the replies would not be influenced by questions subsequently asked about particular qualities and skills.

Because the question was a surprise, and answers were required immediately without time for detailed thought, some significance is attached to what was said first. Moreover, no limit was put on the number of qualities required in an answer. Some members of the survey named one, some two, and some three. A few named more.

Table 25.1 gives the distribution of first choice of qualities, and of both first and second choice combined. In view of the different numbers of Americans, Britons and Germans in the survey, the numerical analysis of replies has been weighted to make all three groups equal, and the replies are expressed as percentages of the total replies.

By far the greater number of qualities mentioned were concerned with the ability to handle people—to select and motivate them, and to develop their abilities. These were 44 per cent of the first choice replies and 40 per cent of the combined choice. The British chose these qualities the least and the Americans the most.

The next most popular range of qualities is concerned with the ability to analyse business problems, determine the right product policy and create new ideas and products. This took

27 per cent of the first choice and 23 per cent of the combined choice. As a first choice it was far more significant for Germans than for Britons or Americans.

Table 25.1

ANALYSIS OF FIRST CHOICE AND COMBINED FIRST AND SECOND CHOICES OF QUALITIES NEEDED BY CHIEF EXECUTIVES

		First choice		Combined first and Second choice	
Handling people, motivation, etc.	British	11	44	11	40
	American	18		16	
	German	15		13	
Analytical skill, creativity, etc.	British	8	27	8	23
	American	6		6	
	German	13		9	
Personal drive, determination, stamina, etc.	British	7	13	4	15
	American	6		4	
	German	0		7	
Knowledge of the business or trade	British	1	9	1	9
	American	3		4	
	German	5		4	
Other needs	British	6	7	5	11
	American	1		3	
	German	0		3	

The third most popular set of qualities covers determination, drive and stamina, at 13 per cent in the first choice and 15 per cent in the combined choice. No Germans mentioned these qualities in their first choice, but they more than made up for this in their second, and took the lead in the combined score.

Next came knowledge of the business or trade, with 9 per cent in both columns and a low figure for the British, the highest figure being for the Germans.

After this came a miscellaneous category.

Is it likely that the qualities described by chief executives as being 'most needed' were in fact the qualities which they, themselves possessed?

Care was taken during the survey not to associate the qualities 'most needed' with those actually possessed. Indeed, there is a case for saying that a person feels 'most need' of those qualities which he does not possess in adequate measure.

A follow-up question was also asked on those aspects of the chief executive's job which were considered to be most in need of the assistance of a very capable colleague.

This question was answered in terms of job functions. Table 25.2 gives the distribution of answers in terms of four major job functions, but the largest group of replies were those denying that this was a problem. The Germans gave the highest number of 'no problem' replies, perhaps partly due to language difficulties. This seemed to be the only question in the survey which had difficulty in crossing the German/English language barrier.

The next largest group were those who replied in terms of the overall co-ordinating job of a chief executive, his need for all-round abilities rather than specialist skills.

As Table 25.2 shows, Finance was the subject area in which the greatest number of chief executives felt most deficient and hence most in need of relying on a skilled colleague. Nevertheless the scores of 13 per cent to 14 per cent are not surprising in view of the importance of finance to a chief executive, and hence the opportunities he would have to feel that he should know more about it.

After finance comes the technical, production and research area, followed by marketing and publicity, then law, then a variety of other subjects.

As the greatest number of chief executives regarded the ability to handle people as the quality they needed most, does not this mean that paramount importance should be given to this in management training?

Possibly it should. But on the other hand, a high level of social skill is of little avail without a good business policy. In the words of MR. ARNOLD, who made analytical skill his first choice: 'I am not talking about the compilation of the data but its analysis. You can have all kinds of carisma, but people are not likely to follow someone who makes consistently bad judgements.'

Table 25.2

ADMITTED DEFICIENCIES OF CHIEF EXECUTIVES

		First choice		First and second choice combined	
			%		%
No problem of deficiency	British	9	33	9	32
	American	11		11	
	German	13		12	
Co-ordinating role of chief executive explained	British	11	28	7	24
	American	7		7	
	German	10		10	
Finance knowledge deficient	British	6	13	7	14
	American	4		4	
	German	3		3	
Technical, production, research knowledge deficient	British	2	10	3	12
	American	3		4	
	German	5		5	
Marketing and publicity knowledge deficient	British	2	6	2	6
	American	4		4	
	German	0		0	
Law knowledge deficient	British	1	2	1	4
	American	1		3	
	German	0		0	
Others deficient	British	4	7	4	7
	American	0		0	
	German	3		3	

REQUIRED QUALITIES

The following is a presentation of the more remarkable quotations in the survey, firstly on the subject of most needed qualities in a chief executive, and secondly on the co-ordinating role of the chief executive.

ABILITY TO HANDLE PEOPLE, MOTIVATE THEM, ETC.—44 PER CENT

MR. AYLWARD: I need a lot of patience. I do a lot of refereeing over differences between philosophies, divisions and colleagues. For every ten decisions I make, I hope that eight are right. Sometimes the decisions are not even fair, particularly where personalities are involved. But someone has to make them.

MR. BLISS: The most important thing is dealing with people, choosing the right people for the job and then keeping them a happy team inspired to work, not to backbite, going whole-heartedly for the job. Spreading it down the line, not just keeping it to a small group at the top. We have tried to preserve in our companies the family spirit that came from the original firms we took over, and this has been made possible because our employees are spread around in about 45 different units averaging less than one thousand employees to each. From head office we try to attend special occasions such as the presentation of long-service awards, and we move around and speak to the staff, having already been carefully briefed so that we have knowledge of them, from a system of annual reporting which gives us the details. It is very difficult for just a few people at the top to do all this, but we encourage the group managers of the different groups of companies down the line to do the same.

MR. ATWELL: Most important is the ability to sum up people. All the impersonal problems are easy. The personal ones are not. It's people that complicate business.

MR. DANNEWALD: The real priorities are selection of people and good communications with people.

MR. ARGENT: We have set up a course and we use it for all from foremen up. They are exposed to the same philosophy of management. We also send employees to the A.M.A. seminars and we have sent a few to the Harvard Business School Advanced Management Programme. You can always buy a good engineer or a good financial man but you can't buy managers who know people and how to work with them.

MR. BAYLISS: One must be able to maintain the balance of a team, so that for example the bully does not always get his own way.

MR. ATTWATER: Motivation is easy when you are ashamed of what you are doing and want to do better, but it is tougher when you are happy and proud of what you are doing. You've got to see that they always want to do more.

MR. DAUTZENBERG: You have to create enthusiasm for a common goal and generate teamwork.

MR. BIGGS: The attitude must be: 'Come on, we can do this, we can knock hell out of them.' There are two types of people running businesses, firstly those who say, we are going to be as good as so and so. They are followers. Secondly, those who say, I want to be a leader. If you are in front, you have to try new ideas. This means getting people to do things that they haven't done before. This is real leadership.

MR. AUBREY: One must have the ability to help people to develop and grow and to motivate them in a way which will support our corporate objectives.

MR. BELLAMY: It is essential to have an interest in, almost a dedication to man-power development. This is the only job that the chief executive cannot delegate. If you delegate it, the divisional heads will keep postponing it. Unless the chief executive does this and is on their backs all the time, it will fail.

ANALYTICAL SKILL AND CREATIVITY—27 PER CENT

MR. DEGENHARDT: You have to make clear analyses, see things without emotion, then convince your colleagues and subordinates that they should be done.

MR. CHILDS: The nearest equivalent to the toy trade is the fashion trade. There is a constant demand for new items. Flair and artistic touch are vital in anticipating what people are going to like.

MR. DOBLER: One must always have new, creative ideas both as regards products and their channels of distribution.

MR. BAYLISS: At the very top, perhaps the most important quality is the capacity to relate apparently separate matters to each other before making a decision.

MR. DILLMANN: I put first technical and economic knowledge.

MR. ALEXANDER: You must have the long view. In my industry this year's profit is the result of decisions made years ago.

MR. DODEN: You need a lot of imagination, particularly at the beginning.

MR. BLACK: One needs the ability to get at the essentials of the problem, the commercial essentials which make it pay.

MR. DECKER: You need the capacity both to recognize the essentials in any problem and to see the possible consequences of any decision.

MR. CASEY: A successful chief executive must spot trends before anyone else.

PERSONAL DRIVE, DETERMINATION AND STAMINA—13 PER CENT

MR. BOWLES: You need physical toughness and the ability to make up your mind on inadequate evidence. For example, yesterday we decided to invest £X million in an overseas developing country. We can't really tell the political future of that country, but we have to have a go. Many people find it extremely difficult to make decisions on this basis, but you have to do it in business. When I make an important decision, I wake up in the night in a cold sweat and wonder whether I have done the right thing. To run a good business you have got to have sensitivity and power of imagination, and if you have these, you are bound to have personality problems that make certain things tough to do.

MR. ASHFIELD: The most important quality is to stick to what you are trying to achieve and never give up. But take the pragmatic approach, have limited goals. Try something and if it doesn't work, try something else.

MR. CHADWICK: If you have a successful formula, stick to it. Don't worry about trivialities, but make sure you do your sums correctly. You can't afford a single error in the costing.

MR. BAILEY: You must have the courage of your convictions. This is half the battle.

MR. ASHBOURNE: One must have good health and a willingness to take a businessman's risks.

MR. BENHAM: It takes a considerable amount of dedication and courage to run a business successfully. It is necessary to do pretty drastic things when a company has taken a hard knock in its markets.

MR. DAHLMANN: A chief executive must have Gesinnung. This German word cannot be translated into English. It comprehends conviction, character, courage, dedication, loyalty. When you look into history you will always find that social, national and economic units deteriorate or die not because of lack of talents but because of lack of Gesinnung.

KNOWLEDGE OF THE BUSINESS OR TRADE— 9 PER CENT

MR. DEDERICHS: One must have a basic understanding of the industries in which one is concerned.

MR. ASCOT: It is important to have a background in the company and the ability to inspire respect and a desire to co-operate.

MR. ASPINALL: One needs a thorough knowledge of the business.

OTHER NEEDS—7 PER CENT

MR. ATTWOOD: Firstly, one must have some of the same qualities as for a junior in the same business, for example the ability to and the willingness to learn. Secondly, one must have the ability to think, to project forward from what you have learnt about what has gone before. Learning is absorbing what went before, thinking is projecting forward from there. This means turning over some flat rocks, looking beyond the obvious. It means coming up with some conclusions that are supportable and viable. Thirdly, one must be able to communicate one's thoughts both orally and in writing, clearly and persuasively. And there is another side to this communication, listening to what the other fellow says in response to what you have said to him. Fourthly, one must be able to deal with numbers, not be a mathematician or statistician but be able to deal with the language of numbers and look at a table or budget sheet or pay out plan and be sufficiently numerate to be able to understand what the figures are saying and spot the frequent errors in the logic of numbers. The numbers can be correct but the information they convey may not be right, assumptions may be false or one aspect may be overstated. Fifthly, one must have the ability to lead, to instill in other people the feeling that you have the capacity for leadership and the willingness to accept it and the responsibilities that go with it.

MR. BLUNDELL: We have many subsidiary and associate companies abroad. It is therefore essential to have a knowledge of the conditions in each country and an ability to deal with people of widely differing nationalities. Having subsidiaries in foreign countries is very different from just having trading posts.

MR. BAKER: It is essential to appreciate the spiritual side of man. Mankind is all the same but at different stages of development. Human beings are capable of exceeding their own thoughts and capacities. You need to feel that way about them and help them to achieve their own national objectives. When you do business in a country, you must think locally, otherwise you are not seeing their country properly.

It isn't difficult to dignify human activity in industry. Industrialists can link the world into one people. Our companies go public in each country where they can because you must allow the local people to participate in the ownership. You have to be a patriot and an internationalist, not a nationalist. You have to have people working with you out of love, not for you out of fear. If you have this kind of motivation, the apparent conflicts in the world can harmonize.

IMPORTANCE OF THE CO-ORDINATING ROLE—28 PER CENT

MR. ARNOLD: The most effective top manager is the generalist. He doesn't substitute for any of the skills, he sees that they are all there, he can tap resources effectively and quickly, both inside the firm and outside it. He knows enough about everything to know what he doesn't know.

MR. BIGGS: The company is a team of people. I delegate everything in the sense that I do not do the detail of anything.

MR. ALLEN: One has to be interested in the lot. If I don't show an interest in something, it gets short change.

MR. BLUNDELL: You can't really dissociate yourself from any of the main functional responsibilities. You have to have enough knowledge of each to understand and interpret what they are trying to convey.

MR. DAHLMANN: The chief should know a lot about a few things, otherwise he becomes someone who just chatters about everything. He must know very clearly what he is not a specialist in. He must be self-critical and humble in the face of all the adulation.

MR. ANSELL: Every major function is important—manufacturing, research, engineering, finance, marketing, sales. If you have a weak one, you are in trouble.

MR. CHRISTIE: You have got to be fairly disciplined to get the most out of the highly qualified people you employ. Most of my ideas about engineering products and markets came from reading magazines. You have to have more facts and figures than your competitors.

MR. AVERY: A chief executive must be careful to have a very good man in every field, so that he retains his ability to delegate in all fields.

MR. CASEY: The chief executive must be allowed to develop his assets and take a special interest in one or two functions. He cannot have a standard yardstick of delegation. Likewise he may tolerate a difficult member of the team if this man contributes well.

MR. BOWLES: What you delegate depends on what people are good at. If there is someone I have almost complete confidence in, I delegate almost full authority to him. By contrast, one of his colleagues may be a very good day-to-day administrator but have relatively poor judgement on major policy matters. I don't follow his advice, and I don't leave him alone on such matters.

MR. DECKER: I depend very much on all my colleagues, but I must have enough technical knowledge to be able to judge whether they are doing right or wrong.

MR. BEST: We have a central research establishment. Controlling scientists is very difficult. One discusses at a quarterly meeting the progress or lack of progress in the various fields that can give us a payoff. One looks at the costs and decides whether to abandon or go on. They have to sell their ideas to me in verbal reports, not written. I have their figures once a month. I ask them why this, why that. Why have your costs risen? How close are you to achieving your objective?

MR. CHISHOLM: Branch operations are our biggest problem, making sure that everything is done right, strictly according to the policies and systems laid down. I have a colleague who concentrates on this. He gets around to the branches frequently.

MR. AUBREY: Having been treasurer before becoming chief, I was forced to be a generalist and to work through people. Those who have a product background tend to want to manage that product instead of managing the company.

MR. AYLWARD: I have 32 extremely competent executives running companies in six divisions. More than 50 per cent of them are former entrepreneurs whose businesses I have bought. I am dealing with a different set of creatures from the usual corporate managers. I prefer dealing with entrepreneurs even though they are stronger people than most salaried executives. Handled properly, they make better executives. They have a fist full of stock in the company and a broad outlook on where the sales and profits come from. They are interested in the whole picture, wanting profits to rise so that their stock rises in value.

26

PHILOSOPHIES OF BUSINESS

What should be the aim of business? Should it be to make better products for the customers, bigger profits for the shareholders, a better living standard for its employees, or what else?

We can all philosophize on this. But the survey asked a specific question on it. Like all the questions in the survey, this one was a surprise, so participants had no time to think out the answers.

Because of the promptness required in replying, some significance is attached to what they said first, and replies have been classified under headings that accord with these first statements.

In view of the different numbers of Americans, Britons and Germans in the survey, the numerical analysis of replies has been weighted to make all three groups equal and the replies are expressed as percentages of the total replies.

Ignoring nationality for a moment, the analysis shows the following overall breakdown:

Thirteen per cent expressed a primary interest in service to their customers.

Eighteen per cent expressed a general philosophic interest in the betterment of mankind.

Eight per cent expressed a primary interest in growth of the business.

Four per cent showed interest in increasing the wealth of their country.

Two per cent were primarily concerned with achieving greater sales.

These together make up 45 per cent who were primarily interested in causes other than the shareholders' personal gains or their own personal aspirations.

Twenty-three per cent were primarily interested in increasing profits.

Thirteen per cent wanted to earn their shareholders a better return on their money.

These together make up 36 per cent who were primarily interested in the firm's profits and the shareholders' return.

Nine per cent put first their own job satisfaction.

Eight per cent put first their own personal success.

These together make up 17 per cent who showed primary interest in themselves.

Finally, one per cent showed primary interest in the security of the firm. As every chief executive and everyone who has ever run his own business knows, this question of security is always at the back of his mind. It is easy to wake in the night and wonder whether everything is locked up properly, whether someone may have been fiddling the till, whether there might be a fire which could ruin the business, lose its customers and put employees out of work.

We all rely so much on the honesty of staff, on the work of the police, fire brigade and insurance companies. The system works on the whole very well, but at the back of the mind is the nagging fear that it might break down. One participant in the survey actually put this matter of security first.

Table 26.1 shows the analysis of primary interest of participants broken down by subject and also by nationality of participant.

Table 26.1

BUSINESS AIMS—FIRST INTEREST EXPRESSED

		National	Sub-total
		%	%
Service to customers	American	10	
	British	1	
	German	2	
			13
General service towards mankind	American	4	
	British	4	
	German	10	
			18
Growth of the business	American	4	
	British	2	
	German	2	
			8
Increased national prosperity	American	0	
	British	2	
	German	2	
			4
Greater sales	American	0	
	British	0	
	German	2	
			2
Greater profits	American	7	
	British	9	
	German	7	
			23
Greater return for shareholders	American	7	
	British	6	
	German	0	
			13
Personal job satisfaction	American	0	
	British	4	
	German	5	
			9
Personal success	American	1	
	British	5	
	German	2	
			8
Security of the firm	American	0	
	British	1	
	German	0	
			1

Are there any real differences in national attitude towards the aims of business?

The survey revealed considerable difference between the Americans and Germans on the one hand, and the British on the other. As Table 26.2 shows, when primary interests are grouped according to whether they are concerned with more idealistic or more self-centred factors, it is seen that the Americans and Germans are far more philosophic and service-oriented than the British.

Table 26.2

BUSINESS AIMS—MAJOR GROUPINGS OF FIRST INTEREST EXPRESSED

		%
Interested in more philosophic and service-oriented causes	American	18
	British	9
	German	18
		45
Interested in the firm's profits and its shareholders	American	14
	British	15
	German	7
		36
Interested in personal career satisfactions	American	1
	British	9
	German	7
		17
Interested in firm's security	American	0
	British	1
	German	0
		1

It becomes clear that in the survey twice as many Americans and twice as many Germans took a service-oriented view of business aims, as did British. The obverse of this is seen in that more British were interested in the firm's profits or in the cause of its shareholders or in their own career satisfactions.

This difference could be at least partly accounted for by the greater tax burden on British profits and incomes up to the time of the survey, but when I mentioned this difference to the chief executive of an American oil company, MR. ALEXANDER, who had just given me a particularly well-stated, service-oriented view of business aims, he expressed no surprise and offered his own explanation. He thought the reason could be found in recent political history. He was speaking in the late summer of 1970: 'You say that you find businessmen more social conscious in Germany and the United States than in Britain. This I have a theory about. In the United Kingdom the Government itself has assumed the goals of social purpose and environmental progress. Therefore the businessman has only economic progress to talk about and concern himself with. Here he must concern himself with all three.'

So there is a numerical difference in the types of aims for business expressed in Britain, America and Germany. But is there a qualitative difference in the way the aims are expressed?

The reader must judge this for himself. The following quotations are analysed in the same way as Table 26.1, and they are selected on the basis of presenting maximum variety of view, eliminating repetitive statements.

SERVICE TO CUSTOMERS—13 PER CENT

MR. ASPINALL: Firstly, to survive a business must fill a need. It must do something for people, making products or services which they want. Secondly, it must be profit orientated. We have 500,000 shareholders and one can't overlook the fact that we must provide a return on the capital invested by this multitude of people. Thirdly, businesses and their staffs must be both good corporate citizens and good industrial citizens. What business does is important to world health, and businesses are in a unique position in their ability to make tremendous contributions to progress, not only technical but sociological progress, both in the way they behave in a community and choose their sites, and in what they contribute towards social welfare. Experience tells us that Government officials are understandably dependent on business for help—for example, the equal employment programme. They can legislate, but the people who have to do this job are the businessmen.

MR. ASHFIELD: Successful business is business in service to mankind. For commercial products, this is obvious, since people pay for what they get. But we also do military products, believing that peace is based on a foundation of strength. We have world markets, but we always sell abroad through the U.S. Government, who make the contract with the other Government and we make a contract with our Government.

MR. COCHRANE: In retail one must maintain absolute cleanliness, keep introducing new lines of products, have nothing a luxury, that is make everything possible for the ordinary housewife to buy, and make things exciting to buy.

MR. DANNEWALD: My aim is to find the most efficient way to sell insurance (my product) to the people.

MR. ARTHUR: Our aim must be to play a useful role in the society that we have in this country, where the basic concept is that free men gather together or sometimes singly in a profession, but usually together, to pool their monies and talents through corporate organization. It is mostly a shareholder pooling, because under our corporate system, management have relatively few shares. The objective is to account for ourselves creditably by providing services and products for the public at large, and to do it in such a way that firstly, it is efficient according to the standards of the day, and secondly, the public like us and buy from us. The result of all this, because my firm is highly computerized, is totalized in a single figure every 90 days, and hopefully this profit figure, which is the yardstick of our performance and our contribution to society, is not gained at the expense of society. It is the determinant of whether we are going to be allowed to go on contributing.

MR. BRADLEY: My first aim is to give service to our customers and thereby make a profit. Secondly, having made the profit, I must use it for three purposes—for the development of the company, to give a return on capital to the shareholders, and give extra reward to the staff above the wage level I've got to pay in order to hire them.

MR. ACLAND: Business is a form of social intercourse, the basic purpose being to supply the wants of people—in our system with the additional stimulus of the profit motive, in other societies perhaps more altruistic.

GENERAL SERVICE TOWARDS MANKIND—18 PER CENT

MR. DECKER: The aim must be to create wealth in general, not my wealth in particular, and to try to give all the people the possibility to develop their personalities, to see a sense of purpose in life and find satisfaction. Profit is only a part of the story.

MR. CONSTABLE: I want material success gained in a happy and exciting environment—for everybody—not just for the chief executive. Atmosphere and environment are vital, one needs them to gain material success.

MR. DILLMANN: I learnt from my grandfather that one is responsible for all the people here, and I have to see that this company gives work and a good living to all the people. I don't like the idea of maximizing profit. Optimum profit is a much better word.

MR. ARROWSMITH: We must do the greatest good for the greatest number—for the owners, the employees and the community.

MR. BANFIELD: Create wealth. If it is properly used, it must be of benefit to the community as a whole.

MR. ALEXANDER: This is not a military or an intellectual country, but a country dominated by business leadership. If business is to deserve that leadership, it has to accomplish the goals people want. They want considerably more than profits per share. They, that is all of us want economic progress, also social progress—to get rid of the ghettos and the poverty, get the best education and adequate medical help, etc. But thirdly, we want environmental goals—to stop the erosion of our cities and not destroy our outside environment.

In the past the economic goal of business has been sufficient, and the businessman didn't care about the other things provided he made economic progress. He must now make decisions on the basis of a three-legged stool. But he must work with the Government because he cannot individually, for competitive reasons, make some of the decisions on his own. He must help the Government to set the rules right.

For example, on the Delaware River there are ten oil refineries, and only one is ours. If we spend a lot of money in getting rid of pollution caused by the refinery, our costs would rise so much that we could not compete. The community of Philadelphia must set the rules and we must help them and work with those who want them set right, so that all the refineries have to get rid of pollution.

MR. DEMMLER: I am a member of Rotary International. My ideals are firstly, youth exchange internationally, and secondly, business mergers on an international basis.

MR. ADAMS: We must aim to stimulate people to think better and put their thinking into action.

MR. DAHLMANN: A big combine is as complex as a human being. One cannot define in one sentence its aim and final purpose. It certainly is not profit. Profit is the result, not the aim. A company has to be profitable to be healthy, but health is not the aim in life of a company, any more than it is of man.

GROWTH OF THE BUSINESS—8 PER CENT

MR. BELLAMY: The purpose of business is growth, embracing profit on a continuing basis. Anyone can run up the profit for a year or two, but you must get it on a continuing basis. The purpose is not to make chocolates or any other product. Nobody is in business to make a particular product. The customers may change their requirements and you have to go with them.

MR. DODEN: We want an expanding business on a solid basis. I am not interested in just doing business from moment to moment.

MR. ASCOT: The fundamental objective is to grow. A company which stands still and is satisfied, is not going to be here for long. Twentieth century corporate investment is based on growth, but the best type of growth is steady.

MR. ANTHONY: We are trying to achieve growth and profitability, each of them continuously and in balance. One can grow quickly at the expense of the short term, and one can make extra large profits at the expense of long-term growth. We must balance. Moreover, there must be market compatibility of products. Because we are in electronics we could now, for example, produce a television set. But we are not a consumer marketing corporation, at least not yet. It would be ridiculous to produce a television set without the marketing capability.

MR. ABBOTT: We are trying to preserve and increase the assets. Unless capital is produced, the Western World can't live. We must aim for the greater utilization of machines, releasing people to do other work and create more assets. For example, with computerisation, the products of a manufacturing firm can go straight into containers and move off in the general directions required and be diverted to specific destinations as required, remaining in the containers which are in effect their warehouse, until required. Under the old system a box car was in motion only 27 hours a month and a vessel was in port for 50 per cent of its time. Goods had to make their laborious journeys and then be warehoused and sorted and redirected. There was no way to re-direct them *en route*. It is now possible to have a through bill of lading, and the original receipt for the goods becomes a financial instrument on which money can be borrowed, as well as a delivery note for the buyer.

INCREASED NATIONAL PROSPERITY—4 PER CENT

MR. BOWLES: My aim is to create something of value. I want this country, which is my home, to be one of the pharmaceutical hearts of the world. If I achieve this, the shareholders of the company will be well satisfied, but I don't start from the shareholders. It takes 10 years to develop a new product now, we have to look way ahead.

MR. DAUTZENBERG: I want to contribute as much as possible to the general economic growth of the company, with the hope that the country's economy grows rapidly.

MR. BAKER: In each country where we operate, I want to serve that country and raise its standard of living. The best form of aid is to put a man in a position where he doesn't need it. The best help from London is to encourage the local management to make their own decisions.

MR. CLIFFORD: To answer what business is about, you have got to ask what will a man do with his success, in money terms? His aim must surely be to use less of the nation's wealth to do his own job. If, for example, you take over a business and it has an overdraft of £10 million, and if you can then run it with no overdraft, you are doing a better job for the community. Basically, what are you doing with every £100 that is entrusted to you? That is what business is all about.

GREATER SALES—2 PER CENT

MR. DENYER: We must aim for better sales results and hence growing business for our concessionaires, so that they can protect their independence, get better production facilities, train their staff better, improve their marketing and their E.D.P. facilities.

GREATER PROFITS—23 PER CENT

MR. COLE: This is a question of responsibility. Without profits there is no future. To get profits you must have the right product in the right place at the right time, be very marketing oriented.

MR. ATTFIELD: One must make a profit, for it is from profits that are generated the funds for research and development, good industrial relations, community service and so forth.

MR. DOBLER: The main job is not to save costs but to make money. One must earn instead of saving money.

MR. BOYD: Unless you maximize profits, you don't get the money, the competition tramps on and you disappear.

MR. ATTWATER: Profit is a score card saying whether you are doing a good job or not—over a period of time, not taking short-term advantage. How do you achieve this? You make sure you are creating something that society needs and has to use.

MR. COOPER: The capital of tomorrow comes from the profit of today.

MR. ARGENT: In our system, everything is pointed towards making a profit. But business has responsibilities to a number of publics—the shareholders, the employees, the community, the country and the world.

MR. BIGGS: Whilst making money is at the back of your mind, you never start off with it. Unless you can give your shareholders a better return than if they had invested in bonds, you are in trouble, but there is a lot more to it than this. Working with people and satisfying customers. You have got to sell them something as good as or better than your competitors.

MR. BLOOMFIELD: Make a profit. That's what I'm here for. My group has made that quite clear.

GREATER RETURN FOR SHAREHOLDERS—13 PER CENT

MR. AYLWARD: I put the shareholders first because they have no protection at all except to remove me, which would be a very drastic step. They do not have any say in the decisions of the corporation, while the employees do.

MR. BOND: The chief executive has three personal responsibilities, all equally important. First, to the shareholders for the servicing of their capital; second to the employees of the group to see that they are rewarded properly and pensioned properly: then third to the customers; unless they are fairly and squarely dealt with, it won't be long before the business begins to go down hill. But this applies equally to each of the three groups.

MR. ARNOLD: The chief executive is responsible for effective long range use of stockholder's equity.

MR. ATWICK: Our aim is to protect and improve the fortunes of our investors. To do that we have to put together the most competitive team.

Who sits in judgement?

MR. AYLWARD: I talk a lot to outsiders, explaining the company's progress and problems, particularly to security analysts and investment fund people.

MR. AUSTIN: My object is to make money—particularly as we are a publicly-held company. Because of our public market, I have to receive quite a few people in the office such as financial analysts who want to know why the share price is going up or down.

MR. BOWLES: There is a special tenseness about running a growth business. We have grown year after year, but how do you keep that up? The stock market is very harsh. If you grow, the market expects you to go on growing, and the moment you hesitate, they slaughter your share price.

MR. BLACK: The great objective is to secure an adequate return on the capital employed. It is the besetting sin of my industry that we have not been doing this.

MR. ARCHER: Every quarter I compare with the same quarter a year ago, in order to report to the security analysts. I keep all the relevant figures handy in case I'm asked a question. The security analysts are now replacing God. Wall Street is so sensitive and the analysts always watch the cycle in this industry.

Who, indeed, sits in judgement on the chief executive? Is God a security analyst?

PERSONAL JOB SATISFACTION—9 PER CENT

MR. DEDERICHS: I am not working to earn money or I would have stopped in lower positions. I like the job. The scope for using money is limited when you are working so furiously.

MR. BOSWORTH: Personal fulfilment in business is measured, in our society, by profit. But if I didn't like what I was doing, I wouldn't do it.

MR. BECKETT: I like the combination of dealing with people, wrestling with problems, having a measurable objective and the freedom to be able to follow whatever one thinks is a profitable line to follow. Though the customer decides it is profitable, if you do the job well the customer will make it profitable for you. It is not a confidence trick by which you sell bad merchandise. The customers are the ultimate test of whether you are doing a good job.

MR. DOEBEL: My job is my life. I have no particular working hours. I just go on and on. My aim is to specialize in certain top advertising problems where I can have more influence on the economy, concentrate on the more important firms in Germany and Europe. But I am not trying to impose any ethical ideas. I merely want to solve the problems of my customers, not try to educate them.

MR. CHILDS: One thing I am clear about is that I am not really in business for the money. The amount of free time we have had since we set this up, we couldn't have spent much money anyway. I want an interest in life, I have to be doing something. This work is worthwhile because it is connected with children. And there is always something new. I get great fun out of it. Also it involves world-wide travel. This suits my temperament. I am fairly quickly bored.

When I talk about doing something for children, I don't mean to be terribly noble about it. I don't feel like a saviour. In fact to cater successfully for children one has got to be one step away from them and take a commercial view, rather than get emotionally involved. This of course rubs off on my own children, who are far more sophisticated than they would otherwise be at their age. I remember taking home one night a new product which was a set of gloves which glowed in the dark if you put them under light first. I went into the bathroom and held them under the strip-lighting. The two boys were already in bed and the room was dark. I put the gloves round the corner of the door and made some funny squiggles with my hands. My six-year-old son, instead of saying 'Oh, how funny' or shrieking with delight, asked me: 'Are they non-toxic?'

PERSONAL SUCCESS—8 PER CENT

MR. BAINBRIDGE: I was brought up to business and I want to be successful and do something I believe in. But I couldn't succeed in anything I didn't like.

MR. DACKWEILER: Business is judged primarily by success. One aims to improve and promote the image of the firm outside to the public and in the market, as a progressive and dynamic and social-minded company and management.

MR. ATKINSON: I have always been a person who likes to win. I grew up trying to be a winner. I was a football player and a leader—that is, a quarter-back. One of the reasons for being in business is trying to achieve the goals I set myself. But I must enjoy the job. I like people, being with them and doing things for them. If I can develop a company, the rewards will be not only mine but for the people in the company.

MR. BAXTER: Eighteen months ago I was assistant managing

director of a big firm and left it to come here to a smaller company in a risky situation. But life before was not what I wanted. I wanted to live in the country, to be number one and to be successful.

MR. CHESHIRE: First, one wants a higher standard of living for oneself. When satisfied to a reasonable degree, one works on because of an obligation to employees and families and shareholders. I cannot now by work improve my standard of living, but I still have a sense of achievement.

MR. CHRISTIE: You must make a lot of money to fulfil the other desires. So making money is primary. In addition, there is the sheer enjoyment of doing a thing and doing it very well. We try to have no grey areas. We try to make it always black or white. Engineering is a compromise anyway, but we must go as close as possible to black and white situations.

MR. CHAMBERS: I came out of big business, with its lack of personal effort. Now I enjoy the challenge of building up a small business, which everybody says is impossible these days.

MR. CHADWICK: I like independence. Success buys me the time to do the things I want to do. I don't like doing anything unless I do it well.

MR. CAVELL: In the thirties, I knew what it was like not to have a job. So I have a special incentive to make money, in case of mishap. There is still the fear at the back of my mind that it could happen again. In spite of having over a million pounds, I still fear losing it. I never waste money. I eat in a self-service cafe if I'm on my own.

SECURITY OF THE FIRM—1 PER CENT

MR. BLUNDELL: One must ensure that the company is secure in all its activities, one must be expanding if at all possible and earning returns for the stockholders that are appropriate and encouraging. The profits in heavy engineering must be large enough to put enough by for reserves to ensure the continuity and development of the business. In heavy engineering this is a very substantial sum.

To conclude this survey of Philosophies of Business, I turn to MR. ATTWOOD, who gives a broader view of security, in terms of the capacity for independent survival. I believe that human freedom and dignity depend very considerably on the capacity of organizations, including business firms, to survive independently of central power. This is what MR. ATTWOOD has to say:

'In a free enterprise system the first objective is to be self perpetuating, and that means the firm must be profitable. But you need a lot more than profit to be self perpetuating. You need standards, philosophies, attitudes to your place in the market and your responsibilities to society, and you need a real concern for and interest in the people who make up the business—their motivations and desires.'

27

SUMMARY AND CONCLUSIONS

Summary of main points

Chapters 1 and 2. Interviews were held with 103 American, British and German chief executives, including those held during the pilot stage of preparing the questionnaire. The object was to look for differences in management techniques between the chief executives of fast and slow growing firms. Because the British economy is slow growing compared with the American and German economies, it was intended to see if the management techniques of the Americans and Germans were superior to those of the British. Some 30 questions were asked in interview, heavily concentrated on specific methods of planning, organizing and controlling business operations.

The surprise result of the survey was that there were no apparent, significant differences in management techniques among the nations or between fast and slow growing firms, but that share ownership by the chief executive appeared to exercise a great influence on company performance and growth.

Because it was not possible for my contacts in America and Germany to spend the same amount of time and attention on selecting fast-growth firms as I had spent in Britain, my sample of fast-growth British firms proved to have a superior growth rate to those of the American and German samples, though of course the British economy has the slowest growth record amongst these three nations.

Closer analysis, however, showed that the really fast growers, almost without exception, were the firms run by founder-owners, the 'original capitalists'. This applied in America and Germany, where there was not the same opportunity for close selection, as well as in Britain.

Analyses of age and education of the chief executive, and of the size of firm, offered nothing of significance to explain differences in growth rates. The overwhelming factor was original share ownership.

Chapter 3. Whereas the popular image of a chief executive is that of a dashing extrovert, in fact just over half those in the survey admitted to being introvert. Because of the awkwardness of this type of question, the real proportion of introverts may have been higher. However, the introverts who rise to the top of the business world learn to develop some of the behaviour patterns of extroversion. They learn to put on a bold face.

A follow-up question was asked on the relative importance of being (*a*) deep thinking and conceptual about long-term problems; and (*b*) observant and quickly responsive to immediate situations. Some 20 per cent said it was more important to be conceptual and another 20 per cent said it was more important to be responsive, and they illustrated their answers with particular business situations where these respective skills were of special significance. However, the most significant result was that 60 per cent emphasized the importance of being both conceptual and responsive.

So our first broad conclusion on the characteristics of chief executives is that a majority of those who reach this position of leadership exhibit characteristics of both introversion and extroversion, and they recognize the importance of exercising both conceptual and responsive skills.

Chapter 4. It was possible to classify from the survey no less than 21 ways in which chief executives keep up to date, 10 of these relating to sources of information internal to the firm, and 11 relating to external sources.

With regard to management training, the survey showed a clear distinction between the non-owning chief executives who believed in it, sent their staff on courses and attended some courses themselves, and the original capitalists who were self-taught, but had the fastest growth rates and clearest product policies, employed the latest management techniques and computer systems, etc. A superficial conclusion might be that management training for those at the top or destined for the top is a waste of time. To abolish it would, however, put everybody in the wasteful position of having to 're-invent the wheel' for himself. A more reasonable conclusion is that good management training is very useful but that its value can be reinforced by the experience and motivation of share ownership and by the opportunity to take on the responsibilities of general management at a reasonably young age, however small the unit of business.

Chapter 5. The average age at which the chief executives in the survey had acquired knowledge of historic accounting was 28, and the average for knowledge of budgeting was 35. The Germans on average acquired such types of knowledge slightly earlier than the Americans, who were earlier than the Britons. Of possibly greater significance is the fact that the fast-growth Britons acquired it several years earlier than the slow-growth Britons.

These average figures, however, cloak a wide range of ages at which individual chief executives acquired accounting and budgeting knowledge, and the main reason for the large range appears to be that most of the chief executives did not acquire accounting and budgeting knowledge until a specific job opportunity or experience, (which they described), made it necessary. Then they set to and learnt it, in some cases on their own.

A general conclusion from this section of the survey is that budgeting falls naturally into line with the thinking of a businessman who is planning ahead for his business, whereas historic accounting does not. Nevertheless, the double entry principles of historic accounting need also to be understood by a business leader—though not the detailed professional practices. The balance sheet is a discipline for ensuring that no items of debit or credit are overlooked, and in planning ahead a chief executive needs to retain a continuing mental picture, in rough approximations, of all the commitments made, both by the firm and to it.

Chapters 6, 7, 8, 9 and 10. Chief executives were asked to describe the ages and circumstances in which they acquired confidence in their possession of four different types of skill, considered to be particularly important in top management—Numerical skill, System skill, Social skill and Policy-forming skill. (The statistical significance of age figures in this section of the study is limited by the fact that this was primarily an interview survey and the total population studied was only 103.)

Numerical skill in this context was taken to mean not merely skill at simple arithmetic, but also including a sense of the economic value of goods and services and an ability to do those quick calculations and make those quick interpretations of a set of figures which mark out the self-informed, numerate decision maker from the person who relies on hunch or simply endorses 'expert opinion' from below.

The average age revealed by the survey for acquiring numerical skill was 26, but the Americans had an average of 25, the British 26 and the Germans 29. Of greater significance, however, was the fact that amongst the large British sample, the super-fast and fast-growing original capitalists had an average age of 20, the non-owning fast growers had an average of 25 and the non-owning slow growers had an average of 28.

System skill was taken to mean skill at delegating specific, detailed tasks concerned with the routine essential functions of a business such as order processing and fulfilment, payment terms, credit and collection terms, accounting and statistics. The average age of acquiring this skill was 29, but it was 28 for the Americans, 29 for the Germans and 30 for the British. Again, looking at the large British sample, it was 27 for the super-fast and fast growing original capitalists, 28 for the non-owning fast growers and 33 for the non-owning slow growers.

Social skill in this context was taken to mean the ability

directly used in getting things done through a significant number of other people. 'Significant' means not just one or two assistants, but a minimum of three or more employees. The average age of acquiring social skill was 24. For the Americans it was 23, for the British and Germans it was 25. Looking at the large British sample, it was 23 for the super-fast and fast-growing original capitalists, 25 for the non-owning fast growers and 24 for the non-owning slow growers. In this case we see that the slow growers had developed social skill almost as quickly as the fast growers. No doubt they needed to. It takes quite a personality to be non-owning chief executive of a company with an unsatisfactory performance, and to justify one's continued survival to stockholders and employees.

As a follow-up to the questions on the social skills involved in employing people, a question was asked on negotiating skill, which was taken to mean the skill required to make a successful agreement with a free and independent person not in a subordinate role. Evidence was collected and presented, with illustrations, on how this skill is exercised, but no figures were obtained.

Policy-forming skill was taken to include decision-making skill but also the creative ability to shape up ideas for products, their sale and distribution, so that the business has a worthwhile flow of sales to customers at worthwhile prices.

The average age of developing this skill was 32, and virtually identical for Americans, Britons and Germans. In the large British sample, however, the super-fast and fast growing original capitalists had an average of 28, the non-owning fast growers had an average of 32 and the non-owning slow growers had an average of 36.

As with all the skills analysed in the survey, these averages cloak a wide range of actual ages and circumstances in which individual chief executives developed their individual skills. Chapter 10 on policy-forming skill contains some of the most important evidence of the survey, contributed to by the experience of every type of chief executive. But the original capitalists tend to dominate the chapter by making far more than their share of the most significant contributions. This chapter was drafted in its present form before the analysis of all participants in the survey revealed how the original capitalists dominated the growth rate tables.

Chapter 11. From the mass of evidence on different criteria for choosing a company's most suitable organization structure, a new principle of organization was evolved based on observation of how the original capitalists in the survey have grown so fast, so successfully. This is the Principle of the Span of Effective Rapport. This says that the chief executive of a business should not be responsible for an organization larger than that in which he can have effective rapport with all who report to him. Effective rapport involves not merely getting on well with a subordinate but working closely enough and often enough with him to have master-minded his job and have such a level of understanding that if the boss is away the subordinate acts in the same ways as the boss would have acted. The Principle of the Span of Effective Rapport recognizes the different requirements for master-minding subordinate jobs in holding companies and in operating companies. Hence it allows for a logical build-up of unit operating and holding companies, each with its chief executive, to make a group structure of any required size.

Chapter 12. From the mass of evidence presented on the frequency and types of top management meeting systems used by the chief executives in the survey, a guide table is presented (Table 12.3) showing nine activities for which meetings need to be held, and in each case for both holding and operating companies the most likely frequency of meeting required is given, also the types of executives probably needed at the meeting, and the forms of information likely to be presented and discussed. This table was developed in keeping with the Principle of the Span of Effective Rapport.

Chapter 13. In the survey it was rare to find a chief executive who claimed virtual infallibility in selection of staff for promotion to senior management positions. A considerable volume of evidence is presented, however, on how participants in the survey try to improve their score of success, and on how readily they try to recognize a failure and make a quick change.

Guidance is also given on how a chief executive can get to know those who are two or more steps below him without being unfair to his immediate subordinates, and how a new chief coming in from outside can speed up the process of getting to know his new team. Finally, the most thorough methods of staff rating and evaluation, used by chief executives in the survey, are described in some detail. Evidence is also given on preparing for the chief executive succession.

Chapter 14. The logic is presented of why the primary measure of business performance must be the return on capital employed, and why the system of operating reports received by a chief executive, their frequency and type, must be derived from a disciplined analysis, in a style given in this chapter, of each item in the income statement or profit and loss account and each item in the balance sheet. Evidence is given from the survey on the frequency with which each type of operating information, e.g. sales, profits, detailed analysis of costs, capital employed, etc. is presented to the chief executives in the survey. Illustrations are given of the best type of operating reports seen in the survey. Finally, the logic is presented as to why the process of budgeting should be carried right through to the pro-forma balance sheet.

Chapter 15. The majority of chief executives in the survey do not have key control figures or ratios which sum up in a nutshell the success or failure of operations in their type of business. For the most part such conventional measures as sales, profits and cash are looked for most frequently. However, evidence is presented on some types of ingenious special indicators that are used in a minority of cases, and there is also evidence on what chief executives would ask about if they phoned the office while on holiday.

Chapter 16. Overall, 73 per cent of the chief executives who were asked if they used charts, said they did, and 27 per cent said they did not. Pungent evidence is presented by the non-users as to why they are satisfied with figures and think charts misleading, but a greater volume of evidence is presented on the advantages of using charts and how they are effectively used in practice.

Chapter 17. An analysis is made of the practices of chief executives in planning and budgeting for the future activities of the business, both for operating revenue and expenditure and for capital expenditure. Criteria are presented for judging and approving capital expenditure, and for subsequent checking on results.

Chapters 18, 19. From the survey it has been possible to analyse and describe the methods used by chief executives to watch over and control staff overheads—or in other words, to come to grips with Parkinson's Law. Evidence is also presented on the different systems used by firms for organizing purchases, budgeting and controlling them. Figures are given on the relative frequency of use of different systems of organization, including those situations where the chief executive himself plays a direct part in purchasing.

Chapter 20. The survey revealed great national differences in the use of cash bonus and share incentive schemes. Whereas only 45 per cent of the British chief executives had cash bonus systems, and these often paid out only 3 per cent to 5 per cent of basic pay—rarely above 12½ to 25 per cent, by contrast 82 per cent of the Americans had cash bonuses and these were more typically 20 per cent to 30 per cent of salary, sometimes much more. All the Germans had cash bonuses and these were rarely less than 25 per cent to 50 per cent of salary, but they ranged up to five times basic salary.

The position with share incentive schemes is different. All the Americans had stock options, 35 per cent of the Britons had recently installed share incentive schemes of one kind or another, and only one of the Germans, whose company happens to have American affiliations, had stock options.

In the light of the success of the original capitalists, the case is presented forthrightly as to why the chief executive and other senior managers of a business should be enabled to become part owners of the business—so that they see the business with 'the owner's eye'. Evidence is also given as to why they should be able to see the business in this way even when their shareholding is only a small percentage of the total.

Chapters 21, 22, 23. The average proportion of their office hours spent by the chief executives in the survey, in meeting with and directly contacting others, is 74 per cent. Evidence is presented on how the participants avoid unnecessary paperwork and concentrate much of their time on gathering information, as a background for decision-making which sometimes has to be fast because events will not wait, and in other cases should be held off until the situation matures.

From the evidence of how much time is spent contacting and meeting with other people, it is concluded that the conventional type of executive desk, which is really only a superior version of a clerk's desk, is most unsuitable for the chief executive. He needs a special design of meeting table, and the best design seen in the survey is presented and described.

Some chief executives have to keep certain key files on special customers, operating reports, standard procedures, etc., ready to hand. Others can pass everything out to their secretary or an assistant or colleague for filing. The reasons why some must file and others not, are given with examples, and an outline design is presented of the best type of chief executive filing cabinet seen in the survey—vastly different from conventional filing cabinets.

Chapters 24, 25, 26. Some 15 per cent of the chief executives in the survey seem to be primarily motivated by enjoyment of their work. Next in order of importance amongst the motivators mentioned were a desire to prove himself, an urge to create something new, and a striving for perfection. These together make up almost half the primary explanations of personal motivation. Only after these comes the desire for more money. It must, however, be noted that chief executives have already arrived at the top and except in some cases in Britain, those included in the survey were certainly not short of money.

The type of personal quality they considered most important in their position was the ability to handle and motivate people. This received a primary score of 44 per cent. Next came analytical skill and creativity, with a score of 27 per cent, and after this came personal drive, determination and stamina, with 13 per cent. Following on was knowledge of the business or trade, with 9 per cent.

The greatest single aim for business, mentioned in the survey, was the achievement of higher profits. This received a score of 23 per cent. Closely allied to it was a greater return for shareholders, with 13 per cent, then in the same category came personal job satisfaction with 9 per cent and personal success with 8 per cent. These four categories of aims together make up 54 per cent, of which 36 per cent is centred on the firm and 18 per cent centred on the individual. These totals must be compared with 45 per cent who ascribed more philosophic and service-oriented aims to business, such as service to the customers at 13 per cent, general service to mankind at 18 per cent and growth of the business at 8 per cent. The Americans and Germans on the whole took a more philosophic and service-oriented view of business aims than did the British. But then they were better off, except in the case of the original capitalists.

Conclusions

The surprise results of this survey were:

(*a*) the vastly superior growth rates of the original capitalists;

(*b*) their generally clearer understanding of their business policies;

(*c*) their earlier, and from the circumstantial evidence, possibly superior grasp of some of the basic numerical and system skills needed for success in business, while at the same time not being short on social skills.

(*d*) their early, and mostly untrained grasp of the significance of capital and the role it plays in a free economic society, and of the responsibilities attaching thereto.

Here we face a 'chicken and egg' problem. Which came first, the outstanding men who decided to set up in business on their own, and were then very successful, or the moderately good men who because they set up on their own and felt the impact of ownership, developed their talents to the full and were outstandingly successful?

There are plenty of owners of businesses who are not successful. Ownership by itself clearly bestows no automatic touch of superior powers. But this survey raises two key questions:

(*a*) is there some combination of ownership, managerial ability and business experience at the general management level which is most likely to create a 'take off' situation, where policies for serving specific types of customers become more clear-cut, where the implications of spending capital in anticipation of customer demands become more precise, where the inspiration to lead a business in pursuit of a specific type of service to customers grows and grows, creating stronger executive drive and greater creative energy, keener attention to the detail of organization and closer rapport with subordinates, so that the system feeds on its own success and there develops a dramatic surge of business activity, serving far more customers and creating far more capital than in the average case?

(*b*) If there is such a 'take off' process, can we simulate it or imitate it or encourage it by bringing together the right combinations of capital ownership, management training and business experience at the general management level, to create a more permanent and reliable source of economic growth and regeneration?

Such questions can only be proposed, not answered here. The evidence so far is quite inadequate. But I can at least conclude this study with a list of propositions which I believe should be considered if answers are to be sought:

1. Business activity is in sheer volume the greatest form of human social activity, and it can make its own unique contribution to a free and democratic society in the way it offers choice of goods and services to its customers, and choice of employment.

2. By and large, choice can only be provided if business firms can survive independently of one another and of central authority, and can produce in anticipation of customer demand, creating facilities for production and service in anticipation of demand.

3. Capital is the amount of money committed in anticipation of customer demand, up to the point where revenue from sales at least equals expenditure.

4. Capital is therefore a measure of the responsibility of a chief executive for ensuring the success of any project entered into, in anticipation of demand.

5. Return on capital employed is the primary yardstick for judging the success of a chief executive in fulfilling his responsibilities—provided of course that he is acting in accordance with the standards and requirements of law.

6. Because those who supply capital to a business expect a return on it, the capital value of any continuing business activity is often measured by taking a multiple of the current net income of the activity, after meeting all expenses.

7. A chief executive who brings in an increasing net income on his business activity is judged as being in charge of an increasingly valuable business, and hence worthy of confidence if he should require more capital to finance further business activity.

8. Because we have an atomized society in which people specialize in particular jobs, and firms specialize in particular products or services, each serving a range of customers and in turn being

dependent on many others to supply most of their wants, it follows that human satisfaction in work must come to a substantial extent from serving others and achieving self-fulfilment through such service.

9. The primary measure of successful service by a firm to its customers is its capital value, as estimated from its current net income. Hence the measurements of service and responsibility are closely allied, for in the case of any new or modified product or service, meeting changing customer needs, the total capital expenditure on it is a measure of the chief executive's responsibility for its successful fulfilment.

10. Capital ownership can be and often is divorced from executive responsibility, both in the 'capitalist' countries where outside shareholders may own most of the capital of a business, and in 'communist' countries where the government or some allied authority may own the capital of business. But there is a prima facie case for saying that when some degree of business capital ownership is put into the hands of those with executive responsibility, this is conducive to the execution of more efficient, faster growing business activity, more responsive to the changing needs of its customers and therefore more in keeping with human aspirations of liberty and the democratic process.

11. Whilst the most dramatic evidence of effective alignment of ownership interests with executive responsibilities is seen in the case of the successful original capitalists, who usually began as sole owners or majority owners of their business, my experience of working with the Greenewalt concept (see Chapter 20) in installing share incentive schemes, suggests that executive aspirations for share ownership are typically more modest. They are related more to the individual's salary position than to the percentage of total common stock or ordinary shares available for purchase.

12. The aspirations of a chief executive and his immediate colleagues can in the vast majority of cases be met within 5 per cent of the total common stock or ordinary share capital of a business.

This leaves 95 per cent in the hands of the existing shareholders, who in capitalist countries will be predominantly:

(*a*) insurance companies and pension funds on behalf of their policy holders;
(*b*) a range of small and large individual shareholders:
(*c*) financial organizations;
(*d*) other business firms; and
(*e*) governments and co-operatives.

It is significant that, whilst a major shift in the composition of ownership of a majority of business corporations in any country could alter its political character—and this is too big a subject to debate here—the type of ownership in any one particular business is not necessarily relevant to the problem of meeting executive aspirations for share ownership. Indeed, experience tells me that a very wide range of business firms—as to size, industry and type of ownership—have no difficulty in this matter.

PROBLEM-SOLVING INDEX

Problem *Page References*

APPENDIX A

QUESTIONNAIRE USED IN THE SURVEY

Strictly Confidential

1.

CHIEF EXECUTIVE INTERVIEWS

Date of Interview ....

Number of Interview ....

Name ....

Position ....

Company ....

Address ....

.... Telephone ....

2.

Age and nationality of chief executive

Professional or academic background, including qualifications.

From which main functional background (e.g. finance, marketing, production, technical, personnel) have you emerged into top management?

....

3.

Size of firm (number of employees).

Main products or services

Rate of growth of both trading revenue and taxable profits over the past five years, expressed as an average annual percentage.

Trading revenue .... Taxable profits ....

What do you consider to be an ideal annual growth rate?

....

What are the main current obstacles to faster growth of your firm? ....

4.

What do you think are the three most important qualities a chief executive needs to have, in order to succeed?

1. ....
2. ....
3. ....

5.

What are the biggest personal difficulties you have faced in becoming a successful chief executive? By 'difficulties' I mean 'weaknesses' in ability that you have had to overcome by personal discipline and training or by delegation to someone who could do these things better?

....

....

....

6.

What do you think business is primarily about, in terms of what a chief executive is trying to achieve?

....

....

....

7.

Now let us assume that business is primarily about money, that the money is obtained from satisfied customers in order to make a profit. At what age-level did the Money Game of Business begin to fascinate you?

I became fascinated by the Money Game of Business at (specify period, and if possible more closely the approximate age):

15–19 .... 30–34 ....

20–24 .... 35–39 ....

25–29 .... 40 and over..............

8.

Assume that you cannot be good at the Money Game unless you have numerical skill, doing quickly on paper or in your head those many little calculations which make all the difference to your ability to judge whether a proposal is a good one, or to assess what is wrong with a situation. Would you broadly agree with that statement?

Yes No

How do you rate your numerical skill?

Good Average Below Average

What particular experiences in your background do you recall as having contributed most to the development of your numerical skill?

....

....

....

9.

In determining price, size of output, market, etc. to what extent do you do little calculations yourself? Please explain.

....

....

10.

How would you describe yourself, as more inclined to introversion or more inclined to extroversion?

More introverted More extroverted Neither Don't know

11.

For running a business, which do you think is more important, to be deep-thinking and conceptual, or to be observant and quickly responsive to the immediate situation around you, to the needs of customers, staff, etc.? Please explain your views, illustrating if possible

....

12.

Assume that the best-made business decisions will not be effective unless you are sufficiently systematic in your work to be able to *delegate* clear responsibility to others, *design* a clear information system linking the team together and check regularly on the results of their activities. Would you broadly agree with this statement?

Yes No

How do you rate your personal skill at doing things systematically?

Good Average Below Average

At what age did you realize that you were really coming to grips with the system skills needed in a successful business manager?

I realized I was coming to grips with the system skills needed in business at (specify period, and if possible more closely the approximate age).

15–19	....	30–34	....
20–24	....	35–39	....
25–29	....	40 and above	....

13.

What particular experiences in your background do you recall as having contributed most to your system skills, either to your ability at delegation and job definition, etc, or to your ability at designing a clear information system?

....

Is your company's system described in a Procedures Manual? Yes/No

If yes, who updates it? ....

What is the present system of organization of your firm? (e.g. by specialist function, by product type, by market area, by production process) ....

How do you go about defining the significant centres of interest when you want to up-date your organization structure?

....

14.

Assume that a well-run business system requires a regular pattern of management meetings suited to the type of business, with a proper agenda, that key reports and results need to be ready in time for discussion at these meetings, that information systems need to be designed for providing the facts in time, etc. Would you agree broadly with this statement?

Yes No

What is the present pattern of meetings you hold for running the business?

Please give the type of meeting, its frequency and the nature of pre-circulated reports (e.g. financial and statistical reports on sales, cash, production).

....

....

....

15.

Assume we can define your social skills as your skills in dealing with people and achieving results through them, assessing their needs and responding to them in a way which gets your message across to them. Would you broadly agree with this statement?

Yes No

At what age did you feel you had acquired an adequate level of skill in dealing with people?

15–19	30–34 ....
20–24	35–39 ....
25–29	40 and over..............

16.

How do you rate your social skills? Good/Average/Below Average

What particular experiences in your background do you recall as having contributed most to the development of your social skills? ....

What is your most effective personal means of communication?

....

Which do you think is more important in 'getting across' to people, to make a logical explanation, step by step, or to associate your message with their own needs and interests?

To what extent do you practise Participative Management, and to what extent Directive Management? Please discuss

....

17.

As regards the social skills, observing and responding to people, what is your particular approach to the task of selecting the right people for promotion to senior management positions?

....

What is your particular approach to training (*a*) your immediate senior executives and (*b*) those who are likely to reach such positions in the future?

....

What plans, if any, do you have to cover your own succession?

....

18.

Assume that your business policy-forming skills are made up of the ability to analyse situations and then synthesize realistic concepts of products or services that customers would be willing to buy, at realistic prices. Would you broadly agree with this statement?

Yes No

How do you rate your policy-forming skills?

Good Average Below Average

At what age were you conscious of having developed policy-forming skills to the point where you felt you must exercise them in a position of general management (in contrast to departmental or functional management)? Specify the 5-year period, and if possible more closely the approximate age level.

15–19 .... 30–34 ....
20–24 .... 35–39 ....
25–29 .... 40 and over..............

19.

What particular experiences in your background do you recall as having contributed most to the development of your policy-forming skills? How, for example, have you been able to develop negotiating or bargaining skill, over big contracts, purchases and sales etc.?

....

....

....

20.

What are the particular ways in which you keep up-to-date in your area of business to help you in policy formation?

....

....

21.

What do you think is the main cause of your higher level of achievement motivation than most people?

....

....

....

22.

What are the main ways in which you have acquired management training and development for yourself?

Magazine reading ....

Book reading......................................

Short courses or seminars ....

Longer courses ....

Other (please state) ....

23.

What do you have in the way of cash bonuses, stock options or incentive shares for your key executives?...................

When reviewing the salaries of key men, which is more important, comparison with colleagues or rate of salary growth relative to his personal development and responsibilities? ....

At what stage of his career do you think a high-flying type of executive ought to be rewarded with capital incentives as well as cash bonuses? ....

24.

The Chief Accountant of a business, trained in the double entry method of book-keeping, must think of the business as a set of different accounts, with money and other items being transferred from one to another. This view of the business is important if the chief accountant is to ensure that all the bills are paid, both in and out, that the books add up, that the firm's property is not stolen and that a fair assessment is made of profit or loss, debit or credit.

By contrast, the chief executive of a business must also think of the business as a dynamic enterprise moving forward through time, with financial budgets to meet, with physical capacity and resources to use, and with time schedules to meet. He needs a system of PERFORMANCE COMPARISON for comparing plans and budgets against actual performance.

In Performance Comparison, what specifically do you compare, e.g. present and previous month, a year ago, budget and actual, month and cumulative, moving 12 months, variation from budget, remainder of budget and revised expectations, variation from expectations?

....

Do the figures come straight off a computer? Yes/No

25.

At what age did you become attuned to the balance sheet and other aspects of traditional accounting, for understanding a business?

15–19	30–34 ....
20–24	35–39 ....
25–29	40 and over..............

At what age did you become attuned to budget accounting and other aspects of performance comparison, for understanding a business?

15–19	30–34 ....
20–24	35–39 ....
25–29	40 and over..............

26.

Please explain briefly how you have rationalized your experience of your present business and reached conclusions as to which are the key indicators that in your industry tell you most, at a glance, about the way things are going. Please name these key indicators and how frequently you need to look at them.

....

....

....

Do you use charts for plotting any of these key indicators?

Yes No

If No, how do you become fully aware of trends?

....

27.

How do you specifically keep control of the following?

Capital Expenditure ....

....

Staff Recruitment ....

....

Major purchases of supplies, etc ....

....

28.

Approximately how would you split your average working day, between time spent talking with people and time spent working alone? Give very rough percentages

....

29.

A normal office desk keeps the visitor at a distance on the other side of the desk. Do you have much need to work alongside people, to sit at a table so that your colleagues or staff or visitors can look at the same sets of figures, diagrams, etc. and work on them with you?

....

30.

The key daily, weekly or monthly control figures that come to you; are they in a form which requires you to keep and file them for a fairly long period, for reference, or are they in a form which enables you to throw them away quickly, knowing that the next set will be cumulative and make all the comparisons you need?

Have to keep Can throw away

Author's Note: Readers may have been surprised to find that this questionnaire in some places asks for approximate age levels when a particular activity occurred, five-year groupings being suggested, and yet the analyses of results are given as precise figures. In practice, however, nearly all participants gave their answers in terms of precise ages, because they associated the activities in question with particular events in their careers which they recalled and in many cases related. No participant answered in terms of a five-year spread of years.

APPENDIX B

OVER 200 PRODUCT AND SERVICE AREAS OPERATED IN BY THE FIRMS OF THE 103 CHIEF EXECUTIVES IN THE SURVEY

Addressing and labelling equipment
Adhesives
Advertising services
Aerospace equipment
Aircraft
Airport equipment
Aircraft services
Aluminium
Agro-chemicals
Asbestos products
Automatic machine tools
Automotive products
Airport services

Baby clothes
Batteries
Beer
Beverages
Bicycles
Boats
Bolts and nuts
Books
Box-making machinery
Building
Bread
Bricks
Building materials
Builders' merchants

Computer peripheral equipment
Chemicals
Cigarettes
Canning
Coal mining
Computers
Confectionery
Copper mining
Control engineering
Cakes
Cables
Construction equipment
Containers
Control cables
Construction
Car cleaning
Carpets
Cleaning equipment
Clay pipes
Cheese
Chain stores
Chemicals
Ceramics
Cement
Copying equipment
Cardboard cartons

Dress fabrics
Discount stores

Department stores
Data transmission equipment
Dairy products

Electrical engineering
Earth-moving equipment
Entertainment products
Electric switchgear
Electricity supply
Electrical controls
Engineering contracting
Electronic components
Expendable tools
Electric generators
Electric domestic appliances
Electronic instruments
Electric generating equipment
Electric traction equipment
Electric stabilizers

Furniture
Frozen foods
Fruit retailing
Formica
Freight transport
Foundry equipment
Furnishing
Fire-fighting equipment
Fertilizers
Finance
Fireproof products

Glass containers
Glass bottles
Graphic systems
Groceries
Garden equipment
Gloves
Games

Hosiery
Housing
Horticultural chemicals
Hotels
Heating oil
Houseware
Hospital supplies
Heat exchangers
Household cleaners

Insulation service to industries
Insurance
Ice cream

Jewellery

Kitchen equipment

Leather goods
Land development
Lighting equipment

Metal products
Mechanical transport equipment
Meat products
Magazines
Motor trucks
Motor tyres
Motor cars
Medical equipment
Milk
Mineral waters
Motor vehicle servicing
Mail order stores
Metallurgical processing
Metal alloys
Marine equipment
Musical instruments
Machine tools

Navigation equipment
Nuclear energy
Nuclear energy products

Office furniture
Optical lenses
Office equipment
Office supplies

Pet foods
Plastic building supplies

Precision moulds
Petrol
Petroleum exploration
Petrochemicals
Paper
Projection equipment
Plastic pipes and fittings
Publishing
Printing
Public relations services
Property development
Plastic containers
Pharmaceuticals
Power transmission equipment
Printing equipment
Packaged foods
Pumps
Photocopying equipment
Photographic products
Plastic closures
Public transport
Plastic cartons
Plastic domestic goods
Perfumes

Retail chemists
Radio and TV retailing
Rubber
Retailing
Rigid PVC
Restaurants
Radio broadcasting transmitters
Radio receivers
Ropes
Refinery

Shipping
Shirtmakers
Satellite tracking equipment
Safety equipment
Steam boilers
Service stations
Space rockets
Spectacles
Sports goods
Steel
Soft drinks
Scientific instruments
Space vehicles
Spectacle frames

Trailers
Toiletries
Transportation fabrics
Textile machinery
Tableware
Tape recorders
Turbines
Tiles
TV receivers
Telephone equipment
TV transmitters
Tractors
Travel
Toys
Travel goods
Telephone services
Tubing
Textiles
Traffic signal equipment
Transistors
Time switches

Under-water marine equipment

Vegetable retailing
Vacuum cleaners
Vibration equipment

Watches
Women's clothing
Water supply
Water treatment equipment
Warehouse services
Wires
Wire
Waste disposal
Wholesalers

Yachts

Pseudonym	*Industry*	*Size*
MR. ASPINALL	Electronics	Super-large
MR. ATKINS	Oil	Small-medium
MR. ATKINSON	Specialist Retail	Medium-large
MR. ATTERBURY	Batch process manufacturing	Medium-large
MR. ATTFIELD	Food processing, etc.	Medium-large
MR. ATTWATER	Household goods manufacturing	Large
MR. ATTWOOD	Advertising	Small-medium
MR. ATWELL	Vehicle manufacturing	Large
MR. ATWICK	Electronics, etc.	Medium-large
MR. AUBREY	Miscellaneous manufacturing	Medium-large
MR. AUSTIN	Transport	Small-medium
MR. AVERY	Food processing, etc.	Large
MR. AYLWARD	Food retailing	Large

Author's Note: The chief executive of one of the super-large firms on this list has requested that it be shown as 'large'.

B = BRITISH NON-FOUNDING CHIEF EXECUTIVES

Pseudonym	*Industry*	*Size*
MR. BACON	Domestic equipment manufacturing	Medium-large
MR. BAILEY	Miscellaneous manufacturing	Medium-large
MR. BAINBRIDGE	Consumer services	Medium-large
MR. BAKER	Mining	Large
MR. BAMBER	Retail	Large
MR. BANFIELD	Equipment manufacturing	Medium-large
MR. BARRATT	Engineering contracting	Small-medium
MR. BASSETT	Machinery manufacturing	Small
MR. BATCHELOR	Hotel and restaurant	Large
MR. BAXTER	Equipment manufacturing	Small-medium
MR. BAYLISS	Batch process manufacturing	Large
MR. BEATTY	Equipment manufacturing	Medium-large
MR. BECKETT	Food processing, etc.	Large
MR. BELLAMY	Continuous process, etc.	Large
MR. BENHAM	Electronics	Medium-large
MR. BERESFORD	Batch process manufacturing	Medium-large
MR. BEST	Electronic, etc.	Large
MR. BIGGS	Machinery manufacturing, etc.	Medium-large
MR. BISSETT	Engineering goods	Large
MR. BLACK	Miscellaneous manufacturing	Medium-large

Pseudonym	Industry	Size
MR. BLISS	Consumer goods manufacturing	Large
MR. BLOOMFIELD	Specialist wholesaling	Small-medium
MR. BLUNDELL	Heavy engineering	Large
MR. BLYTH	Industrial equipment manufacturing	Large
MR. BOLTON	Chemical	Large
MR. BOND	Consumer supplies	Large
MR. BOSWORTH	Furniture	Small-medium
MR. BOOTH	Food retailing	Large
MR. BOWLES	Chemical	Large
MR. BOYD	Specialist retail	Large
MR. BRADLEY	Specialist retail	Small-medium
MR. BRIDGES	Vehicle manufacturing	Large
MR. BURKE	Building supplies manufacturing	Large

C = CAPITALIST BRITISH CHIEF EXECUTIVES—ORIGINAL FOUNDERS OR REORGANIZERS OF A BUSINESS—HOLDING A SIGNIFICANT SHARE STAKE

Pseudonym	Industry	Size
MR. CAIRNS	Building supplies manufacturing	Small-medium
MR. CALDER	Finance	Medium-large
MR. CAMERON	Finance	Small-medium
MR. CARLISLE	Specialized consumer manufacturing	Medium-large
MR. CASEY	Chemical	Small-medium
MR. CAVELL	Construction	Large
MR. CHADWICK	Furniture	Small-medium
MR. CHAMBERS	Specialized construction	Small-medium
MR. CHANDLER	Hotel and Restaurant	Medium-large
MR. CHAPMAN	Electronic	Small-medium
MR. CHARLTON	Building supplies manufacturing	Medium-large
MR. CHATFIELD	Vehicle servicing	Small-medium
MR. CHESHIRE	Equipment manufacturing	Small-medium
MR. CHILDS	Specialist consumer manufacturing	Small
MR. CHISHOLM	Specialist retail	Medium-large
MR. CHRISTIE	Construction equipment manufacturing	Small-medium

Pseudonym	*Industry*	*Size*
MR. CLARK	Industrial services	Small-medium
MR. CLEMENTS	Engineering	Super-large
MR. CLIFFORD	Manufacturing and retailing	Medium-large
MR. COCHRANE	Food retailing	Large
MR. COLE	Machinery manufacturing	Small-medium
MR. CONSTABLE	Construction	Small-medium
MR. COOPER	Building supplies manufacturing	Medium-large

D = DEUTSCH (GERMAN) CHIEF EXECUTIVES

Pseudonym	*Industry*	*Size*
MR. DACKWEILER	Specialist consumer manufacturing	Medium-large
MR. DAHLMANN	Engineering	Super-large
MR. DAMM	Specialist consumer manufacturing	Medium-large
MR. DANNEWALD	Finance	Medium-large
MR. DAUTZENBERG	Consumer supplies manufacturing	Medium-large
MR. DECKER	Heavy engineering	Large
MR. DEDERICHS	Engineering and chemical	Large
MR. DEGENHARDT	Retail	Large
MR. DEMMLER	Consumer supplies manufacturing	Small-medium
MR. DENYER	Consumer supplies manufacturing	Large
MR. DERKUM	Consumer supplies manufacturing	Large
MR. DILLMANN	Chemical and Metals	Medium-large
MR. DITTMER	Electrical engineering	Large
MR. DOBLER	Building equipment manufacturing	Small-medium
MR. DODEN	Communication	Small
MR. DOEBEL	Advertising	Small-medium

APPENDIX C

LIST OF PSEUDONYMS OF PARTICIPANTS TOGETHER WITH BROAD INDICATION OF THEIR INDUSTRY AND SIZE OF FIRM, SHOWN IN NATIONAL GROUPINGS

Size Notation: Small = up to 200 employees; small to medium = Over 200 and up to 1,000 employees; Medium to Large = Over 1,000 and up to 10,000 employees; Large = over 10,000 and up to 100,000 employees. Super large = over 100,000 employees.

A = AMERICAN CHIEF EXECUTIVES

Pseudonym	*Industry*	*Size*
MR. ABBOTT	Transport	Medium-large
MR. ACLAND	Miscellaneous manufacturing	Medium-large
MR. ADAMS	Retail	Large
MR. ALEXANDER	Oil	Large
MR. ALLEN	Textile manufacturing	Medium-large
MR. ANDERSON	Chemical	Medium-large
MR. ANSELL	Machinery manufacturing	Large
MR. ANTHONY	Machinery manufacturing	Medium-large
MR. ARCHER	Machinery manufacturing	Medium-large
MR. ARGENT	Machinery manufacturing	Medium-large
MR. ARMSTRONG	Equipment manufacturing	Large
MR. ARNOLD	Food processing, etc.	Large
MR. ARROWSMITH	Aerospace manufacturing	Large
MR. ARTHUR	Oil	Large
MR. ASCOT	Retail	Large
MR. ASHBOURNE	Aerospace manufacturing	Large
MR. ASHFIELD	Aerospace manufacturing	Large
MR. ASKEW	Consumer goods manufacturing	Large